100 THINGS
ELVIS FANS
SHOULD KNOW & DO
BEFORE THEY DIE

100 THINGS ELVIS FANS SHOULD KNOW & DO BEFORE THEY DIE

Gillian G. Gaar

TRIUMPH
BOOKS

Copyright © 2014 by Gillian G. Gaar

No part of this publication may be reproduced, stored in a retrieval system, or transmitted in any form by any means, electronic, mechanical, photocopying, or otherwise, without the prior written permission of the publisher, Triumph Books LLC, 814 North Franklin Street, Chicago, Illinois 60610.

Library of Congress Cataloging-in-Publication Data

Gaar, Gillian G., 1959– author.
  100 things Elvis fans should know & do before they die / Gillian G. Gaar.
    pages cm. — (100 things...fans should know)
  One hundred things Elvis fans should know and do before they die
  Includes bibliographical references.
  ISBN 978-1-60078-908-3 (paperback)
  1. Presley, Elvis, 1935-1977—Miscellanea. I. Title. II. Title: One hundred things Elvis fans should know and do before they die.
  ML420.P96G33 2014
  782.42166092—dc23

                       2013050917

This book is available in quantity at special discounts for your group or organization. For further information, contact:
  Triumph Books LLC
  814 North Franklin Street
  Chicago, Illinois 60610
  (312) 337-0747
  www.triumphbooks.com

Printed in U.S.A.
ISBN: 978-1-60078-908-3
Design by Patricia Frey
Photos courtesy of AP Images unless otherwise indicated

To Patricia Doheny
(and Gracie, Indy, and Tidbit)
Thanks for all you do.

Contents

Introduction

I grew up a committed Beatles fan. I knew little about Elvis Presley other than his name. His movies were occasionally shown in the 3:00 PM slot on afternoon television, but they always seemed to be the mid-1960s ones that co-starred Bill Bixby (the same way that *Star Trek* re-runs always seemed to show that episode about Apollo). The women waiting in line to buy tickets to his shows all seemed so, well, old (they must've been at least 30). What did Elvis have to do with rock 'n' roll?

One day I found out. In the fall of 1973, I saw a TV commercial for a box set of Elvis' recordings that opened with the vibrant blast of "Hound Dog." Wow. What was *that*? I'd never heard anything like that before. I immediately rushed out to buy the single; a big deal for me, as I usually only bought albums (since a single was inevitably on the album, buying the album was better value). I was mesmerized by everything about the song: Elvis' raucous vocal, the machine-gun attack of the drums, that stinging guitar. If I'd known then that I would later speak with that guitarist (Scotty Moore) and drummer (D.J. Fontana) on numerous occasions, I would have been flabbergasted. Not to mention that I'd also get the chance to interview producer Sam Phillips, Steve Binder (director of the Elvis Comeback Special), Elvis' costume designer Bill Belew, Egil "Bud" Krogh (who facilitated Elvis' meeting with President Richard Nixon), the Jordanaires' Gordon Stoker, and a wide range of musicians who had the good fortune to work with Elvis (Reggie Young, Jerry Carrigan, Ronnie Tutt, Jerry Scheff), among others, over the years.

Because Elvis had such a long career, there are many different facets you can explore: the '50s rock 'n' roll years, the '60s movies, the '70s live shows, the gospel recordings, the Memphis '69 sessions—an Elvis for every taste. So although innumerable

Elvis books have already been published (and more are surely on the way), in some ways it feels as if the surface has hardly been scratched. This is my third book on Elvis (after *Return of the King: Elvis Presley's Great Comeback* and *Elvis Remembered 1935–77*), and I sure don't feel I've run out of things to say about him and his music.

But this book was an interesting challenge. How to distill everything about Elvis into 100 key items, and then rank them in order? Some choices were pretty obvious: the *Ed Sullivan* appearances, Comeback Special, and *Aloha From Hawaii* concerts were all historic performances; "Hound Dog"/"Don't Be Cruel" was a hugely popular single; and surely every Elvis fan needs to visit Graceland at least once. But I also wanted to bring to light other aspects of his career, such as some of the excellent non-soundtrack, non-religious recordings he did in the '60s (his cover of Bob Dylan's "Tomorrow is a Long Time" is one of my very favorite Elvis songs). Or reexamining all of his '60s films in defiance of the common perception that Elvis' '50s films were good and his '60s films were not. And I of course wanted to convince people they needed to read Peter Guralnick's masterful two-volume biography of Elvis, *Last Train to Memphis* and *Careless Love*.

As for the order of the 100 Things, that's always going to be seen as somewhat subjective; you could probably do another book listing a completely different set of 100 Things. My hope is that you find this listing fun and entertaining, and that it gives you a few new things to think about. Elvis rocks on!

—Gillian G. Gaar
Seattle, Washington, November 2013

1 Let's Meet Elvis

Elvis Presley was the world's first rock star, whose fame and influence was such that it led to his being proclaimed the King of Rock 'n' Roll. He became so famous that even today, more than 35 years after his death, you only have to say his first name—Elvis—and everyone knows exactly who you're talking about. No last name is necessary.

One reason why Elvis' rise was so remarkable is because his roots were so humble. Elvis was born on January 8, 1935, at the home of his parents, Vernon and Gladys Presley, in East Tupelo, Mississippi (the town was later incorporated into the town of Tupelo itself in 1946). The two-room house was the kind of small structure dubbed a "shotgun shack" because you could shoot your gun from the front door straight through the house and right out the back door without hitting anything else. There was no electricity, no running water, and an outhouse in the backyard.

It was a difficult pregnancy for Gladys, and she eventually had to quit her job. She could tell she would probably give birth to twins, as she grew bigger and bigger, not to mention her being able to feel two babies moving around inside her. She went into labor on the night of January 7, and Dr. William Robert Hunt arrived at the Presley home in the early hours of January 8. Around 4:00 AM, Gladys' first son was delivered, a stillborn birth; the arrival of a second baby about half an hour later helped alleviate some of the pain. The twins were named Jessie Garon and Elvis Aaron. Elvis was Vernon's middle name, and Aaron was in honor of his friend, Aaron Kennedy; Jessie was Vernon's father's name, and Garon was to rhyme with Aaron. It had been a hard delivery, and Gladys

Elvis between takes at his first RCA Victor recording session in Nashville, Tennessee, in January 1956. (AP Photo)

Aron or Aaron?

Elvis' middle name has been spelled differently over the years. His birth certificate spelled it as "Aron." On his tombstone, it's spelled "Aaron." But a 1980 box set went back to the original spelling for its title: *Elvis Aron Presley.*

Much has been made about the different spellings. Some even think that the spelling of Aaron on Elvis' tombstone is meant to be a clue that Elvis isn't really dead.

The simplest explanation is that it was likely that the Aron spelling was an error. Memphis journalist Bill Burk said that Vernon told him he didn't know the correct spelling of Aaron. But Burk's own book, *Early Elvis: The Tupelo Years,* says it was the mistake of the doctor who delivered Elvis and his twin, stating that Dr. William Hunt not only misspelled Aron on Elvis' birth certificate, but also recorded the twin's name as Jesse Garion instead of Jessie Garon.

According to Elvis Presley Enterprises (EPE), the company that looks after Elvis' business interests, Elvis was planning to start using Aaron as the official spelling of the name in the 1970s. After Elvis' death, Vernon, knowing Elvis' wishes, used Aaron on his tombstone, and EPE has since designated that Aaron is now the official spelling of Elvis' middle name.

and her newborn son were sent to the hospital; afterward, she was unable to have another child. Jessie was buried in an unmarked grave in the nearby Priceville Cemetery.

The loss of one baby made Vernon and Gladys treasure Elvis all the more, and Gladys in particular fussed over him. Though Elvis sometimes resisted his mother's attentions ("Mama never let me out of her sight," he later recalled), there was nonetheless a strong bond between the two, and it was undoubtedly the most important relationship of his life.

The Presleys were poor and moved throughout Elvis' childhood. The family unit was broken up for a time in 1938 when Vernon was sent to prison for nine months for forging a check. But Elvis' parents were always devoted to their son and encouraged his growing interest in music. Elvis first began singing at church, and avidly listened to country music on the radio. He made his public debut at the Mississippi-Alabama Fair and Dairy Show in 1945, and soon after received a guitar for his 11th birthday. He became a regular visitor at Tupelo radio station WELO, where he'd watch local musician Mississippi Slim perform, then shyly ask him for tips on playing the guitar after the broadcast. He could soon play well enough that he could be coaxed into performing for his school-mates during lunch breaks.

In November 1948, the Presleys moved to Memphis in search of better job opportunities. It was an exciting city to be in for someone as interested in music as Elvis was. He could find every-thing from country to pop to R&B on the radio; listen to the gospel music he loved so much at one of the city's many churches or at all-night Gospel Singings; or hang out on Beale Street, the main thoroughfare in Memphis' African American neighborhood, and hear the exciting music emanating from its many nightclubs.

By the time he graduated from Humes High School in 1953, Elvis was determined to become involved in music somehow. He wasn't sure how to make it happen. But in just a year's time, he would finally get the break he was longing for.

2 Recording in Memphis: The First Single

The events of July 5, 1954, did more than bring about dramatic changes in Elvis Presley's life. What happened that evening would also alter the course of popular music—forever.

In 1953 and 1954, Elvis made two demo records at the Memphis Recording Service (later renamed Sun Studio). Though he later said he just wanted to hear what he sounded like, he also wanted to make sure he was heard by Sam Phillips, the studio's owner. Phillips eventually decided to see what Elvis was capable of, asking him to come to the studio on June 26, 1954, to work on a song Phillips was considering recording, a ballad called "Without You."

Nothing resulted from that session, but Sam mentioned Elvis to a guitarist he knew, Scotty Moore, who was in a local band called the Starlite Wranglers. Sam asked Scotty if he'd get together and work with Elvis on some numbers, and Scotty duly arranged for Elvis to come by his house on July 4, also inviting a fellow Wrangler, bassist Bill Black, to join them. They worked on a number of songs, primarily ballads, and when Scotty called Sam and told him how the evening went, Sam suggested the three come by the studio the next night, July 5.

The musicians started out working on ballads, recording versions of "Harbor Lights" and "I Love You Because." They were pleasant enough, but there was nothing terribly original about them. Then during a break, Elvis picked up his guitar and began to do a rocked-up version of Arthur "Big Boy" Crudup's "That's All Right." Though unfamiliar with the song, Scotty and Bill quickly joined in. "And Sam stuck his head out and said, 'Hey, what are you guys doing?'" Scotty said when talking about the famous session. "And Elvis told him, and Sam said, 'Well, that sounds pretty good, let me hear it again.' Of course, it was up-tempo and everything from what we'd been doing before. And so we went through it, we rehearsed it two or three times, and made a record of it."

Just like that, Elvis and his backup musicians had managed to create music that was new, different, and innovative. Crudup's original was laid back and drenched in the blues. Elvis took that bluesy beat and injected a bit of country & western swing, giving the song a high-spirited energy with a vocal performance that's positively joyous.

Sam knew he'd found the new sound he'd been looking for, even if he couldn't quite define what Elvis had done. "It's not black, it's not white, it's not pop, it's not country," he later recalled. He couldn't wait to share it with his friend, DJ Dewey Phillips—no relation to Sam, though the two men were as close as brothers. Sam cut an acetate of the song for Dewey, who played it on his *Red, Hot and Blue* radio show later that week (either July 6 or July 8). The phones lit up, and Elvis was brought down to the station for an interview—his very first.

Sam was now anxious to get out a single and capitalize on the growing excitement, so the musicians returned to the studio that week and recorded a B-side for "That's All Right," a cover of Bill Monroe's "Blue Moon of Kentucky." This time, they took a country number and gave it a dose of the blues. "Hell, that's different," Sam said approvingly during the session. "That's a pop song now, nearly about!" Lightning had managed to strike twice.

On July 19, the single was ready to go, released on Sam's Sun Records label. It wasn't the first rock 'n' roll record—people are still debating about that one—but it showed that from the beginning, Elvis had an instinctive grasp of how to meld two seemingly disparate musical genres to create music that was fresh and exciting. As *Billboard* commented in its review of "That's All Right," "Presley is a potent new chanter who can sock over a tune for either the country or the R&B markets." Elvis was on his way.

3 Recording in Memphis: The Sun Sessions

The 19 surviving tracks Elvis recorded at Sun form the cornerstone of his musical career and are undeniably some of his best work.

We've already mentioned "Harbor Lights" and "I Love You Because," both recorded at the "That's All Right" session. Bing Crosby recorded the former, while the latter was a country hit for Leon Payne. Both reveal the affinity Elvis had for ballads from the very beginning of his career.

Sam Phillips set up another session for Elvis in August, probably the week of August 15-21, 1954 (the dates are uncertain). Elvis recorded a haunting version of the Rodgers and Hart standard "Blue Moon," that becomes positively eerie when he goes into a wailing falsetto; the song's melancholy feeling is heightened by the fact that Elvis leaves out the final verse, which brings the song to a happy ending. Instead, Elvis is left alone under that blue moon.

But Sam didn't feel the song would work on a single, so Elvis returned to the studio on September 12 (and probably other days that week). He recorded a diverse array of songs, beginning with a lovely, languid version of Lonnie Johnson's "Tomorrow Night." Jimmy Wakely's "I'll Never Let You Go (Little Darlin')" also starts out as a ballad then segues awkwardly into a faster tempo toward the end.

This wasn't the new sound Sam wanted to capitalize on. The band's lively rendition of "Just Because"—popularized, among others, by Frankie Yankovic—was a step in the right direction, but Sam found Elvis' next single in the two best songs of the session. "I Don't Care If the Sun Don't Shine" was a top 10 hit for Patti Page in 1950 and had appeared in the Dean Martin/Jerry Lewis film *Scared Stiff*, and Elvis gave it a bright country swing. But the standout was a cover of Roy Brown's "Good Rockin' Tonight." Elvis sings with an appealing confidence from the very beginning, making this invitation to a big night out an instant classic. "Good Rockin' Tonight"/"I Don't Care If the Sun Don't Shine" was released in October 1954.

Elvis was back in to the studio in November (or possibly December), to record his next single. Sam took the country song

"Milk Cow Blues" and renamed it "Milkcow Blues Boogie," to make it sound livelier. Elvis then gave it one of the most memorable openings of any of his songs, singing slowly, stopping to announce, "Hold it, fellas. That don't *move!* Let's get *real, real, gone* for a change!" then launching into a brisk rockabilly beat. He also recorded his first original number, the sweet "You're a Heartbreaker." The two songs were released as a single at the end of December 1954.

There are no exact dates for Elvis' remaining Sun sessions. In late January or early February '55, he recorded "Baby Let's Play House," a hit for Arthur Gunter, and here featuring a terrific hiccupping vocal from Elvis.

At some point between November '54 and April '55, Elvis recorded a slow version of "I'm Left, You're Right, She's Gone." Drummer Jimmy Lott also remembers working on the song "How Do You Think I Feel" at the same time. And a second, faster (and superior) version of "I'm Left..." was done possibly as late as mid-April. The faster version became the B-side of the "Baby Let's Play House" single, released in April '55. The song was the first Elvis recording to feature drums.

The next session was held in mid-July. Elvis recorded another original, the lyrically playful "I Forgot to Remember to Forget," as well as an impassioned "Tryin' to Get to You." But the highlight was a terrific rendition of Junior Parker's "Mystery Train," Elvis turning in a spirited performance that ends with a happy "Woo!" in the fade out that Sam rightly declared "A fucking masterpiece." "I Forgot to Remember to Forget"/"Mystery Train" was released in August '55. During Elvis' final Sun session, in November '55, the band recorded Billy "The Kid" Emerson's laidback "When It Rains, It Really Pours." But the session was cut short when word came that Elvis was signing to RCA.

The most comprehensive package of Elvis' Sun recordings is the *A Boy From Tupelo: The Complete 1953–55* box set (2012) from the collector's label Follow That Dream; *Sunrise* is a cheaper collection with fewer outtakes.

Further reading: *Good Rockin' Tonight: Sun Records and the Birth of Rock 'n' Roll* by Colin Escott and Martin Hawkins.

The Man With the Vision: Sam Phillips

Sam Phillips was the visionary producer who recognized Elvis' potential as a singer and had the capability to draw it out of him. His belief in the redemptive power of music, and his desire to seek out undiscovered talent and share it with the world, led to his working with a range of legendary musicians in addition to Elvis.

Samuel Cornelius Phillips was born on January 5, 1923, in Florence, Alabama. His parents were sharecroppers, and it was while working alongside his family in the cotton fields that he became fascinated with the songs the field hands sang as they worked. He also absorbed the music he heard in local churches, both the white Baptist church he attended and the black Methodist church nearby.

His first job in the music industry was at radio station WLAY in Muscle Shoals, Alabama, where he worked as a DJ and engineer. After briefly working in Nashville, he arrived in Memphis in 1945, landing a job as an engineer at WREC. His desire to seek out new and different types of music led to his opening the Memphis Recording Service at 706 Union in January 1950, helped in no small measure by Marion Keisker, a radio show host who worked with Sam at WREC.

Sam initially leased his recordings to other labels. One of his most notable recordings was "Rocket 88," recorded by Ike Turner's

Who First Recorded Elvis?

As with many incidents in Elvis' life, there's been a debate over who was the first person to record Elvis when he came to the Memphis Recording Service in 1953 to make his personal recording.

For years, Marion Keisker said that it was she—because Sam Phillips was not at the studio at the time. She took Elvis into the studio, and while the cheap acetate was being recorded direct-to-disc, she also turned on the studio's tape recorder so Sam could hear the singer when he returned. She played the tape for Sam later that day, and he was interested, asking if she'd taken down the singer's name and phone number, which she had.

Then in 1979, Sam began telling his version of the story. He stated that it was he who operated the disc-cutting lathe on that first session, thus making him the first person to record Elvis.

Sam and Marion remained at odds over this issue for the rest of their lives. Marion eventually began relenting a bit, saying that Sam had returned to the studio while Elvis was still making his recording. Sam never changed his version.

It's a small matter that's only assumed greater importance because it's Elvis we're talking about. As Peter Guralnick wrote in his Elvis biography, *Last Train To Memphis*, "Who flicked the switch simply should not represent an issue of earthshaking importance."

band and credited to the singer, Johnny Brenston; it's considered by many historians to be the first rock 'n' roll record. He was also the first person to record Howlin' Wolf. In 1952, he decided to launch his own label, and Sun Records was born. His biggest success before Elvis came with the single "Bear Cat" by Rufus Thomas, an "answer record" to Willie Mae "Big Mama" Thornton's R&B hit "Hound Dog," though its success was marred by a lawsuit for copyright violation—the melodies of the two songs were exactly the same. He had better luck with "Mystery Train" by Little Junior's Blue Flames and "Just Walkin' in the Rain" by the Prisonaires (a group actually serving time in Tennessee State Penitentiary). Then, in 1954, came Elvis.

The underlying principle of Sun Records was to allow artists creative freedom; as Sam told me, "I was attempting to just give people an opportunity to innovate and be heard." Following Elvis' success, numerous other artists came to Sun to try their luck, including Carl Perkins, Jerry Lee Lewis, Johnny Cash, Billy Lee Riley, and Roy Orbison. Sam did a little innovating himself, using a tape delay technique while recording (running the tape through a second recorder head) to create what was called "slap back echo."

"It just brought that liveness to [the recording]," Sam told me. "I just knew sound and I didn't over-doctor it—even if I'd had the equipment to do that! I believed in the essence; I wanted to hear the warmth of the human voice or a sax solo or whatever. The electronic equipment that's available now, as far as the actual audio sound is concerned, is incredible. But this overdubbing stuff, it's okay for some things, but to punch in a vocal here because something went wrong, that is not the spirit of it. People get where they feel like there is a net under them all the time. I want 'em to feel like man, this is a tightrope and this is gonna be it! Because that's the spirit of the thing. You can't substitute the warmth of that human body, and that's got to come over on a record."

Sam used the money he got from selling Elvis' contract to RCA to invest in other projects, including WHER, a radio station with an all-female air staff. He also made a great deal of money through his investments, investing in the Holiday Inn hotel chain and radio stations. In 1957 he started the label Phillips International, and in 1960 he opened the Sam Phillips Recording Studio. In 1969 he sold the Sun catalogue to Shelby Singleton. He received numerous awards over the years for his achievements, and he was always on hand to offer Elvis advice and suggestions. He died of respiratory failure at age 80 on July 30, 2003.

The King's Manager: "Colonel" Tom Parker

The most controversial figure in Elvis' life was his manager, "Colonel" Tom Parker. He wasn't a colonel. He wasn't even really named Tom Parker. The man who oversaw the career of one of the most culturally influential performers in rock history was born Andreas Cornelis van Kuijk on June 28, 1909, in Breda, Holland.

Even before embarking on his career in show business, "Dries," as his family called him, had a colorful life. As a child, he was fascinated by the circus and managed to pick up a little work doing odd jobs whenever a small troupe came to town. At 16, he left for Rotterdam, and the following year he made his first visit to America where he worked for a traveling show called a Chautauqua. He returned to Holland in 1927, but in 1929 he went back to America for good. It's been suggested he left Holland suddenly because he'd been involved in a murder there, though there's no hard evidence to support this theory.

Parker was always careful to cover his tracks. It's believed he sailed first to the Dutch West Indies before entering America, which he did illegally. He then joined the United States Army and was initially stationed in Hawaii, very possibly the reason he saw to it that Elvis later made numerous appearances in the islands. While in the service he began to bury his Dutch past, taking on the name Thomas Andrew Parker, possibly after a Captain Thomas R. Parker who also served in Hawaii. Back on the mainland, he was arrested after going AWOL and subsequently suffered a mental breakdown; he was discharged from the service in 1933.

He then worked for different circuses and carnivals, and it was while working at the Royal American Shows carnival in the 1930s that he met and married Marie Frances Mott, though there's no official record of a wedding date. He later got a job working for the Humane Society in Tampa, Florida. Always on the lookout for new promotional opportunities, he designed and opened a popular pet cemetery.

He'd met singing star Gene Austin while working for Royal American, and began working for him in the late '30s, booking

This is a 1961 photo of Colonel Tom Parker, Elvis Presley's manager. (AP Photo)

shows and doing promotion. He later managed country singer Eddy Arnold, as well as doing concert promotions through his company, Jamboree Promotions. In 1948, Louisiana Governor Jimmie Davis, a former country singer himself, gave Parker the honorary title of "Colonel."

Arnold broke with Parker in 1953, feeling his manager was spending too much time working with other performers, including Hank Snow; Parker only let him go after a buy out of $50,000. He next briefly worked with singer Tommy Sands. In 1954, he heard about Elvis from Oscar Davis, who did advance promotion for Parker's shows and had seen Elvis at the Eagle's Nest club in Memphis in October '54. The following January, Parker saw Elvis perform on the *Louisiana Hayride* radio show and began booking concert appearances for him jointly with Snow through Hank Snow Attractions/Jamboree Promotions.

He then maneuvered his way into becoming Elvis' full-time manager, something that became final on March 2, 1956. Snow assumed that he was also part of the managerial team but found that Parker had edged him out. Snow later denounced his former partner as the "most egotistical, obnoxious human being I've ever had dealings with."

Parker's skill in promotion helped make Elvis the top entertainment star in the country. But by keeping his gaze so firmly fixed on the bottom line, he stunted Elvis' creative growth. The endless movies Elvis was contracted to do in the 1960s gave him little artistic satisfaction—and that eventually did affect the bottom line. Returning to live performance in the '70s did jumpstart Elvis' career for a time. But without any further challenges to engage him, Elvis again became dissatisfied with the direction of his career.

After Elvis' death, Parker became embroiled in legal disputes with Elvis' estate, which were finally settled in 1983 when Parker was paid $2 million for giving up all claims to any of Elvis' future earnings. He spent his remaining years in Las Vegas, marrying a second time in 1990 after the death of his first wife. Parker died on January 21, 1997, of a stroke at age 87.

Further reading: *The Colonel: The Extraordinary Story of Colonel Tom Parker and Elvis Presley* by Alanna Nash.

6 Elvis' Biggest Single

"Hound Dog"/"Don't Be Cruel" is Elvis' most successful single. It was No. 1 for 11 weeks and sold more than 4 million copies.

"Hound Dog," written by Jerry Leiber and Mike Stoller, was a slice of raw R&B originally written for Willie Mae "Big Mama" Thornton and released in 1953 when it topped *Billboard's* Rhythm & Blues charts for seven weeks. Sam Phillips had Rufus Thomas record an "answer song" called "Bear Cat" for Sun Records.

A keen record fan, Elvis knew Big Mama's version of the song, as well as Rufus Thomas' answer to it. But it wasn't until he heard Freddie Bell and the Bell Boys doing a very different version of the song that he decided to record it himself. He heard the group doing the number during his first Vegas appearance in April and May 1956. When Elvis wasn't working he was eagerly checking out all the shows at the casinos on Las Vegas Boulevard—the famous Strip. Freddie Bell had released his version of the song in 1955 and made it a good deal more playful by speeding it up and changing the lyrics. In the original, Big Mama was giving the boot to her man; the remake added such lines as, "You ain't never caught a rabbit," which lyricist Leiber thought were nonsensical.

Elvis added the song to his act and created a sensation when he first performed it on television on *The Milton Berle Show* in June 1956. His gyrations provoked such outrage that when he appeared the next month on *The Steve Allen Show*, Allen tried to calm the furor by having Elvis dressed in a tux and tails.

Perhaps his irritation at being straightjacketed on the Allen show fueled his ferocious performance of the song when he recorded it the following day, July 2. He worked his way through 31 takes before he was satisfied with the song; time very well spent. "Hound Dog" opens with a blast from D.J. Fontana's drums, and the excitement never lets up throughout, with Scotty Moore playing an especially stinging guitar line.

"Don't Be Cruel" was also recorded at the same session. It was the first song Elvis recorded by Otis Blackwell, who was a singer but was also developing a strong reputation as a songwriter. Elvis liked the demo of the song as soon as he heard it. Its laidback beat (emphasized by bassist Bill Black in the opening measures) made a nice contrast to the frantic feel of "Hound Dog." Elvis again took his time to get it the way he wanted it, recording 28 takes. Blackwell was induced to give up half of his publishing, as well as letting Elvis have a co-songwriting credit, and he agreed, rightly guessing that the single's success would give his own career a big boost.

With the publicity "Hound Dog" had generated due to Elvis' TV performances of the song, the single, released in July 1956, had little trouble topping the charts. Though it's been said that only "Don't Be Cruel" reached No. 1 while "Hound Dog" stayed at No. 2, in fact both songs are considered to have topped the charts; the latest edition of *Top Pop Singles 1955–2012*, compiled from *Billboard*'s own charts, lists both songs at No. 1, and they're both included on the 2002 release *ELVIS: 30 No. 1 Hits*. More unusually, the single not only topped the pop charts, it topped the country and rhythm & blues charts. The single's success firmly established that Elvis wasn't destined to be a one-hit wonder; he was a bona fide star.

7 The Comeback Special

Elvis' 1968 television special, simply entitled *Elvis*, couldn't have come at a better time. When it first aired, on Tuesday, December 3, at 9:00 PM on NBC, Elvis was on the verge of becoming irrelevant. But just one hour later, he was reborn, his career rejuvenated, and everyone was excited about Elvis again. As a result, the show has come to be known as the "Comeback Special."

The special was announced on January 12, 1968. It would be Elvis' first television appearance since he'd appeared on *The Frank Sinatra Timex Show: Welcome Home Elvis* back in 1960. Parker had nothing more creative in mind than having Elvis spend the hour singing Christmas carols—a bland TV counterpart to the uninspired movies he'd been making. But the show's executive producer, Bob Finkel, suggested otherwise, as did Elvis himself, telling Finkel in a meeting that he wanted the special "to depart completely from the pattern of his motion pictures and from everything else he has done," as Finkel recalled.

And Finkel knew just who to approach for the job: the two men who ran Binder/Howe Productions. Steve Binder was the director of the landmark rock concert film *The T.A.M.I. Show* (for "Teenage Music International") and had also directed the rock TV variety series *Hullabaloo*. His partner, Dayton Burr "Bones" Howe, began his career as a recording engineer and had worked with Elvis before at some of his recording sessions in L.A.; more recently he'd been producing The Fifth Dimension and The Association.

Steve, who wasn't much of an Elvis fan at the time, was inclined to turn down the job, but Bones convinced him otherwise, telling Steve he was sure to enjoy working with Elvis. The two passed muster with Parker and then met with Elvis. The two men impressed Elvis with their frankness; Steve bluntly told Elvis his career was in a rut and that while doing the special gave him a shot at changing that, it was also a risk. "I think those kind of conversations hit home," Steve told me. "Elvis even said later on that he totally trusted me because I was giving him straight answers, whereas I'm sure he was surrounded by other people just stroking him all the way."

Steve was hired as the show's director with Bones in charge of music production. The two pulled in most of the creative team who had worked on Steve's last TV special, *Petula*, starring British singer/actress Petula Clark, and crafted a show that played to Elvis' strengths. In the stunning opening sequence, Elvis sang a medley of "Trouble" (from *King Creole*) and his 1967 single "Guitar Man" with a menacing power in front of large red letters that spelled out E-L-V-I-S. A gospel sequence highlighted his love of that genre. "Guitar Man" also served as the theme song for a rags-to-riches production number that charted Elvis' rise to fame through song. The closing number had Elvis, resplendent in a white suit, singing "If I Can Dream," an impassioned plea for peace and understanding that was especially timely in a year that had seen the assassinations of Rev. Martin Luther King Jr. and presidential candidate Senator Robert Kennedy.

The show's most inspired moments came as a result of Steve's observing Elvis unwind after a day's work by playing guitar and singing with his buddies in his dressing room. Steve wanted to get some of that intimate feel into the show, and filmed four short live concerts of Elvis performing "in the round" for a studio audience. In the first two, he sat down and was backed by two of his original musicians, Scotty Moore and D.J. Fontana; in the second two he performed solo, stalking the small square stage like a panther with an orchestra backing him. He wore one of his most iconic outfits for these concerts, a form-fitting black leather suit. They were the first live shows Elvis had done since 1961.

"If I Can Dream," the first single released from the show, and the soundtrack album were both released in November 1968, reaching No. 12 and No. 8, respectively. They were Elvis' highest-charting releases since 1965. The show's ratings were also good, and offers for more appearances came pouring in. The show's success primed Elvis to go on and create some of the best work of his career.

8 Recording in Memphis: The American Sound Sessions

In January and February 1969, Elvis recorded in Memphis for the first time since his days at Sun. Working in a new studio with new musicians and a new producer, Elvis recorded a number of his most notable—and successful—albums and singles.

The sessions were his first non-soundtrack sessions in more than a year, and feeling newly energized after the success of the *Elvis* TV special, Elvis wanted to do something different. When it became apparent that he wasn't anxious to return to RCA's studios in Nashville, it was suggested that he consider recording at a small studio in north Memphis that had been making a name for itself, American Sound Studios. The studio was run by Lincoln "Chips" Moman, who'd previously worked for Stax Records producing a number of the label's early hits. Since opening American in 1964, acts like the Box Tops, Merrilee Rush, Wilson Pickett, and Dusty Springfield had all recorded hit records at American.

Chips himself was interested in working with Memphis' biggest star and had often asked members of Elvis' entourage about doing so, in his typically frank style: "When's Elvis gonna get some good songs, man? When's he gonna quit cuttin' that crap?" When the opportunity finally arose, Chips readily postponed a Neil Diamond session that had been scheduled at American; Diamond also agreed to the postponement on the condition that Elvis record one of his songs.

The dates of the American sessions were January 13–16, January 20–23, and February 17–22. Elvis was also fortunate to work with American's in-house musicians, a group nicknamed the 827 Thomas Street Band after American's street address, later rechristened the Memphis Boys: Reggie Young on guitar, Tommy Cogbill and Mike Leech on bass, Bobby Emmons and Bobby Wood on keyboards, and Gene Chrisman on drums.

The Memphis Boys gave the music recorded at American a distinctive sound. The musicians also had greater autonomy than at other studios. "We'd write our own charts and come up with our own arrangements," Reggie Young told me. "We'd worked together long enough to where we sort of all thought alike. And there was no time restraint on us. Like Nashville, a session is every three hours. Whereas in Memphis it was really loose. We had time to really work out the arrangements."

As in Elvis' sessions at Sun, and the Comeback Special, the musicians and producer provided a truly creative environment for Elvis to work in. But there were a few bumps along the way. When Elvis asked the musicians what they thought of the demos that had been submitted for the sessions, they had no hesitation in saying they didn't like a particular song—only to be pulled over by Felton Jarvis, Elvis' regular producer who was also at the sessions, and told to keep their opinions to themselves.

Chips was equally outspoken. When he told Elvis he was singing flat during a take, Jarvis quickly told him not to talk to Elvis like that. "And Chips just ignored him," Mike Leech told me. "And of course Elvis didn't mind a bit; he said, 'Oh, okay, I'll do it again, no problem.' Of course, I think that scared Felton to death because he had never talked to Elvis like that." Publishing disputes also arose over a few songs.

Elvis himself clearly enjoyed the sessions; on the way home after the first night, he told his friends, "Man, that felt really great. I can't tell you how good I feel." And the 32 songs he recorded, spread over four albums and six singles, capture a performer at the peak of his interpretive powers. People remember the hits "In The Ghetto," "Suspicious Minds," and "Don't Cry Daddy," which all reached the Top 10. But there are other songs on *From Elvis in Memphis* (1969, No. 13) and *Back In Memphis* (1969, and initially released as part of the two-album set *From Memphis to Vegas/From Vegas to Memphis*, which reached No. 12) that are just as strong. Blues and soul ("Wearin' That Loved On Look," "Long Black Limousine"), country ("Gentle On My Mind," "If I'm A Fool"), heartfelt ballads ("Without Love"), pop ("Any Day Now"); the American sessions produced an impressive, mature body of work that reestablished Elvis' validity as a contemporary recording artist.

Further reading: *Memphis Boys: The Story of American Studios* by Roben Jones.

9 A Home Fit for a King

Elvis owned a number of different homes during his life, but there's no doubt that the residence he was proudest of was Graceland. As he once told a friend, "I never feel like I'm really home, until I get back to Graceland." He'd probably be pleased to learn that his home has been officially designated as a National Historic Landmark.

The first house that Elvis bought in May 1956 was a three-bedroom ranch-style house at 1034 Audubon Drive in Memphis. But the neighbors soon began complaining about the crowds of fans that showed up hoping to see Elvis. So he decided he needed a home that would give him and his family some more privacy.

In early 1957, Elvis' parents had met a real estate agent while he was in Hollywood making the film *Loving You*, and she had shown them Graceland. The 13-acre property had a colonial mansion sitting on top of a hill, and it was located eight miles south of downtown Memphis in the city's Whitehaven neighborhood. The original property, owned by S.E. Toof, was a 500-acre spread called Graceland Farms, named after Toof's daughter, Grace. Grace's niece, Ruth Moore, and her husband, Dr. Thomas Moore, built the mansion itself in 1939.

Elvis' parents told him about Graceland as soon as they'd seen it, and when Elvis arrived back in Memphis on March 18, he went over to see the property the next day. He quickly decided to buy it, and by the end of the month, Graceland was his with a final price tag of $102,500. In the first of many renovations, Elvis built a wall across the front of the property, made of Alabama fieldstone; today, fans from all over the world write messages on the wall (which is spray-washed regularly, so fans can leave new messages). He also installed the famous music gates, specially made of wrought iron and featuring a music staff, notes, and Elvis' own silhouette; it's another spot where fans like to pose for photographs.

Fans were always hanging around Graceland's gates during Elvis' lifetime, and Elvis would occasionally come down to visit with them, signing autographs and posing for photos. When he was out of town, the guards, who were usually Elvis' relatives, would sometimes escort a few lucky fans up the driveway to get a closer view of the house.

At the time, most people thought they'd never be able to get any closer to Graceland than viewing it from the outside. But on June 7, 1982, Elvis' home was opened to the public. You're not able to see everything; no one's allowed on the second floor where Elvis' bedroom was. (Before you go inside, look at the second floor

Elvis Presley with his girlfriend, Yvonne Lime, at Graceland in Memphis, Tennessee, April 19, 1957. (AP Photo)

windows on the right; that's where Elvis' bedroom was. And when you stand in the entry hall, you're right beneath Elvis' bathroom.) But there's still much to see, including the most famous rooms in the house: the yellow and black TV Room with its three sets; the Pool Room with a pool table and 400 sq. ft. of multi-colored fabric draping the walls; and the Jungle Room with its dark shag rug, Polynesian-style furniture, and animal figures atop every surface. Elvis' trophy room and the racquetball building have been redesigned to display artifacts from his career, including some of his

A Street of One's Own

The Presley family undoubtedly drove up and down U.S. Highway 51 South innumerable times after they moved to Memphis. They could not have imagined that one day they would not only live in the pleasant countryside that Hwy. 51 S. passed through, but that the road would also be named after their famous son.

Throughout the years, there had been various suggestions to name something in Memphis after Elvis. One suggestion was to name the Mid-South Coliseum after him, though the idea was turned down—fortunately, because the Coliseum closed in 2006.

Instead, Elvis received a more lasting tribute. On June 29, 1971, the Memphis City Council voted to rename the section of the highway that runs from S. Parkway East to the Tennessee state line "Elvis Presley Boulevard." Elvis' home address of Graceland then became (and remains) 3764 Elvis Presley Boulevard. A formal ceremony in honor of the event was held in January 1972, attended by Elvis' father, Vernon, and the mayor of Memphis, Wyeth Chandler.

Twenty-three years earlier, the Presleys arrived in Memphis as just another anonymous family; the street renaming was a sign of just how far the family had come—and how much Elvis in particular had accomplished.

most famous costumes as well as personal items. The racquetball building also has an impressive display of gold records.

Elvis, his parents, and his grandmother, Minnie Mae Presley, are all buried in the Meditation Garden, a lovely area on the property that was built in 1965, featuring a brick wall set with stained glass windows that curves around a lighted fountain. From 7:30 to 8:30 AM every day, fans are allowed to walk up to the Meditation Garden free of charge.

Graceland Plaza, across the street, has museums where you can see more of Elvis' personal belongings, including his cars and planes. You can opt to just tour the mansion, but it's well worth seeing the other exhibits, too, so go for the Platinum tour. The Elvis Entourage VIP tour adds a few extras if you feel like splurging.

The one Elvis-related site all fans should see is Graceland. The home reveals a lot about the man who lived there.

Further reading: *Graceland: The Living Legacy of Elvis Presley* by Chet Flippo; *Elvis Presley's Graceland the Official Guidebook* by Todd Morgan; *Elvis Presley's Graceland Through The Years 1957–1977* by Joseph Pirzada, Rhonda Marsden, and John Michael Heath.

10 The First Hawaiian Film

Blue Hawaii was not only one of Elvis' most successful films, it also had a profound effect on the rest of his movie career.

Elvis' 1950s movies had depicted him as a troubled young man and a bit of a rebel. But *Blue Hawaii* created the template that would be used for most of the subsequent films he did—what you might call the Elvis Movie Formula—casting Elvis as an ambitious young man who lives in an exotic (or at least picturesque) locale, gets the girl by the final reel, and naturally (if somewhat improbably) is also a singer.

In *Blue Hawaii*, Elvis plays Chad Gates, who returns to home to Hawaii after his army service, but declines an offer of working in his father's pineapple company as being too much of a "ready-made set-up" for his liking (the desire to be fully independent was another key motif of most of Elvis' 1960s films). Instead, he opts to become a travel guide, though romantic complications ensue when his girlfriend becomes jealous of his first batch of clients—an attractive schoolteacher and four teenage girls. But all is resolved by the film's end.

The film was shot in the spring of 1961, with location shooting on the islands of Oahu and Kauai. Hawaii had just become a U.S. state in 1959, and *Blue Hawaii* served as a wonderful introduction to the island paradise, as Elvis drives his charges from one lush green locale to another. "I think *Blue Hawaii* did more to promote Hawaii tourism than anything," Tom Moffatt, a Hawaiian DJ who knew Elvis told me. "It opened Hawaii up to the world. Up to then, Hawaii was only promoted in travelogues, and Bing Crosby had made a movie called *Waikiki Wedding.* But this was in color. And this was Elvis Presley. And all of a sudden a young demographic became aware of Hawaii." Angela Lansbury plays Elvis' mother complete with a broad Southern drawl, and well-known Hawaiian performer Hilo Hattie also appears in a small role.

The film's soundtrack had an unprecedented 14 songs, the most of any Elvis movie. The music is all Hawaiian-themed, and while there's some undeniable silliness ("Ito Eats," "Slicin' Sand"), there are also lovely performances of the traditional song "Aloha Oe" (which means "Farewell to Thee," written by Queen Lili'uokalani, the last reigning queen of Hawaii) and the title track, first recorded by Bing Crosby. The romantic "Can't Help Falling in Love" became Elvis' signature song. The only nod to rock 'n' roll comes in "Rock-a-Hula Baby," which Elvis performed during a party sequence.

Blue Hawaii was released in November 1961 and proved to be an immediate success. The soundtrack, released in October 1961, stayed at No. 1 for 20 weeks and became Elvis' biggest-selling album during his lifetime. Both sides of the accompanying single, "Can't Help Falling in Love"/"Rock-a-Hula Baby," also charted— the former at No. 2 and the latter at No. 23.

Blue Hawaii is one of the better films in Elvis' filmography and, aside from some painfully dated moments (the portrayal of the Gates family's Asian butler, Ping Pong, is especially embarrassing), is largely pleasant to watch. It's easily the best of the

"Hawaiian trilogy" of movies Elvis filmed in the islands. But its greater importance is that its success charted the future course of Elvis' film career.

11 Visit Memphis

When Elvis returned from the army and was asked what he missed most about Memphis, he was quick to reply, "Everything!" And there's much to enjoy in the city; good food, great music, and friendly people.

After visiting Graceland, most Elvis fans head over to Sun Studio, where tours run every hour. The studio (with an adjoining office and control room) isn't very big—you can see the entire space in a few minutes—but as a historic landmark it can't be beat. Remember, Sun wasn't just the place where Elvis made his first records; a number of other musical legends stepped through its doorway. As you stand in the middle of the studio, it's amazing to consider the wealth of talents that stood right where you are, and it's a thrill to be able to touch the actual microphone that Elvis used when he recorded at Sun.

Soulsville USA: Stax Museum of American Soul Music is on the site where the Stax Records recording studio and Satellite Record Shop once stood. Elvis recorded at Stax in 1973, and one block away from the studio is the former site of the First Assembly of God Church that Elvis attended during the early 1950s where he met his first serious girlfriend, Dixie Locke.

You'll also find Elvis on display at the Memphis Rock 'n' Soul Museum. The museum is located on Beale Street, which was once known as "the Main Street of Negro America." Elvis spent a lot of time hanging out on Beale as a teenager, absorbing all the sights and sounds, gazing longingly into the windows of Lansky Brothers' Men's Store, and stopping by to check out new releases at the Home of the Blues Record Shop.

Beale is in downtown Memphis where there are a number of Elvis-related sites. The Peabody Hotel on Union Avenue, famous for its ducks swimming in the lobby fountain, is where Elvis attended his senior prom. It's also where Sam Phillips and Marion Keisker worked at radio station WREC before setting up the Memphis Recording Service. Lansky Brothers now has four clothing and gift shops in the Peabody, including "Clothier to the King," which sells Elvis-inspired fashions. The Chisca Hotel on South Main was once home to WHBQ Radio where DJ Dewey Phillips first played "That's All Right" on the radio (the building is currently under redevelopment).

If you want to hunt down every place where Elvis lived, ate, shopped, and played in Memphis, you'll want to pick up a copy of *Memphis Elvis-Style* by Cindy Hazen and Mike Freeman, which is an interesting read even if you're not planning to visit the city (the book has easy-to-follow driving directions). When the couple was married, they were lucky enough to live in the house Elvis lived in right before he moved to Graceland, at 1034 Audubon Drive. The two restored the home to how it looked during Elvis' day and often opened it to the public. Unfortunately, after the couple divorced, the property was sold to Rhodes College, and tours are no longer available.

The only other home where Elvis lived that you can go inside is the apartment he and his family lived in from 1949 to 1953 in what was then called Lauderdale Courts. The area was redeveloped in the early twenty-first century and is now called Uptown Square, and you can stay in Elvis' apartment—#328—for up to four nights. During Elvis' "Birthday Celebration" in January and "Elvis Week" in August, public tours are offered. Elvis attended nearby Humes High School (now Humes Middle School), and the building is occasionally open for public tours.

It's pretty easy to get around Memphis, but there are also numerous tours offered by different companies. I recommend Mike's Memphis Tours, owned and operated by Mike Freeman (www.mikesmemphistours.com, and "Mikes Memphis Tours" on facebook); as an Elvis historian, his tours give you a more in-depth look at Elvis sites than other tour companies and you can specify which sites you're interested in seeing.

Further reading: *Memphis Elvis-Style* by Cindy Hazen and Mike Freeman.

12 Elvis' Favorite Film Performance

In the debate over which of Elvis' films is his best, *King Creole* ranks right up there at the top. And it's not just a fan favorite—it's the film Elvis felt featured his best performance.

Elvis' fourth film was based on the Harold Robbins novel *A Stone for Danny Fisher*, about a young man in 1920s America who takes up boxing as a profession against his parents' wishes. When Elvis was cast in the lead role, Danny became a singer, and the story was relocated from '20s-era Brooklyn to 1950s New Orleans—specifically the French Quarter, a colorful and appropriate setting for a performer.

The film certainly has the most striking beginning of any Elvis film. Street vendors are seen singing about their wares, with Elvis eventually joining one vendor, portrayed by jazz singer Kitty White, in singing the haunting song "Crawfish." In the story,

Danny pursues his singing career in the face of opposition from his father, gets mixed up with gangsters, and (as would often happen in an Elvis film) is torn between two women, the young, innocent Nellie and the older, world-weary Ronnie.

King Creole had a strong cast, including Walter Matthau as the head mobster Maxie Fields, Carolyn Jones (who later played Morticia Addams in the 1960s sitcom *The Addams Family*) as Ronnie, and character actors Dean Jagger and Paul Stewart. Jan Shepard, who played Elvis' sister, later co-starred with him in *Paradise, Hawaiian Style*; Dolores Hart, who played Nellie, had co-starred with Elvis in *Loving You* (in 1963 she left show business, became a nun, and joined the Benedictine Abbey of Regina Laudis in Bethlehem, Connecticut). The film was directed by Michael Curtiz, who'd directed such classics as *Mildred Pierce* and *Casablanca*. It was the last Elvis movie to be shot in black and white, which enhanced the stark feel of the film as location shooting in New Orleans added to the seedy atmosphere.

With Elvis playing a singer, the film's songs are naturally slotted into the film's nightclub sequences. The tougher, edgier numbers like "Trouble," "Hard Headed Woman," "New Orleans," and "King Creole" are the highlights; the more light-hearted "Lover Doll" is also used to good effect with Elvis singing the number as he strolls through a department store, providing a distraction so his hoodlum friends can burglarize the place.

Danny Fisher is straight out of the *Rebel Without a Cause* mode (and it's been said the film was originally planned as a vehicle for James Dean); a troubled youth who's good with his fists but has a sensitive side underneath. Elvis clearly relishes the part and is given some great dialogue in his steamy scenes with Jones, yet he's also believably vulnerable in his scenes with Hart. Perhaps the knowledge that he was about to enter the army added to his vulnerability; Elvis had been drafted after signing the contract to do *King Creole* and requested a deferment from his draft board in order to complete work on the film. It was granted, and 13 days after shooting ended, Elvis began his military service on March 24, 1958.

"Hard Headed Woman" was released as a single in June, reaching No. 2 in the charts, followed by *King Creole*'s release in July, and the release of the film's soundtrack album in September (the album also reached No. 2). The film was well received, and the critics, including *The New York Times* and *Variety*, gave Elvis some of the best notices of his career. The strength of Elvis' performance was such that it should've been a stepping-stone to greater things. Instead, it was—far too soon—the dramatic peak of his film career.

13 The Satellite Concert

Elvis' 1973 *Aloha from Hawaii via Satellite* concert was one of the most memorable shows he ever did—a true high point of his career.

What made the show different was that it was also broadcast live; not quite the "worldwide event" it's been hailed as, but impressive enough for that time. Parker had been contemplating such an event for Elvis for some years, possibly as a way to address the many requests he received for Elvis to tour internationally.

Dates were initially arranged for November 17 and 18, 1972, at the Honolulu International Center (today the Blaisdell Center Arena) in Hawaii but were later pushed back, as the documentary *Elvis On Tour* was scheduled to be released at the same time. The new date at the same venue was January 14, 1973, with a rehearsal show on January 12. The previously scheduled November shows went ahead as regular concerts.

Marty Pasetta, who'd directed television shows for acts ranging from Frank Sinatra to the Smothers Brothers as well as the

Academy Awards, was asked to direct. Marty saw Elvis perform at Long Beach Arena in November '72 and wasn't impressed. "He stood there like a lump," he later recalled. But he nonetheless met with Elvis and shared his ideas for the show, concluding by saying, "And you've got to lose weight, because you're too fat." Elvis threw back his head and laughed, then went over and hugged the startled director, telling him, "I'll do whatever you want me to do."

The stage set jazzed up Elvis' standard show, placing the band on a riser; Elvis' name and the silhouette of a guitar player projected on a rear screen; strips of mylar hanging from the ceiling to make the stage seem larger; and a runway that went into the audience, allowing Elvis to get closer to the fans. Parker had initially objected to the runway, but Pasetta insisted it was needed to enhance the show's visual appeal.

And Elvis had a terrific new outfit to show off his slimmed-down figure. He'd asked his costume designer, Bill Belew, to design a white jumpsuit studded with jeweled eagles—Elvis' way of saying "America" to the world. During rehearsals, Elvis impulsively gave away the jumpsuit's ruby-studded belt to the wife of *Hawaii 5-0* star Jack Lord, and Belew had to hurriedly round up enough jewels to create a new one and ship it over in time for the shows.

The January 14 show began at 1:00 AM in order to be seen in prime time by the countries that were carrying the live broadcast: Australia, Japan, Korea, New Zealand, the Philippines, Thailand, and South Vietnam. The following night, the show was broadcast in Europe, and it aired in America on April 4.

The show featured some rock 'n' roll ("Hound Dog," "Blue Suede Shoes," "Johnny B. Goode"), but it was the more dramatic numbers that drew the most powerful performances from Elvis: "You Gave Me a Mountain," "My Way," "I Can't Stop Loving You," and "What Now My Love." There were also sensitive performances of "I'm So Lonesome I Could Cry" and Kui Lee's "I'll Remember You" (the show was a benefit for the late performer's cancer fund). After "American Trilogy" (a dramatic medley of "Dixie," "All My Trials," and "Battle Hymn of the Republic") he was so caught up in the emotion of the song he threw his studded belt into the audience. "Can't Help Falling In Love" closed the show, after which Elvis hurled his cape into the audience. After the crowd left, he recorded five further songs, which were inserted into the U.S. broadcast of the show.

The ratings for the show were impressive, but the claim that the concert was seen by more than a billion people is exaggerated. It's been pointed out that the total population of all the countries that broadcast the show was 1.3 billion, meaning that everyone in those countries would have had to be watching the show for the billion-plus viewing figure to be accurate.

But there's no denying *Aloha From Hawaii* was a milestone in Elvis' career. The soundtrack album, released in February, reached No. 1; it was the last chart topper during Elvis' lifetime. The *Aloha From Hawaii Deluxe Edition* DVD (2004) has both concerts and bonus footage.

14 The Backing Musicians

In the 1950s, Elvis was backed by a great group of musicians: guitarist Scotty Moore, bassist Bill Black, and drummer D.J. Fontana.

Winfield Scott Moore III was born on December 27, 1931, on a farm outside of Gadsden, Tennessee. His father and brothers played music in their spare time; Scotty received his first guitar from one of his older brothers. His first performing experience came while he was in the navy; while stationed in Bremerton, Washington, his group had their own show on a local radio station.

Elvis Presley is seen on his theater tour in the summer of 1957. Scotty Moore is on guitar, and Bill Black is playing the stand-up bass. (AP Photo)

After leaving the service in 1952, he settled in Memphis, working at his brother's dry cleaning store. He played guitar with different bands, eventually forming his own, the Starlite Wranglers, in 1954. The bassist in the group was Bill Black.

William Patton Black Jr. was born on September 17, 1926, in Memphis. He grew up listening to his father play guitar; his first "instrument" was a makeshift guitar his father made for him out of a cigar box and strings. He was playing guitar in local bands by age 16; after his army service, he switched to upright bass. As a teenager, Elvis knew Bill's younger brother, Johnny, and may have seen Bill on occasion, although by then Bill was married and living in his own home. In contrast to Scotty, who was more reserved, Bill was prone to cracking corny jokes during performances and riding his bass like a bull.

Moore approached Sam Phillips about recording the Starlite Wranglers, and in May 1954 Sun Records released a single by the group, "Now She Cares No More For Me"/"My Kinda Carryin' On." The record didn't generate much excitement, but Scotty knew that Sam was the kind of person who could make things happen and made a point of coming by the studio regularly to chat and hang out.

As a result, when Sam was looking for someone to work with Elvis, he naturally turned to Scotty. Scotty had heard Sam and Marion Keisker talking about Elvis and was curious about the singer. Bill was also brought in to keep the instrumentation spare and better highlight Elvis' voice.

After recording the first single, Elvis appeared as a guest performer with Scotty and Bill backing him at two Starlite Wranglers shows at the Bon Air club in Memphis. But the other Wranglers were jealous of Elvis' rising success, and the group soon fell apart. Scotty also served as Elvis' manager for a brief period, until Memphis DJ and promoter Bob Neal took over in January 1955. It was Bob who dubbed Scotty and Bill "The Blue Moon Boys."

On Sun's singles, the records were credited to "Elvis Presley, Scotty and Bill."

As the group toured further and further afield in 1955, they decided they needed to add a drummer, and turned to D.J. Fontana, who was in the house band for the *Louisiana Hayride* radio show. Dominic Joseph Fontana was born on March 15, 1931, in Shreveport, Louisiana (where the *Hayride* show broadcast originated). He first played drums in his high school band then moved on to play in local groups. After Fontana's army hitch, he played drums at a Shreveport burlesque club. He later said following the movements of the strippers as he drummed was good practice for working with Elvis.

After playing occasional live shows with Elvis, D.J. officially joined the band in August 1955. The three musicians backed Elvis until 1958 and also appeared with him in the films *Loving You*, *Jailhouse Rock*, and *King Creole*.

But none of them were sharing in the financial rewards Elvis was enjoying, and despite Elvis' success, they were often in debt. Scotty and Bill resigned in September 1957 (D.J. had always been on a straight salary and didn't feel as aggrieved). Elvis hired them back the next month, but the feelings were never the same. The last time all three worked with Elvis was a recording session on February 1, 1958.

There's no doubt that Elvis was always the star of the show. But it was Scotty and Bill who helped him there. Add D.J. to the mix, and you get classic recordings like "Hound Dog" and "All Shook Up." Elvis was well served by his musicians.

Further reading: *Scotty & Elvis: Aboard The Mystery Train* by Scotty Moore and James L. Dickerson; *The Blue Moon Boys: The Story of Elvis Presley's Band* by Ken Burke and Dan Griffin.

15 The Best Dance Number in an Elvis Movie

Out of the 31 feature films that Elvis made during the course of his career, there's no doubt that *Jailhouse Rock* features the most memorable dance sequence.

Compared to the sunny atmosphere of his later films, *Jailhouse Rock* is surprisingly dark—even menacing. Elvis plays Vince Everett, who's sent to prison for manslaughter after accidentally killing another man in a bar fight. His cellmate, Hunk, is a former country singer, who gives Vince the idea to take up singing himself. After being released from prison, Vince meets Judy, a music promoter; the two start a record label and have an on-again/off-again romance. Further complications arise when Hunk is released from prison and expects Vince to help promote his career.

Jailhouse Rock is no lightweight entertainment. Vince's time in prison is harsh; in the film's most startling scene, he's stripped to the waist and his wrists tied to a bar above his head so he can be whipped. Nor is the realm of show business seen in a glamorous light. If not exactly run by mobsters (as in the brilliant rock 'n' roll satire *The Girl Can't Help It*, released the year before *Jailhouse Rock* and featuring performances by Little Richard, Gene Vincent, and Eddie Cochran), it's certainly unscrupulous, as seen when a record company executive blatantly steals the arrangement of one of Vince's demo recordings.

And Vince himself isn't especially nice. He's surly and rude in the beginning and arrogant and egotistical once he becomes a star, though he learns his lesson in the end. It's the only time Elvis ever played a character who's frankly unsympathetic at times, making you wonder how he would have fared if he'd had the opportunity

The Crowning of the King

Elvis was dubbed "The King of Rock 'n' Roll." But when did he get that title?

Promoters used a number of colorful phrases in describing Elvis in their advertising, including "the Hillbilly Cat," "the Memphis Flash," and "the Atomic Powered Singer." And it might have been a woman who first tied the word *king* to Elvis. In an article for the *Waco News Tribune* published on April 19, 1956, reporter Bea Ramirez described Elvis as "the 21-year-old king of the nation's rock 'n' roll set."

A month later, the key phrase appeared in an article in the *Memphis Press–Scimitar*. Robert Johnson covered Elvis' first appearance in Las Vegas in a May 4, 1956, article entitled, "The Golden Boy Reaches for a Star While The Music Goes Round and Round and—... oh, ho, ho-ho!" In noting that the more adult Vegas crowd wasn't overwhelmed by Elvis' performance, Johnson wrote, "The applause was scattered. A cold audience and the fledgling king of rock 'n' roll was in a foreign land."

It made sense for Elvis to be called the King of Rock 'n' Roll. He wasn't the first person to make a rock 'n' roll record, but he was the first rock 'n' roll singer to have such phenomenal success. But Elvis didn't like the designation. During the press conference following his opening in Vegas in 1969, he pronounced Fats Domino as the real king of rock 'n' roll. And when people called him the King, he'd respond, "The only King is Jesus."

to play a genuine bad guy all the way through a film. But he's also allowed to have some fun. In one scene, after storming out of a party Peggy's parents are hosting, Vince grabs Peggy and kisses her harshly. "How dare you think such cheap tactics would work with me!" Peggy fumes. Vince's response is perfectly timed: "That ain't tactics, honey. That's just the beast in me."

The "Jailhouse Rock" number was featured in a sequence where Vince rehearses for an upcoming television special. The song references Vince's time in the pen and has him performing in front of a stylized row of prison cells, then sliding down a pole to dance with the other cons. Alex Romero, the choreographer, showed Elvis the routine he'd devised for the number but quickly realized the dance moves wouldn't work for Elvis. Thinking fast, Alex asked Elvis to play some of his records and move to the songs as he would on stage; he re-choreographed the sequence using Elvis' own movements. Elvis got some further dance tips from future *West Side Story* star Russ Tamblyn, who was introduced to Elvis by a mutual friend.

While filming the dance number, Elvis' enthusiasm was such that he loosened one of the caps on his teeth, and then accidentally inhaled it. The surgery to retrieve it involved using an instrument to part Elvis' vocal cords to get into his lungs and remove the cap, which had a parallel in *Jailhouse Rock*'s plotline when Vince's own vocal cords become injured during a fight.

Jerry Leiber and Mike Stoller wrote all of *Jailhouse Rock*'s best numbers, starting with the title song itself; they also wrote "I Want to Be Free," "Treat Me Nice," and "(You're So Square) Baby I Don't Care." "Jailhouse Rock" was released as a single in September 1957, and it gave Elvis another chart-topping million-seller. There was no soundtrack album, although a five-track EP was released in October that topped the EP charts.

Jailhouse Rock had its premiere in Memphis on October 17, 1957, and the film was released nationally the following month. Sadly, co-star Judy Tyler, a *Howdy Doody* regular who played Peggy, didn't live to see the film; she and her husband were killed in a car accident on July 3, 1957. The film was an immediate commercial success and, like *King Creole*, it isn't just a great Elvis movie; it's also a great rock 'n' roll movie.

16 The Breakout Single

"Heartbreak Hotel" was the song that made Elvis a national star. He'd previously had records on regional charts and the country charts, but "Heartbreak Hotel" was an across-the-board smash and his first million selling record.

The song was co-written by Mae Boren Axton and Tommy Durden, who both lived in Jacksonville, Florida. Mae worked as a high school teacher but was also a songwriter and freelance writer. She also did publicity for Parker's tours in the area, which is how she met Elvis when he played a number of Florida dates in May 1955. Mae interviewed Elvis during his trip and took an instant liking to him, somewhat brashly telling him that she would write his first big hit.

Four months later, Durden, a local musician and songwriter, showed Axton an article in the *Miami Herald* about a man who'd committed suicide, leaving behind a note with the sole line: "I walk a lonely street." Both of them were struck by the dramatic possibilities of the incident and decided to write a song about it, quickly coming up with the title, "Heartbreak Hotel." They wrote the song just as fast—in 22 minutes by Durden's account. As the two were working on the song, a local DJ, Glenn Reeves, stopped by. He was asked to help write the song for a third of the writer's credit but was put off by the title. Reeves did agree to record a demo of the song and was again offered a songwriting credit as payment. To his eternal regret, he turned it down a second time.

In November, Mae headed to the Country Music Disc Jockey Convention in Nashville determined to present it to Elvis. They met up on November 10, and Elvis flipped when he heard the song, saying, "Hot dog, Mae, play it again!" Mae's dream came true when, after listening to the number over and over, Elvis told her, "That's gonna be my next record." Mae rewarded him by giving him a third of the writer's credit. By December, Elvis had added the song to his set list, announcing that it would be his next record.

"Heartbreak Hotel" was recorded at Elvis' first session for RCA on January 10, 1956, at the label's studio in Nashville. It's hard to appreciate today just how strange the song sounded back then. Its cold opening (there's no instrumental introduction, Elvis simply starts singing), the stark instrumentation, the brooding picture painted of the broken-hearted lover shedding his tears at the ominously named hotel with its desk clerk dressed in black as if in mourning, and Elvis' gulping, stuttering vocal made it quite different from the warm buoyancy of his Sun releases. Sam Phillips called it a "morbid mess," and Steve Sholes, the A&R executive who'd signed Elvis to RCA, was told he should get Elvis back into the studio to record something else for his debut single.

Sholes declined, and "Heartbreak Hotel"/"I Was The One" was released at the end of January. The single took some time to catch on, not entering the charts until the beginning of March, which certainly didn't calm any nerves at RCA. But it rose steadily over the next seven weeks and finally reached the top of the pop charts, No. 1 on the country charts, and No. 5 on the R&B charts. By the end of April, "Heartbreak Hotel" had sold more than 1 million copies.

17 The Comeback Single

It was the record that put the cherry on top of Elvis' success during his "comeback" period of 1968–69, his first No. 1 single since 1962 and the last 45 to top the charts during Elvis' lifetime. And yet it almost didn't happen.

During Elvis' first round of recording sessions at American Sound in January 1969, Chips Moman had brought in a song he was sure would be a great fit for Elvis, "Suspicious Minds." Mark James, a songwriter with Moman's publishing company, Press Music, had released the song himself as a single on Scepter (produced by Moman) the previous year, and it was not successful. But Chips felt the song had the potential to be a big hit, and after listening to it, Elvis agreed.

But then business problems arose. Chips owned publishing rights to the song, and he refused to give up any of them—a demand that Elvis' publishers required before the song could be cut. Representatives from Elvis' publishing companies applied considerable pressure, but Chips refused to budge, saying, "You can take your damn tapes and get the hell out of my studio. Don't ask me again."

"I think they were kind of shocked when I stood up to them," he later recalled. "They probably had never had anyone ask them to leave the studio before but I did, and it turned out to be better for Elvis." Indeed it did. RCA executive Harry Jenkins finally stepped in and said Chips didn't have to give up any of his publishing rights.

The song is about a relationship on the verge of falling apart due to suspected infidelity. Mark James' version has a plaintive, pleading vocal but lacks urgency. Elvis, using the same arrangement and the same musicians, created something far more powerful, a performance that only becomes more passionate as it goes on, especially in the song's unique extended ending. Elvis debuted the song during his season in Las Vegas in the summer of 1969, extending the number by singing the "caught in a trap/can't walk out" lines repeatedly, intently caught up in the song's emotions, lowering and raising the volume as he thrust his body to accentuate the beat, finally ending in a dramatic crescendo of sound.

The single, released in August 1969, tried to emulate the live performance by fading the song out, then fading it back up and continuing for another minute before the final fade out with horns and backing singers wailing alongside Elvis. "Suspicious Minds" had quickly become the high point of Elvis' live show, and fans were just as excited about the record; the single became another million seller and Elvis' first chart topper since "Good Luck Charm" in 1962.

But neither Chips nor the musicians liked the song's "false ending," which had been added after the sessions at American Sound by Elvis' regular producer, Felton Jarvis. "It sounded like a technical mistake is what it sounded like to me," keyboard player Bobby Emmons told me. Chips might have won the battle over the song's publishing rights, but he ended up losing the war; the wrangling over publishing, not receiving a producer's credit on the record, and now the altering of his work all rubbed the producer the wrong way. Although Elvis recorded some of his best work with Chips, he never returned to American Sound again.

18 The First Post-Army Album

The first album Elvis released after returning from the army was titled, naturally enough, *Elvis Is Back!* Though hardly a failure—it quickly reached No. 2 in the charts—it's nonetheless one of Elvis' most underrated albums.

In a sense, it was the first album that gave Elvis a chance to show what he could really do as a singer. Both the *Elvis Presley* and *Elvis* albums captured Elvis at the height of his rock 'n' roll years, *Elvis' Christmas Album* was limited to holiday music, and his other albums were soundtracks or hodge-podge collections like *For LP Fans Only* and *A Date With Elvis*.

The album could've been subtitled *Elvis Is Back And He's All Grown Up.* When Elvis recorded the album, he'd just turned 25 years old. And he now had greater command over his voice than he did when he first entered the recording studio. This is most apparent in "Fever," where the only instrumental accompaniment is provided by bass guitar, congas, and finger snaps, which really brings Elvis' voice to the forefront of this smoky, sultry number. His performance of "Reconsider Baby" (the album's closing track) is superlative, with the song's bluesy quotient underscored by Homer "Boots" Randolph's accents on saxophone. And there's the smooth sweetness of "I Will Be Home Again," which Elvis had discovered on an album by the Golden Gate Quartet, a group he'd learned about through Charlie Hodge, whom Elvis had met in the army; Hodge also provides a harmony vocal on the number.

Of course, Elvis hadn't forgotten how to cut loose, as he does on "Dirty, Dirty Feeling," originally written by Jerry Leiber and Mike Stoller for *King Creole* (but not used in the film), and the kind of number Elvis could breeze through with his eyes closed. "Make

Me Know It," by Otis Blackwell (Elvis had previously recorded Blackwell's "Don't Be Cruel" and "All Shook Up") also has the kind of upbeat good spirits that would've made it a good contender for a single.

Elvis Is Back! hits all the bases. There's the light pop of "Such A Night" and the catchy "Girl Next Door Went A' Walking." A mellower mood is conjured up by the romantic dilemma presented in both "The Girl of My Best Friend" and "Soldier Boy," a 1955 hit for the Four Fellows that was an obvious nod to Elvis' recent service (and a number he'd actually been practicing while he was in the service).

But it's the blues and rhythm & blues numbers that draw out the most emotive performances from Elvis; pop songs like "Stuck on You" (recorded during the same sessions) might provide the hits, but "Thrill of Your Love," "It Feels So Right," and "Like A Baby" showed that he could do so much more.

Elvis Is Back! sold 300,000 copies at the time of its release in April 1960; not bad, but it didn't compare to 700,000-plus sales for the *G.I. Blues* soundtrack released the same year (and which also performed better on the charts, reaching No. 1). It was an ominous sign of things to come; when commercial concerns outweighed artistic satisfaction, Elvis' career began to suffer. But *Elvis Is Back!* stands as a testament to what Elvis could achieve when the material he was given was equal to his talents.

19 Visit Tupelo

If you've made it to Memphis, it's well worth making the trip to Tupelo, Mississippi, to see where Elvis was born and spent the first 13 years of his life. It's not too far away; Tupelo is just 109 miles south of Memphis. Though it's certainly changed from when Elvis lived there in the 1930s and '40s, it still retains much of its small-town flavor.

The first place most Elvis fans head for when they reach Tupelo is the Elvis Presley Birthplace and Museum (www.elvispresleybirthplace.com). In addition to the (refurbished) two-room "shotgun shack" where Elvis was born, and a museum, the grounds also have a chapel, a commemorative statue, a gift shop, and other attractions; the actual building that once housed the Assembly of God church that the Presleys attended has also been moved to the grounds. Special events are occasionally held at the Birthplace throughout the year, and there's an Elvis Presley Festival held each June.

Be sure to take time to walk around the neighborhood; the Presleys lived on nearby Berry, Kelly, and Adams streets. Elvis' first school, East Tupelo Elementary (now Lawhon Elementary) is a 10-minute walk down the hill. It's a great way to get a better sense of what the area was like when Elvis lived there.

The Tupelo Convention & Visitor's Bureau has an Elvis Driving Tour map you can download from their website (www.tupelo.net) with directions to other local Elvis sites: Tupelo Hardware, where you can see the very display case that held the guitar Elvis' mother bought him for his 11th birthday; the courthouse, which was also the location of radio station WELO, where Elvis performed on Mississippi Slim's show; the fairgrounds where Elvis performed three times, commemorated with a new statue, as well as other sites. The Tupelo Automobile Museum and Oren Dunn City Museum have Elvis items on display and can fill you in on Tupelo's history.

Stop by the Visitor's Bureau to pick up a map if you have time; the staff is friendly and helpful. In fact, be sure to take the time to talk to people you meet at your various stops around town; Tupelo citizens are very proud of their native son and often have interesting anecdotes to share.

The books *The Field Guide to Elvis Shrines* (Bill Yenne) and *Roadside Elvis* (Jack Barth) have information about some more obscure sites, such as Elvis' various homes (both books are out of print, but can be found online). The website www.welovetupelo.com also has useful information and links. If you want to leave the driving to someone else, Mike's Memphis Tours (www.mikesmemphistours.com; the company is also on Facebook) offers day trips to Tupelo.

20 On Top on *Ed Sullivan*

Throughout 1956, Elvis was on various national television shows. But he knew he'd finally made it when he appeared on the top variety show in the country, *The Ed Sullivan Show*.

Sullivan had previously declined to book Elvis because of his price. And after Elvis' second, controversial appearance on *The Milton Berle Show*, Sullivan staunchly asserted that his program was for family audiences. But when Elvis drew top ratings on the rival program *The Steve Allen Show*, Sullivan changed his mind, and Elvis was quickly booked for three appearances.

Elvis first appeared on *Ed Sullivan* on September 9, 1956. Sullivan was recuperating from a car accident, so the show was hosted by actor Charles Laughton; Elvis' segment was broadcast from L.A., where he was filming *Love Me Tender*. Laughton showed off a selection of Elvis' gold records on the New York set, then introduced Elvis with a jaunty, "Away to Hollywood—to meet Elvis Presley." Elvis strolled out onto the set wearing a plaid jacket, modestly saying, "This is probably the greatest honor I've ever had in my life," then going into "Don't Be Cruel," strumming his guitar lightly, the camera focused above his waist. He then debuted "Love Me Tender," a slow ballad that wasn't going to make any TV censor nervous.

He was finally able finally cut loose during his second appearance on the show with "Ready Teddy," though the camera was quick to cut away when his body movements became too uninhibited (check out his facial expression during the song's instrumental break). Elvis then sent out a greeting to Sullivan ("We know that somewhere out there you're looking in…") before concluding with a short rendition of "Hound Dog."

Elvis next appeared on the show on October 28, 1956, in the New York studio with Sullivan hosting. After Sullivan's introduction, Elvis stood for a moment taking in all the screams, then he went into "Don't Be Cruel," laughing and cutting a few moves to get the girls in the audience screaming. But it's a playful performance, and the camera actually dared to show a few full-body shots. Then "Love Me Tender" again soothed the audience. He had two further spots in the show, first singing "Love Me," a country & western send-up by Jerry Leiber and Mike Stoller that Elvis delivered with perfect sincerity, and closing with "Hound Dog," with the usual jokey intro ("We're gonna do a sad song for you; this song here is one of the saddest songs we've ever heard") before doing an abbreviated version of the song, the camera daringly pulling back to capture his leg movements. Afterward, Elvis plugged the upcoming opening of *Love Me Tender* and his next appearance on *Ed Sullivan*, waving goodbye as he said, "Until we meet you again, may God bless you as He's blessed me."

Both shows got good ratings, but generated plenty of complaints, as well, causing concern that Elvis might be too hot for *Ed Sullivan* to handle. It was decided that for his next appearance, the camera would stay firmly focused above his waist. Perhaps that was why Elvis adopted a more exotic look for the show, wearing a velvet shirt and sparkling gold vest; maybe he knew that's all the home viewers would be able to see.

Elvis' third *Ed Sullivan* appearance was on January 6, 1957, and he opened with short renditions of "Hound Dog," "Love Me Tender," and "Heartbreak Hotel," then he took another spin through "Don't Be Cruel." Tantalizingly, the audience' screams revealed that Elvis was doing *something* with his body out of the camera frame, but no one at home could tell exactly what. In his next spot, he romped through "Too Much" and a more unusual choice, "When My Blue Moon Turns to Gold Again." The screams continued, but for his final number, Elvis looked suitably reverential as he performed "Peace in the Valley."

And then, Ed Sullivan gave Elvis his seal of approval, coming out to shake hands and state, "I wanted to say to Elvis Presley, and the country, that this is a real decent, fine boy." It was a moment of vindication for Elvis, and one that helped end the controversy about his "vulgar" movements.

Further reading: *Impresario: The Life and Times of Ed Sullivan* by James Maguire.

21 "My Best Girl": Gladys Presley

Elvis and his mother, Gladys, were especially close. More than one relative or friend observed that Elvis might have lived his life quite differently had his mother not died when he was only 23 years old.

Gladys Love Smith was born on April 25, 1912, in Pontotoc County, Mississippi, one of eight children. Her father was a tenant farmer, and Gladys grew up doing farm work too. Later as a young adult, she got work "in town," operating a sewing machine at the Tupelo Garment Factory for $2 a day.

Despite the hard financial times, Gladys had a spirited nature and loved to go out dancing. She was also deeply religious and attended the Assembly of God church in East Tupelo, where she met her future husband, Vernon Elvis Presley, who was born on April 10, 1916, in Fulton, Mississippi. Gladys first dated Vernon's brother Vester, while her younger sister, Clettes, dated Vernon. But the two couples soon switched partners. Gladys and Vernon married on June 17, 1933, two months after they met. (Clettes and Vester soon married, too.) Gladys was 21 but said she was 19; Vernon was 17 but said he was 22.

Because Elvis' twin had died at birth, Gladys was especially protective of her surviving son, and they grew even closer when Vernon was sent to prison. During the nine months he was away, Gladys and Elvis were forced to live with different relatives who had a spare bed. This shared adversity made the bond between mother and son especially tight.

Elvis recalled his mother continually watching over him, but he was just as concerned with her well-being. The two communicated in what seemed to others to be a secret language; Elvis called his mother "Satnin'" or "baby," and the two spoke of "sooties" (feet) or "iddytream" (ice cream). It was another sign of the closeness they felt for each other.

Elvis also felt a keen responsibility toward both his parents. When he graduated from high school and began full-time work, he gave most of his paycheck to his parents; as he explained to one of his girlfriends, they were getting older, and he needed to take care of them. As he began playing out-of-town dates, he sent the money he earned on the road back to his parents and faithfully called them every night.

If Gladys worried about Elvis as a child, she became increasingly concerned as his career took off. Prior to leaving for a tour,

Elvis' parents, Vernon and Gladys Presley. (AP Photo)

Gladys would ask Scotty Moore and Bill Black to "Look after my boy." Though she was glad when Elvis started taking his friends on the road to accompany him, she was alarmed at the frenzied reaction of the fans. When hearing that fans had stormed his dressing room after a show in Jacksonville, Florida, in 1955 and torn most of his clothes off, she was upset at the thought that he might get hurt. And when Elvis' career exploded in 1956, she was distressed at all the criticism he received for what critics called his "vulgar" and "obscene" stage antics.

Mostly, the intensity of Elvis' fame seemed to overwhelm her. As the money came in, Elvis never hesitated to lavish gifts on her

Elvis' Girlfriends: Anita Wood

The longest relationship Elvis had with a girlfriend before he met Priscilla was with Anita Wood, a young woman from Jackson, Tennessee.

Elvis first saw Anita in the summer of 1957 when the 19-year-old was a co-host on the Memphis TV show *Top 10 Dance Party*. He had Lamar Fike, a member of his entourage, call her to see if she was available for a date, but to Lamar's astonishment, Anita said she already had a date for the evening and couldn't break it. She worried she'd blown her chance with Elvis but was also not about to compromise. But Elvis was not put off, and when he had Lamar call her the next week, she agreed to go out with him. She was with Elvis for the next five years.

She found that Elvis could be possessive. He wanted her by his side when he was in Memphis and at Graceland with his family when he was out of town. He discouraged her from pursuing an acting career in Hollywood. And his manager wanted Anita to stay in the background so that Elvis would seem "available" to his fans.

Elvis had told Anita they would marry, but as the years passed, Anita became impatient. The breaking point came in the summer of 1962 when Anita found a letter Priscilla had sent to Elvis. Elvis had sworn to her that Priscilla meant nothing to him. But now Anita knew otherwise, and she broke up with Elvis soon afterward. She later married football player Johnny Brewer.

and hoped that Graceland would be her dream home. Instead, she only felt more isolated from her family and friends. Gladys would have been happier if Elvis would have settled down in Memphis, got married and started a family, and used the money he'd earned from singing to buy a nice little business.

When Elvis was drafted, Gladys became depressed at the thought of him going overseas. In the summer of 1958, Elvis' parents moved to Texas where Elvis was undergoing basic training, but they returned to Memphis on August 8 when Gladys became ill. She was diagnosed with hepatitis, and Elvis was given emergency leave August 12. He was able to see her before she died on August 14.

Elvis was devastated. A picture taken of him and Vernon on the steps at Graceland after Gladys' death with their arms around each other shows their faces etched in grief. His mother's death was a blow that Elvis never really recovered from.

Further reading: *Elvis and Gladys* by Elaine Dundy.

22 The Only Mrs. Elvis Presley

Elvis was linked with innumerable different women throughout his life. But he only married one of them: Priscilla Beaulieu.

Priscilla Ann Wagner was born on May 24, 1945, in Brooklyn. Her father was James Wagner, a navy pilot, who was killed six months after her birth in a plane crash while returning home on leave. In 1948 her mother, Ann, married Joseph Paul Beaulieu, an officer in the Air Force, with whom she had five more children.

Priscilla grew up a typical "military brat" and was used to moving every few years with her family. When she learned in 1959 that her father was being stationed in Germany, she joked with her friends that maybe she'd meet Elvis. The family arrived in Wiesbaden in August, and soon after, Priscilla met a mutual friend of Elvis' at the Eagles Club, a local hangout for military personnel and their families. The friend, Currie Grant, said he would take Priscilla to Elvis' home to meet him.

Their first meeting was on September 13, 1959. Elvis was instantly smitten, and Priscilla quickly became a regular visitor. The two spent hours in his bedroom talking (Priscilla has insisted they didn't do much beyond kissing), Elvis sharing his sadness over

Elvis and Priscilla Presley share a kiss for photographers just after their wedding on May 1, 1967, in Las Vegas. (AP Photo)

his mother's death and his fears about how his career would fare after his army service.

When his army hitch was up in March 1960, Elvis promised he'd stay in touch. Priscilla hoped that he would, but even at age 14 she was not completely naïve. She knew he already had a steady girlfriend, Anita Wood, waiting for him in Memphis, and he was constantly rumored to be dating the co-stars in his movies.

But Elvis did call Priscilla, and the two spoke regularly over the phone for the next two years. In June 1962, Elvis arranged for Priscilla to visit him in Los Angeles for two weeks. When she visited again at Christmas time, Elvis said he wanted her to stay for good. Priscilla had to return to school in Germany, but Elvis called her father and pressed his case. It's not known why he insisted on having Priscilla come over right then; she was already in her last year of high school and after graduation in June '63, she would have been free to return. Perhaps he just relished the challenge.

In any case, he was successful; Priscilla returned to Memphis in March 1963. She attended Immaculate Conception High School, an all-girls school, and was "officially" living with Elvis' father Vernon and his second wife, Dee, at their home around the corner from Graceland. In reality, she moved into Graceland and lived with Elvis. No reporter ever broke the story.

There are conflicting accounts of why Elvis finally decided to marry Priscilla. Some say there was pressure: from Captain Beaulieu, who reminded Elvis of his promise to marry Priscilla; from Elvis' manager, who wanted to avoid scandal; and from Priscilla herself. But in her autobiography, Priscilla wrote, "It was [Elvis'] decision and his alone." Though she admitted neither of them was happy with the quick wedding ceremony Elvis' manager arranged for them in a suite at the Aladdin Hotel in Las Vegas.

The couple was married on May 1, 1967, and became a family when Lisa Marie Presley was born the following year. But Elvis didn't change his ways. He'd seen other women before marrying Priscilla and continued to do so after he was married, especially when he returned to live performance and touring. Priscilla was also realizing what an insular life they lived, writing in her autobiography about Elvis' increasing dependence on "chemical aids" and being surrounded by an entourage "who distanced us from reality."

"There was a whole world out there, and I had to find my own place in it," she wrote elsewhere in the book. An affair with her karate instructor, Mike Stone, was her first step away from Elvis' world. The two separated at the end of 1971 and divorced on October 9, 1973. Priscilla later enjoyed a career as an actress (in the TV show *Dallas* and *The Naked Gun* film series). And she's also been instrumental in helping to keep Elvis' legacy alive, starting with her decision to open Graceland to the public in 1982.

Further reading: *Elvis and Me* by Priscilla Beaulieu Presley.

23 "Hound Dog" On *Milton Berle*

Elvis' first national television appearances in 1956 on *Stage Show* introduced him to the nation. But it was his second appearance on *The Milton Berle Show* that made him a sensation.

Elvis first appeared on Uncle Miltie's program on April 3, 1956. The show was broadcast from the deck of the aircraft carrier the USS *Hancock*, docked in San Diego. Elvis performed "Shake, Rattle and Roll," "Heartbreak Hotel," and "Blue Suede Shoes" before an enthusiastic audience of sailors and their screaming dates. Elvis was more confident and relaxed than he'd been on *Stage Show*, and Bill Black was so carried away during "Blue Suede Shoes" he turned his stand-up bass on its edge and rode it like a bull to wild cheers and applause (afterwards, Elvis' manager sternly told Black to never pull such a stunt again). Elvis also joked around with Berle, posing as Elvis' "twin brother" Melvin, and sang a reprise of "Blue Suede Shoes" while Berle tried to imitate Elvis' dancing style.

The show's success was such that Elvis was readily welcomed back for a second appearance on June 5, this time broadcast from NBC's studios in Los Angeles. Elvis first performed his latest single, the ballad "I Want You, I Need You, I Love You," after which Berle presented him with a Triple Crown award from *Billboard* for "Heartbreak Hotel." (The Triple Crown was awarded when a record topped the Best Sellers in Stores, Most Played on Jukeboxes, and Most Played by Disc Jockeys charts in the same week.)

The Elvis returned to do "Hound Dog," a song he hadn't recorded yet. Elvis romped through the song then paused at the end, stretched his arm out, and went into a slower paced vamp through the song's chorus, bumping and grinding his way around the mike stand, and knocking his knees together. He'd been making the same moves throughout the song, but slowing the tempo greatly emphasized them.

Berle bounded out on stage afterward, exclaiming, "How about my boy? I love him!" and getting the band to play a bit of "Hound Dog" again so he could get in a little dancing himself. He then engaged in some jokey patter with Elvis. At one point Elvis said he'd like to date a nice, quiet girl like Debra Paget, who was another guest on the show (she would soon be Elvis' co-star in his first film, *Love Me Tender*). Berle tried to dissuade him, saying Paget was "too sophisticated" for him, and bringing Paget out on stage to meet Elvis. Unsurprisingly, on being introduced, Debra ended up screaming, flinging her arms around Elvis, and giving him a big kiss.

It was all in good fun—at least until the reviews started coming in the next day. He was pilloried for his "grunt and groin" antics, "primitive physical movement difficult to describe in terms suitable to a family newspaper," as the *New York Journal-American* put it, a style "primarily identified with the repertoire of the blond bombshells of the burlesque runway," in the words of *The New York Times*.

It was the moment when Elvis fully realized the power of television. He'd been shaking and gyrating in performance for a few years now, generally in theaters and auditoriums and a few ballparks on occasion. And until 1956, most of those venues had been in the South. But television took him into every home across America. And by June of that year he'd become a star, meaning that more people probably watched him on *The Milton Berle Show* than had seen his *Stage Show* appearances.

It was also at this time Elvis acquired the nickname "Elvis the Pelvis," which he found embarrassing. He also insisted to the media he wasn't trying to be obscene in his act. And certainly when you watch him perform, it's clear there's a good deal of fun in his performance; he's the first to laugh at the fans' reactions to his movements. It was the first controversy of Elvis' career and, for better or worse, it did help boost his national profile.

24 Elvis and Las Vegas

Along with Memphis and Tupelo, the city of Las Vegas has a lot of associations with Elvis. When he returned to live performance in 1969, he played more shows in Vegas than in any other city.

Elvis first went to Vegas in 1956 when he appeared at the New Frontier Hotel's Venus Room from April 23 to May 6. But Elvis' brand of rock 'n' roll was too newfangled for Vegas, a city then steeped in the more traditional entertainment offered by the likes of Frank Sinatra and Dean Martin. More crucially, teenagers, Elvis' fan base, weren't allowed in the casinos or the lounges, though a special matinee performance was later scheduled for teens. So during his first Vegas season, Elvis was facing an audience primarily made up of adults more interested in seeing the subsequent acts on the bill—comedian Shecky Greene and Freddy Martin and his Orchestra.

But when he was offstage, Elvis found Las Vegas to be a terrific playground. He saw every show he could. And from 1960 to 1968, Elvis visited Vegas regularly. Sometimes it was for work, such as when *Viva Las Vegas* was shot there in 1963. And he got married in Vegas in 1967. But most of his visits were recreational, with Elvis and his friends enjoying all the nightlife Vegas had to offer.

In the wake of the *Comeback Special*, offers for Elvis to perform live came pouring in. But his manager was cautious. Instead of sending Elvis out on a major tour, he made Elvis' return to live performance a bona fide event by booking him at Las Vegas' newest hotel, the International. At the time the hotel opened in 1969, it had the biggest casino in town, and it was also the tallest building in the state. Elvis would not only generate buzz for his shows but also benefit from the publicity surrounding the opening of the hotel itself. Still, Parker chose not to let Elvis be the first act to perform at the International; he let that honor go to Barbra Streisand so all the bugs in the new venue would be fully worked out by the time Elvis took the stage.

Opening night was July 31, 1969, before a star-studded audience that included Pat Boone, Petula Clark, Phil Ochs, Ann-Margret, and Dick Clark, among others. Elvis got a standing ovation before he'd sung the first song, and the response at the show's end was nothing short of ecstatic. At the press conference following the show, Elvis happily stated, "This has been one of the most exciting nights in my life."

For the rest of the run through August 28, Elvis performed two shows a night, seven days a week. He was quickly booked for a second engagement at the International from January 26–February 23, 1970, and would return to the hotel every year through 1976: August 10–September 7, 1970; January 26–February 23 and August 9–September 6, 1971; January 26–February 23 and August 4–September 4, 1972; January 26–February 23 and August 6–September 3, 1973; January 26–February 9 and August 19–September 2, 1974; March 18–April 1 and August 18–August 20, 1975; December 2–December 15, 1975; and December 2–December 12, 1976. It was a remarkable run of 837 shows.

Elvis' Vegas seasons were documented on the albums *Elvis In Person at the International Hotel* (1969), *On Stage* (1970), and the film and soundtrack of *Elvis: That's The Way It Is* (1971). The former International Hotel (later the Hilton and now the Las Vegas Hilton) has a 6', 400-lb. bronze statue of Elvis in the lobby with a plaque that reads in part: "All of us at the Las Vegas Hilton were always proud to present Elvis in our showroom. The decorations in the hotel, the banners, the streamers, 'Elvis, Elvis' always created excitement with his loyal fans and friends. The Las Vegas Hilton was Elvis' home away from home."

25 The First Documentary Film

The 1970 documentary film *Elvis: That's The Way It Is* captures Elvis at the height of his Las Vegas years.

Though albums had been released drawing on Elvis' 1969 and 1970 winter Vegas seasons, nothing had been filmed. In fact, Elvis hadn't been filmed in a live concert situation since his 1956 dates in Tupelo. He was also planning to tour again, having tested the waters with some dates in Houston, Texas, in February and March 1970, and a concert film would provide some excellent promotion for future touring.

Filming began on July 14, 1970, at MGM's studio in Culver City, California, with a film crew shooting a few days of rehearsals. Elvis tends to play to the camera, and the rehearsing doesn't always seem all that serious. But it's nonetheless fascinating watching Elvis at work. More rehearsal footage was shot in Vegas. The cameras were also there on opening night, August 10, and continued filming through August 13; a total of 17 songs from the live shows appear in the film. Live footage from a September 9 date in Phoenix was also included in the film's opening sequence.

There is no voice-over narration, which keeps the viewer at something of a distance. You never know what Elvis is thinking or why he chooses the songs he does. His thoughts on how performing has changed since the 1950s would also have been interesting to hear, for example. Director Denis Sanders attempted to flesh out the story by including interviews with fans and employees of the International Hotel. But there's no interview with anyone close to Elvis, such as his musicians. It's simply a straightforward record of how his show comes together.

Elvis: That's The Way It Is opened on November 11, 1970. The album of the same name was released the same month. But despite its name, it wasn't exactly a soundtrack. Only four live songs from the Vegas season were featured; the remaining songs were studio recordings from sessions in Nashville in June 1970 with applause dubbed in. It reached No. 21 in the charts and soon sold more than half a million copies. The single "You Don't Have to Say You Love Me," released in October '70, did even better, reaching No. 11 and selling more than 800,000 copies.

In 2001, a special edition of the film was released on DVD. Instead of compiling unreleased material separately, it was decided to re-edit the entire film. The new version does have more songs from the live shows (21). But it also cut all of the interview footage. It's true that the fan footage in particular can seem hokey, at times odd (as in listening to two fans describe how their cat likes Elvis), and even a little alarming (as when one fan threatens to send the filmmakers "a dirty little letter" is he doesn't like the movie). But in context, it makes sense; the film is about the Elvis phenomenon as much as it is about the show. And given that the director didn't speak to Elvis or any of his musicians or associates, the only interviewees available were fans and hotel employees; outside observers, just like those who'd later see the movie.

Cutting these scenes left the impression that the team that worked on the reissue was embarrassed by the footage. It was also disrespectful to Sanders' original work (Sanders died in 1987). A better compromise would have been to reissue the original film along with a supplementary bonus film of outtakes.

Fortunately, the 2007 DVD reissue includes both edits (the first time the 1970 edit had appeared on DVD). This is the edition to get, as each edit has songs that don't appear in the other version, and there are bonus outtakes to boot. Watch both edits yourself and see which version you prefer. The album was also reissued in a special edition in 2000, featuring more rehearsal material, and as well as an entire show.

Considering how many live shows Elvis did, especially in the '70s, there's surprisingly little official live footage of him. This alone makes *Elvis: That's The Way It Is* (the 2007 reissue) essential. What you see is Elvis in his '70s concert prime: vigorous, enthusiastic, and wonderfully athletic.

26 The Death of Elvis

Elvis' death on August 16, 1977, came as a great shock to his fans around the world. And there is still controversy over the actual cause of his death.

Elvis woke up around 4:00 PM on August 15, as was his habit by that time; he stayed up all night and slept during the day. He tried to arrange for a private screening of Gregory Peck's new film, *MacArthur*, but no prints could be located. So he and his girlfriend, Ginger Alden, went out for a late night dentist appointment at 10:30 PM. They were back by 12:30 AM, and a few hours later, Elvis

Elvis' Girlfriends: Ginger Alden

Ginger Alden was Elvis' last serious girlfriend and the last person to see him alive.

Elvis met Ginger on November 19, 1976, when Elvis' friend, George Klein, brought Ginger and her two sisters, Rosemary and Terry, out to Graceland to meet him. It was Ginger, that year's Miss Mid-South Fair winner, who caught Elvis' fancy. She had just turned 20. They'd actually met when she was five, on one of the nights he rented out the Mid-South Fairgrounds; Ginger's father had also been a public relations officer for the army and was present at Elvis' induction.

By the end of the month, Ginger was accompanying Elvis on tour. But their relationship was a bumpy one. She already had a boyfriend and took her time in breaking up with him. She sometimes balked at going on Elvis' tours, saying she missed her family (Elvis often ended up flying her relatives out to accompany them). She spent time at Graceland but refused to move in. Elvis persisted in trying to win her over, buying her jewelry and cars. And in January, according to Ginger, he proposed to her. Whether he would have gone through with the marriage is a subject of dispute.

Elvis occasionally still went out with other women, but Ginger was his main girlfriend; she can seen briefly in the *Elvis In Concert* TV special when Elvis introduces her to the audience. It was Ginger who found Elvis on the floor at Graceland and first summoned help. But it was too late for the man she'd known just nine months.

summoned his cousin, Billy Smith, and his wife, Jo, who lived at Graceland, to join him and Ginger for a game at Graceland's racquetball court. After knocking around a few balls, Elvis entertained everyone by playing a few songs on the piano in the lounge of the building; the last number was said to be Willie Nelson's "Blue Eyes Crying in the Rain" (which he'd actually recorded at Graceland the previous year).

Elvis and Ginger then retired to his bedroom to try and get some sleep; they were flying out later that day in advance of Elvis' next tour, scheduled to start August 17 in Portland, Maine. But sleep didn't come easy. Elvis took three packets of prescription medication, then told Ginger he was going into the bathroom to read. When she awoke and checked on Elvis in the bathroom around 2:00 PM, she found him lying face down on the floor; he'd also vomited.

Elvis was rushed to the hospital, but despite resuscitation efforts, it was clear it was too late. Elvis had been dead when he was found on the floor in the bathroom at Graceland; he was officially declared dead at 3:30 PM.

At a press conference that evening, Shelby County medical examiner Dr. Jerry Francisco stated that Elvis' death was "due to cardiac arrhythmia due to undetermined heartbeat." Dr. Eric Muirhead, chief of pathology at Baptist Memorial and also present at the press conference, was surprised at Francisco's remarks, not least because Elvis' autopsy was still going on. But for many this would be the final word: Elvis died of a heart attack.

Still, stories that Elvis' death was drug-related began to circulate. Blood samples had been sent to two different laboratories for testing, and both revealed the presence of up to 14 different drugs in his system, leading to a belief that the true cause of death was polypharmacy (a fatal drug interaction). Some of Elvis' associates continued to deny he had a problem with drugs, even though the lab results indicated that he was a heavy user. "We respected his privacy no matter," Joe Esposito explained. "I was with him for 17 years, and for me protection was an automatic thing."

At the time, drug abuse was seen as more of a character flaw than a medical and psychological problem. Some of Elvis' fans didn't want to believe he used drugs, let alone that they played a role in his death. The debate continued, to the point that in 1994 the autopsy was reexamined.

Toxicologists who participated explained that improved testing would show that the actual amount of drugs in Elvis' system was lower than previously established. And Dr. Joseph Davis, former chief medical examiner of Dade County, Florida, who looked at all the autopsy materials, explained to the authors of *Down at the End of Lonely Street* that Elvis' death was indeed due to a heart attack. He pointed out the position of Elvis' body when it was discovered indicated a sudden, violent seizure; that it takes hours to die of a drug overdose and Elvis had been dead for some time when he was found; and that pulmonary edema is an "almost certain" sign of a death by drug overdose, but that Elvis had a very dry set of lungs.

So Elvis' death wasn't due to an overdose. But could it still have been drug-related? Possibly. Elvis was in poor health due to a number of factors, including his weight, his diet, his lack of exercise, and his drug abuse. As Priscilla put it, "The last year of his life was rough.... He wasn't happy. As a result, he abused his body. It was that abuse that killed him."

Further reading: *The Death of Elvis* by Charles C. Thompson II and James P. Cole; *Down at the End of Lonely Street: The Life and Death of Elvis Presley* by Peter Brown and Pat Broeske.

27 Soldier Boy

Elvis' army service disrupted his career at its height. But it could have turned out quite differently.

In the 1950s, all men in the U.S. were required to register for military service and, once drafted, serve for two years. Elvis went through his pre-induction physical on January 4, 1957, and was informed he would be drafted in December of that year. He picked up his induction papers himself on December 20, 1957.

Parker insisted that Elvis not ask for any special treatment during his hitch. But Elvis didn't have to ask—each branch of the military readily offered different ways in which Elvis could do

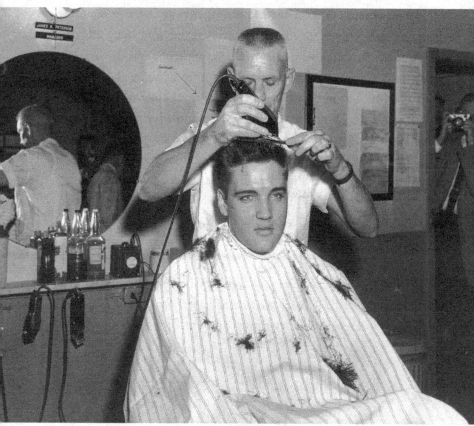

Elvis Presley gets his hair cut at Fort Chaffee in Barling, Arkansas, on March 25, 1958. According to the U.S. Army, Presley entered the service on March 24, 1958. (AP Photo/File)

his service. The navy suggested setting up a special Elvis Presley company. The air force's idea was to send Elvis on a tour of recruitment centers as a means of encouraging people to enlist.

Had Elvis accepted such a deal, it certainly would have drawn some criticism. But would it have mattered? The United States was not at war at the time, making his presence in the field less essential. And even during times of war, numerous entertainers had served their country in a similar fashion in the Special Services division without facing disapproval. And those who would've complained the most about Elvis taking such a route were hardly his target audience.

Nonetheless, Elvis agreed to take his manager's advice; Elvis would do his service like an ordinary soldier, though he did ask for, and receive, a deferment so he could complete work on the film *King Creole*. But "ordinary soldiers" are hardly subjected to the unpleasant treatment Elvis received when he was inducted on March 24, 1958, when he was paraded before reporters during his physical while wearing nothing but his underwear, being photographed, and having to be a "good sport" about it all. He was also photographed the next day when his hair was cut—seen as the symbolic shearing of the one-time rebel. It wasn't until Elvis arrived at Fort Hood in Killeen, Texas, on March 28 that he was finally shielded from the media.

After completing basic training, Elvis was allowed to live off base with his legal dependents, his parents, which gave him a place to relax in private when he was off duty. When he learned he was being assigned to the 3rd Armored Division, stationed in Friedberg, West Germany, he also arranged for his family to accompany him there. Having his family around helped to make him a little less homesick.

Elvis left Fort Hood by train on September 19, 1958, en route to Brooklyn. It was during the trip he met fellow soldier and musician Charlie Hodge, a member of the Foggy River Boys; Charlie helped keep Elvis' spirits up in the wake of his mother's death, and quickly became a member of Elvis' inner circle. He sailed for Germany on September 22, walking up the gangplank of the USS *Randall* eight times for the benefit of photographers; excerpts of the press conference held that day were soon made available on the EP *Elvis Sails*.

He arrived in Germany on October 1. His father, grandmother Minnie (Vernon's mother), and friends Red West and Lamar Fike arrived three days later, first living at a hotel in Bad Nauheim, later renting a house. Elvis frequently invited his friends over for meals and parties; it was at one such party that he met his future wife, Priscilla Beaulieu. Another new friend he met in the service was Joe Esposito, who also became a member of Elvis' entourage.

When on leave, Elvis took his friends to Munich and Paris where they spent the time nightclubbing. The rest of his time in Germany was largely uneventful, as he focused on being a good soldier. "He did what you asked him to do," then-lieutenant William Taylor told me. "And he did it better than most people. He was a good guy." Elvis was nonetheless glad when his hitch was up. He was promoted to full sergeant a month before he was finally mustered out on March 5, 1960.

When Beatle John Lennon was asked for a comment in the wake of Elvis' death, he famously responded, "Elvis died when he went into the army." And while that's certainly an exaggeration—Elvis made a lot of great music after he left the service—it's true that his career never again had the momentum that it did in the '50s.

Further reading: *Elvis In The Army* by William Taylor; *Sergeant Presley: Our Untold Story of Elvis' Missing Years* by Rex and Elisabeth Mansfield, Marshall and Zoe Terrill.

28 The Singles that Charted a New Course

A few ballads aside, Elvis was mostly associated with rock 'n' roll in the 1950s. But when he got out of the army, it didn't take long for him to assert that he was interested in taking his music in a completely new direction.

"Stuck On You," the first single Elvis released after he left the army, definitely had a rock swing. But his next two singles, "It's

Now or Never" and "Are You Lonesome Tonight?," revealed a more adult singer, a mature performer who was in full command of his vocal prowess.

This was especially true of "It's Now or Never." The song's melody was based on the classic Italian aria "O Sole Mio," written in 1898; Enrico Caruso's version of the song was a big favorite of Elvis' mother. In 1949, singer Tony Martin recorded the song with new English lyrics, entitled "There's No Tomorrow." Elvis heard Martin's version when he was stationed in Germany and liked the song so much he added it to the impromptu sing-a-longs he held around the piano in his Bad Nauheim home (he recorded some of these sing-a-longs; a brief bit of "There's No Tomorrow" can be heard on the 1997 box set *Platinum*).

Elvis told his publisher, Freddy Bienstock, he wanted to record the song. The song was in the public domain, meaning new lyrics could be written for it, and Bienstock commissioned Wally Gold and Aaron Schroeder to write them. (Schroeder had previously co-written songs for Elvis, including "I Was the One" and "Stuck On You.") Elvis showed a masterful control of his voice; delicate and gentle during the verses, stronger and more forceful during the chorus. A fan of film and singing star Mario Lanza, "It's Now or Never" gave Elvis a chance to have his own operatic moment.

But he had trouble reaching the song's final high note, and said in despair to Schroeder, who was in the studio when the song was being recorded, "I'm sorry, Aaron. I don't know if I can do this song justice." Elvis was told they could simply splice on a better take of the final notes, but he was determined to do the song straight through, telling the engineer, "I'm going to do it all the way through, or I'm not going to do it." And on the fourth take, he got it right.

"Are You Lonesome Tonight?" was also an older song, first recorded in 1927. Elvis recorded it at his manager's request—it was said to be his wife's favorite song—though there's some indication it was another song he played during those home sing-a-longs in Germany. He may have heard Jaye P. Morgan's version of the song that was released in 1959.

In another performer's hands, the song's sentimentality could've become mawkish. But there was no hint of parody in Elvis' approach; it was straightforward, heartfelt, and unabashedly romantic. And he likewise delivered the song's spoken word bridge with the utmost sincerity. The song had minimal instrumentation—just guitar and bass—with the Jordanaires providing backing vocals. Elvis also asked that the lights be put out in the studio, which greatly enhanced the atmosphere. Even so, he was again initially uncertain if he could do a good enough job, and again worked until he could sing the song all the way through.

"It's Now or Never" was released in April 1960, and "Are You Lonesome Tonight?" was released in November 1960, Elvis' second and third post-army singles. Both singles were immediate hits and strong sellers, topping the charts not only in the U.S. but around the world. And those who thought of Elvis solely as a rock 'n' roll singer realized that he was capable of much more.

29 Elvis' Daughter: Lisa Marie

Lisa Marie Presley is Elvis' only child.

Priscilla became pregnant very soon after her marriage to Elvis. She was initially a little dismayed. Although the couple wanted to have children, Priscilla had hoped to spend more time with her husband on their own before starting a family. Elvis sensed her apprehension; when she briefly considered having an abortion, Elvis told her, "I'll back you up whatever you want to do." "He

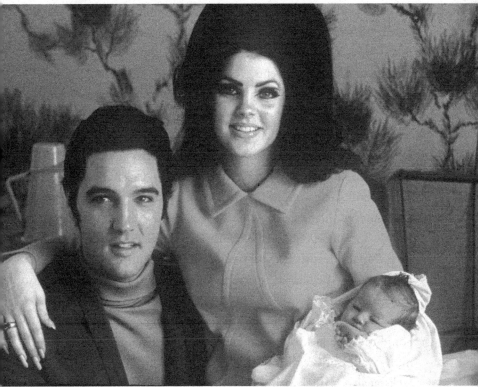

Lisa Marie Presley was born on February 1, 1968, to Elvis and Priscilla Presley. (AP Photo)

was leaving the decision up to me," Priscilla wrote in her autobiography. "'It's our baby,' I said, sobbing. 'I could never live with myself, neither could you.'"

When the news Priscilla was pregnant was publicly announced, Elvis proclaimed that he was "ecstatic," though some apprehension remained for him. Seven months into her pregnancy, Priscilla was stunned when Elvis said he wanted a trial separation. Instead of pressing him for reasons why, Priscilla swallowed her anxiety and agreed. But Elvis never brought up the subject again.

Both parents were thrilled when Lisa Marie was born on February 1, 1968; "She's a little miracle," Elvis proclaimed enthusiastically. The two doted over the child, and when Elvis began traveling more after he returned to performing live, Priscilla made sure to send him plenty of photographs of his growing daughter. After her parents' marriage ended, Lisa primarily lived with her mother, though she regularly visited her father. Priscilla later commented that their parenting differed—Elvis was far more lenient with their daughter than she was.

Lisa, like her mother, became a Scientologist and met her first husband, Danny Keough, at the Scientology Celebrity Centre in Hollywood. The couple married on October 3, 1988, and had two children, Danielle (now an actress, she uses her middle name, Riley), born in 1989, and Benjamin, born in 1992. They divorced in 1994, and less than three weeks later, Lisa surprised her family by marrying Michael Jackson on May 26, 1994. The marriage was not immediately announced, and when the news became public, there was skepticism about the union being a "real" marriage. Some thought Jackson was merely trying to rehabilitate his image in the wake of the child abuse allegations that had erupted in 1993; Jackson had settled with the family of his accuser in 1994. In an interview on the TV show *Prime Time*, the couple was even asked if they had sex. "Yes! Yes! Yes!" Lisa responded.

Lisa later said she felt sorry for Michael and had hoped she could "save" him. But the marriage ended in 1996. Her next marriage was even shorter; she married actor Nicholas Cage on August 10, 2002, and on November 25, 2002, Cage filed for divorce (the divorce was finalized in 2004). On January 22, 2006, Lisa married musician Michael Lockwood, and in 2008 she gave birth to twin girls, Harper and Finley.

When Elvis announced his wife's pregnancy, his manager had stated, "I've already got a contract drawn up for the new Presley singer." Lisa did indeed become a singer, starting her career in music with a bang, unveiling a video of the song "Don't Cry Daddy," which showed her singing with her father at the first *Elvis In Concert* performance held August 16, 1997, in Memphis. (She did another similar duet with her father in 2007, performing the song "In The Ghetto.") But she didn't release her first album, *To Whom It May Concern*, until 2003; it reached No. 5 in the charts. *Now What*, released in 2005, reached No. 9. And though 2012's *Storm & Grace* fared less well on the charts, the rootsy album received stronger reviews in contrast to her previous more pop-oriented releases. Lisa's husband, Michael, also plays guitar on the album.

In 2010, Lisa and her family moved to England where she bought a home in Tunbridge Wells, 40 miles south of London. While she sold a majority interest in Elvis Presley Enterprises in 2005, she retains full ownership of the Graceland property and her father's personal effects.

30 How to Have It All

In the 23 years Elvis was a recording artist, he released an amazing amount of records: 105 singles, 29 EPs, and 75 albums. That's 209 different releases. You needn't buy them all; many of the EPs simply duplicate material on an album, for example. But it can be tricky to compile a complete collection of Elvis recordings.

You could get it all in one fell swoop by purchasing the box set *The Complete Elvis Presley Masters*, which includes everything Elvis officially released during his lifetime. It's a lovely set, but it comes with a prohibitive price tag: $749.00, not counting tax and shipping.

But it's still possible to assemble a complete collection by buying other releases. Here's one way to do it (all albums are on CD and released by RCA, unless noted).

The '50s are the easiest; just buy the box set *The King of Rock 'n' Roll: The Complete '50s Masters* (1992) that contains every song officially released during that decade. You might want to add *Sunrise* (1999) if you want the four songs Elvis recorded before he signed with Sun Records.

I Believe: The Gospel Masters (2009) has nearly all of Elvis' religious recordings, and compilations like *If Every Day Was Like Christmas* (1994) or *Christmas Peace* (2003) have all of Elvis' holiday recordings.

On to the '60s. *From Nashville To Memphis: The Essential '60s Masters* (1993) has all of Elvis' non-soundtrack, non-religious recordings. As for those soundtracks, *G.I. Blues* and *Blue Hawaii* were released in expanded editions in 1997. Songs from Elvis' other movies were released in the *Double Features* series: *Harum Scarum/Girl Happy; Viva Las Vegas/Roustabout; Kid Galahad/Girls! Girls! Girls!; It Happened at the World's Fair/Fun in Acapulco* (all 1993); *Frankie and Johnny/Paradise Hawaiian Style; Spinout/Double Trouble; Kissin' Cousins/Clambake/Stay Away Joe* (all 1994); *Flaming Star/Wild in the Country/Follow That Dream; Easy Come, Easy Go/Speedway; Live a Little, Love a Little/The Trouble With Girls/Charro!/Change of Habit* (all 1995). *The Complete '68 Comeback Special* (2008) has all the songs featured in the special, including all four of the live concerts.

In the '70s, *Elvis Country: Legacy Edition* (2012) has songs that appeared on *Elvis Country, Love Letters From Elvis,* and *Elvis Now. Elvis At Stax: Deluxe Edition* (2013) has all the songs Elvis recorded at Stax in 1973 that appeared on *Raised On Rock/For Ol' Times Sake, Good Times,* and *Promised Land.* The expanded edition of *Moody Blue* (2000) has songs from the albums *From Elvis Presley Boulevard* and *Moody Blue* (though not the live tracks that appeared on the original edition of the latter album). The compilation *Burning Love* (1999) collects key tracks from the period, and CD reissues of *Elvis Now, Elvis* (also known as the *Fool* album, to

Before the Colonel

Once "That's All Began" began generating acclaim, Sam Phillips suggested Scotty Moore become Elvis' manager, and the two signed a contract on July 12, 1954. It was only a temporary measure. Elvis needed a buffer between him and other promoters, and Scotty was happy to fill that role until someone more suitable could be found.

That person ended up being Bob Neal, a DJ on WMPS in Memphis, who also booked shows. Neal first saw Elvis when he added him to the bill of a Slim Whitman show at the Overton Park Shell in Memphis on July 30, 1954. Neal was instantly impressed by Elvis, and soon began booking shows for him. He officially became Elvis' manager on January 1, 1955.

Neal set up appearances for Elvis all over the South. He also booked Elvis' first date outside the South, in Cleveland, and secured an audition for *Arthur Godfrey's Talent Scouts* in New York City.

But Neal also began an association with Tom Parker in 1955, arranging to have Elvis join tour packages Parker was booking, which would lead to the end of his managerial role in Elvis' career. As Parker ingratiated himself with Elvis, Neal was pushed to the side. And when Neal's contract with Elvis expired in 1956, he lost Elvis for good.

distinguish it from the 1950s album of the same name), *Raised On Rock/For Ol' Times Sake* and *Today* and will pick up the stray tracks.

As for the live albums, *On Stage: Legacy Edition* (2010) has both *Elvis In Person* and *On Stage*; *Elvis: That's The Way It Is: Special Edition* (2000) is an expanded version of that live release; *Prince From Another Planet* (2012) is an expanded version of *Elvis As Recorded At Madison Square Garden*; *Aloha From Hawaii Via Satellite: Legacy Edition* (2013) is an expanded version of the Hawaii shows. The Follow That Dream edition of *Elvis As Recorded Live On Stage In Memphis* (2004) features the entire concert. (Follow That Dream is an official collector's label we'll talk about later.)

That's 31 different releases. It's still not quite everything Elvis released during his lifetime. It doesn't include the spoken-word releases *Elvis Sails* or *Having Fun With Elvis On Stage*, the *Elvis: A*

Legendary Performer series that featured some rarities, or *Welcome to My World* (1977) that features an alternate take of "Make the World Go Away." Some people might add *Elvis In Concert*, recorded on his final tour, though it wasn't released until November 1977. But it's certainly enough to qualify as the core collection. And while some of these releases are no longer in print, they're fairly easy to find on resale sites like Amazon or eBay.

31 The Memphis Mafia

As soon as Elvis began touring extensively, he developed an entourage. He liked having people around him who he could trust, and he had first asked members of his family to accompany him on the road. His entourage steadily expanded over the years and was eventually given a nickname: the Memphis Mafia.

Before his army hitch, the primary members of Elvis' entourage were his cousins Gene and Junior Smith, high school friend Robert "Red" West, DJ Cliff Gleaves, Lamar Fike (who knew both Gleaves and another high school friend of Elvis' who was also a DJ, George Klein), and Alan Fortas, another of Klein's friends. The entourage didn't just hang out with Elvis; they sometimes lived with him, and when they traveled together, Elvis would pick up the tab for their room and board.

While in the army, Elvis met Joe Esposito and Charlie Hodge, who would both become key members of the group. After the army, West's cousin, Delbert "Sonny" West, Marty Lacker, another of Klein's friends, Elvis' cousin Billy Smith, and Jerry Schilling, who first met Elvis as a young teen in the '50s, became members of the gang. The number of people in the group fluctuated over the years, and the line between "entourage" and "good friend" could be a thin one. George Klein, for example, was very much a member of the inner circle, but due to his job as a DJ in Memphis, he didn't travel with Elvis as much as other core members of the group.

It was in the early '60s that the gang became dubbed the Memphis Mafia because of their uniform appearance when they'd hit a hot spot like Las Vegas, all attired in dark mohair suits and wearing dark glasses; they're also sometimes jointly referred to as "the Guys." The Memphis Mafia was like an extended family—most of them lived with Elvis, joined in on all of his activities, and stayed with him whenever he traveled.

Because most people saw Elvis surrounded by the Memphis Mafia when he was in public, the Guys were often seen as simply hangers-on and yes-men, sycophants who hung around to indulge Elvis' every whim. Actually, the Mafia all had various duties, which could range from making travel arrangements, to booking the local movie house for private screenings, to working on stage lighting for Elvis' shows, to serving as bodyguards and providing general security. They served as intermediaries between Elvis and the public, and their first loyalty was always to Elvis.

But the fact that the Mafia was around Elvis all of the time did provoke some consternation. Women who went out on a date with Elvis were surprised to find that often meant being accompanied by the Mafia. And once Elvis got married, Priscilla frequently expressed frustration at not being able to be alone with her husband. As she told Becky Yancey, a secretary who worked at Graceland, "Somebody's always there, everywhere we go. A bunch of guys and their wives are always around. We never have any privacy."

The Guys each received a salary, though it was never very much; $250 a week in the '60s, up to $425 a week in the '70s. But they also received room and board, and the occasional lavish gift from Elvis—jewelry, cars, and in some cases, a house. This occasionally resulted in jealousy; if one person was given a car, the others would want one, too. Members of the Mafia have also talked about constantly vying with each other for Elvis' attention.

Toward the end of his life, most of the original Memphis Mafia members were no longer with Elvis, some leaving by choice, others having been fired. Elvis' father, for one, always thought Elvis spent too much money keeping his friends around and was never sorry to see anyone go. But Elvis continued to need to have people around him that he could unwind with. Gordon Stoker of the Jordanaires referred to the Memphis Mafia as "just friends that moved in, so to speak. Elvis needed those guys to say, 'Hey man, you look great this morning, your hair is beautiful, your eyes are beautiful, oh man, that's a beautiful shirt you've got on.' He needed that all the time."

32 The "Bodyguard Book"

When *Elvis: What Happened?* was first published on August 1, 1977, it was shocking to many fans. Elvis was viewed by the public as an all-American boy who was respectful to his elders, had served his country proudly, and held an abiding faith in God. Then came a startling expose from members of his own inner circle, depicting Elvis as a compulsive womanizer, a drug addict, and someone dangerously prone to violence, as in the book's opening chapter where he contemplates hiring a hit man to kill his ex-wife's new boyfriend.

Co-author Sonny West asserted that the book was really meant to help Elvis. "He will read [the book] and he will get hopping mad at us because he will know that every word is the truth," Sonny explained. "But maybe, just maybe, it will do some good...if he can realize what he is doing to himself." Good intentions aside, it's unlikely what was later dubbed the "bodyguard book" would have been written in the first place if the book's authors, which included Red West and Dave Hebler as well as Sonny, hadn't been fired by Elvis the previous year.

Red attended high school with Elvis, earning his friendship by stepping in on two occasions to prevent Elvis from being beaten up by fellow students. It was useful training for a future bodyguard. Red introduced his cousin, Sonny, to Elvis shortly before he went into the army, and Sonny became a full-fledged member of the Memphis Mafia when Elvis returned to Memphis after his army service. Dave Hebler joined the group later; he was a karate instructor Elvis met in 1972.

There had been disagreements between the men and Elvis in the past—Sonny had left after having an argument with Elvis in the early '60s, and Red had left when he wasn't invited to attend Elvis' wedding—but everyone had always come back to the fold. And prior to being let go in 1976, no one had any sense that Elvis might be unhappy. So all three men were stunned to be told on July 13, 1976, that they were being fired.

Adding to the shock was that the three were given the bad news not by Elvis, but by his father, Vernon, over the telephone; they were also given only one week's severance pay. The official reason the men were told they being were fired was that Elvis wanted to cut back on expenses. There had also been lawsuits over the bodyguards' roughness with overly eager fans. But the men were nonetheless bitter. "We were like brothers, man," said Red in the book. "But in the end it just worked out that we meant nothing to him."

By August, the three men were shopping a book proposal and signed a contract with the World News Corporation, who then landed a deal with Ballantine Books. Steve Dunleavy of the tabloid *The Star* was hired to write the book, receiving an "as told to" credit.

It didn't take long for Elvis to hear about the book. He arranged for a private detective to offer the men money to not do it (calling it "overdue severance pay"), but the offer was rebuffed. As the book's publication neared, Elvis became increasingly upset, and according to his cousin, Billy Smith, spoke about having the men killed. Smith recognized it was an empty threat; Elvis' real fear was what people would think about him if they read the book.

Elvis: What Happened? did present a disturbing portrait of Elvis, and when Elvis died, sales of the book skyrocketed; indeed, Elvis' death seemed to substantiate the claims of drug abuse. And the bodyguards earned the enmity of many Elvis fans for breaking the code of silence around their idol.

Sonny, in his later memoir, *Elvis: Still Taking Care of Business*, still insists the book's main intention was "to help Elvis get his life straightened out." In George Klein's memoir, *Elvis: My Best Man*, he writes that Red told him he was sorry for writing "the damned book," which had been "nothing but a nightmare for him." George added he felt Elvis would have eventually renewed his friendship with the men, and Sonny made the same observation in his own book.

33 Elvis and Drugs

After Elvis' death, fans were surprised to learn he had been a drug user, and some refused to believe it. But in fact, Elvis used drugs for half of his life. Drugs may have played a role in his death, and they certainly contributed to his ill health.

Elvis rarely touched alcohol or smoked. But he began using drugs recreationally in his twenties. Elvis' girlfriend, Anita Wood, recalled that while visiting him in Hollywood in 1957 they visited a pharmacy and, "The pharmacist said, in effect, 'Help yourself.'" Elvis had always enjoyed staying up late, and he and friends would take amphetamines—speed—to give them energy in their late-night carousing. While in the service, amphetamine was also given to the soldiers to help them stay awake when they pulled guard duty, and Elvis also made sure he had a hefty supply for his off-duty hours. One of his friends observed him picking up four large bottles of amphetamines from a dispensary clerk after giving the clerk a sizeable tip.

The drug was very much a part of Elvis' post-army years—everyone in the entourage took speed when they partied in Hollywood or Las Vegas. "None of us slept more than a few hours at a time," Joe Esposito later recalled. "We lived on amphetamines." As the drug culture took off during the '60s, Elvis experimented with other drugs. Priscilla wrote in her autobiography about a night when she, Elvis, and some other friends took LSD together. He also tried marijuana. Some accounts say that in the '70s he used liquid cocaine.

But in general, Elvis stayed away from "street" drugs. In addition to amphetamines, he was also increasingly using sleeping pills in the '60s. And he encouraged those around him to partake as well, sometimes with near-catastrophic results. When Priscilla visited Elvis at Graceland for Christmas 1962, he gave her "two large red pills" to help her sleep—they knocked her out for two days.

By 1967, his drug use was beginning to alarm his friends. Jerry Schilling felt things changed when the group was staying at a ranch Elvis had bought near Graceland, and Elvis rustled him out of bed at 2:00 AM to accompany him to the home of a pharmacist to pick up a prescription—this was something he'd previously been discreet about doing. A month later, in L.A., when Elvis fell in his bathroom one night and hit his head on the tub, it was suspected that drugs were to blame.

Elvis' Girlfriends: Linda Thompson

After Elvis and Priscilla separated at the end of 1971, Linda Thompson was Elvis' next serious relationship.

The two met on July 6, 1972, at the Memphian Theatre where Elvis was hosting one of his private late-night screenings. Linda, who was 22 years old, was a beauty queen, having recently won the Miss Tennessee Universe Pageant among other titles, and had been invited to the screening by a mutual friend. Elvis took an instant liking her, saw her the following evening, and invited her to join him in Vegas at the end of the month. After the Vegas run, Linda moved into Graceland and stayed with Elvis for the next four years.

Linda was a friendly, down-to-earth woman who was well-liked by Elvis' entourage. Being Elvis' girlfriend was demanding, as he wanted her with him 24 hours a day. "I realize it wasn't healthy, but he was my first great, great love," she told biographer Peter Guralnick. "I thought it was natural to be with someone all the time." As his drug use increased, she also ended up saving his life on more than one occasion; when he'd nod off in the middle of a meal, she was able to keep him from choking.

But by the end of 1976, she was worn down. "He was going to go ahead and slowly kill himself, no matter what I did. I couldn't make him happy, and I knew he wasn't going to change. So I left." She later became an actress and songwriter.

One reason for Elvis' rising drug use may have been the boredom he felt in making movies. The next few years, which saw the making of the '68 Comeback Special, the American Sound sessions in Memphis, and his return to live performance, engaged Elvis more creatively than he had been in some time. But as the touring regimen took over in the '70s, his drug use again escalated.

When he was hospitalized in 1973 with breathing problems, it was discovered he'd become addicted to Demerol, a pain medication. He was detoxed from the drug but refused any follow-up consultations. This was Elvis' usual response when anyone tried to address the subject. He was shocked when, in January 1976, friends in the Denver Police Department spoke to him about his drug use (they'd been tipped off by a police surgeon who mentioned that Elvis had requested Dilaudid, a powerful painkiller, on a previous visit). They recommended he get treatment at a private sanatorium. Elvis rebuffed their efforts. "You don't think I can handle it, do you?" he told them, adding, "I can get off this stuff any time I want." He then promptly left town.

Elvis did know he had a problem. But it was something that he refused to deal with. He admitted to his girlfriend, Linda Thompson, that his biggest character flaw was that he was "self-destructive," yet in the same breath told her "but there's not a lot I can do about it." This attitude, more than drugs themselves, prevented Elvis from getting help. "People have asked, 'Why didn't you initiate an intervention?'" Priscilla later wrote. "People who ask that don't know Elvis. Elvis would no more have responded to an intervention than a demand to give up singing."

34 Jumpsuits

Among the outfits that Elvis is most associated with are the jumpsuits he wore as his stage costumes in the 1970s.

When Elvis returned to live performance in 1969, he wore two-piece suits during his first Las Vegas season; trousers and a tunic-style top modeled on a karate gi. But by his next season at Vegas, in January 1970, he began wearing one-piece jumpsuits. Elvis felt a one-piece costume gave him greater freedom of movement, and he didn't have to worry about his shirt becoming loose.

Early jumpsuits were very simple. The jumpsuit Elvis is seen wearing on the cover of the 1970 album *On Stage* has no

Elvis wears one of his trademark jumpsuits in concert in New York's Madison Square Garden on June 9, 1972. (AP Photo/Ray Stubblebine)

ornamentation whatsoever, aside from a macramé-style collar. Another 1970s jumpsuit had a brocade collar as its only decoration. But even in 1970 there were signs of things to come; some jumpsuits had fringe on the arms (in one case the fringe went nearly to the floor), and another, seen on the cover of the 1971 album *I Got Lucky*, had studs on the outside of the legs and arms.

And from 1971 on, Elvis' jumpsuits always had studs in increasingly elaborate designs; stars on the legs, arms, and back for example. Studs then gave way to semi-precious stones, and embroidery. Dramatic images were often featured; tigers, birds of prey, dragons, or flames rising up Elvis' legs. Besides white, jumpsuits were also made in primary colors like red, blue, and black.

The suits were then accessorized with jeweled belts featuring large, ornamental belt buckles (check out the American Indian head belt buckle you see Elvis sporting on the cover of the 1976 album *From Elvis Presley Boulevard, Memphis, Tennessee*) and capes. The jumpsuits were made of wool gabardine, and once a belt and cape were added, the entire ensemble could be quite heavy; when Elvis finished a show, he was always drenched in sweat.

In 1972, Elvis' primary wardrobe designer, Bill Belew (who'd also designed costumes for the *Elvis* television special) created some more restrained stage wear, white trousers, jacket, and cape with color accents on the pockets and cape lining. But in general, Elvis' costumes became more and more extravagant over the course of the decade. "I started out simple," Belew said in *Elvis Fashion*, "but the fans really dictated where we went because they demanded more opulent things from Elvis and he was willing to go along with it." Elvis had even spoken with Belew about designing a suit that would shoot out laser beams operated by a remote control.

The last jumpsuit Elvis ever wore in concert was a white suit that had a large golden sundial design on the front and back; in the center of the sundial was the face of Huitzilopochtli, the Aztec god of war. The suit also featured heavy gold studs and a chain. Outrageous and over-the-top as the jumpsuits often were, they were still nonetheless quintessentially Elvis.

35 From Coast to Coast

Elvis made his national television debut on January 28, 1956. It was the first of six appearances he'd make on *Stage Show*, hosted by Big Band legends (and brothers) Tommy and Jimmy Dorsey.

Elvis' manager recognized that television exposure would be just as important as radio exposure for his client. *Stage Show* wasn't the top variety program on the air, but it was a start. It was to be something of a slow start; bad weather meant the theater, CBS Studio 50, wasn't full, even though free tickets were passed out in Times Square. But the Dorseys gave Elvis a nice build up, bringing in DJ Bill Randle, who'd recently made a short film with Elvis, to introduce him. Randle made the bold claim "We think tonight that he's going to make television history for you" before turning things over to the young hopeful: "We'd like you to meet him now—Elvis Presley, and here he is!"

If Elvis was suffering from any nerves, it didn't show as he strode out to the microphone, let out a short "W-e-l-l-l," and launched into a lively "Shake Rattle and Roll," seguing neatly into "Flip, Flop and Fly" at the song's end. "I Got A Woman" came next and was just as fresh and invigorating. The audience was equally caught up in the excitement, bursting into a smattering of applause during the instrumental breaks when Elvis stepped back from the mic and began moving his body around. He then bowed and left the stage.

He was back in action the next week on February 4, getting off to a brash start with the hiccupping beat of "Baby Let's Play House." "Go wild!" he shouted before the instrumental break, during which girls' screams could be heard for the first time. He followed up with "Tutti Frutti," racing through the song and prompting a few more screams.

Given that "Heartbreak Hotel" was released in January '56, it would've seemed logical for Elvis to plug his new single on *Stage Show*. But rehearsals of the song had not gone well, so Elvis didn't perform it until his February 11 appearance. He first rocked his way through "Blue Suede Shoes," then finally unveiled "Heartbreak Hotel." He was backed by the *Stage Show* orchestra on the latter song, in a rather lumbering arrangement that had a trumpet solo during the instrumental break making the song a sort of rock/jazz hybrid.

On his February 18 appearance, Elvis again sang "Tutti Frutti," lapsing into a jokey voice on occasion and getting the audience to clap along. Then, a surprise: Elvis took off his guitar to perform "I Was the One," the flip side of "Heartbreak Hotel." Elvis had so far done nothing but rock; now he showed he was capable of delivering a smooth ballad, as well.

Elvis had originally only been scheduled for four appearances on *Stage Show*, but his growing popularity ensured that he was brought back two further times. On March 17, Elvis was greeted by rapturous screams when he walked out, and the screaming continued from the first notes of "Blue Suede Shoes" on, particularly when he began jiving around the stage during the instrumental breaks, throwing his body around more than he had on previous appearances. They screamed again when Elvis introduced "Heartbreak Hotel," performed with his band this time (the orchestra only came in after the instrumental break), and Elvis was clearly more relaxed.

His final *Stage Show* appearance came on March 24. He opened with the loping beat of "Money Honey," then announced,

"Now we'd like to do one side of my latest record. We did it last week and we had a lot of mail to do it again. So we're going to do it again, and it's called 'Heartbreak Hotel.'" It's a confident, self-assured performance, with the orchestra again staying musically in the background.

By then, "Heartbreak Hotel" was heading up the charts; the next month, it would reach No. 1. Elvis' *Stage Show* appearances had boosted the single's sales. But more important was the fact that they introduced Elvis to America, giving teenagers across the country their first look at the rising star.

36 The Ultimate '50s Box Set

The release of *The King of Rock 'n' Roll: The Complete 50's Masters* in 1992 was a turning point in the development of Elvis' posthumous legacy. For after a decade and a half of scattershot releases, this thoughtfully compiled release provided a forceful reminder of just what a revolutionary artist Elvis was when he first burst onto the music scene in the mid '50s.

The set was the idea of Ernst Jørgensen, managing director of BMG in Europe, and Roger Semon, RCA's marketing director in the UK. The two had worked together on Elvis reissues for the European market, such as the *Essential Elvis* series (originally available only overseas, with U.S. release of the series delayed until 1988). In 1991, the two were asked if they wanted to focus on Elvis' catalogue full time.

It was a terrific opportunity to change things. Since Elvis' death, there had been some good compilations (such as the *Essential Elvis* and *Elvis: A Legendary Performer* series) and box sets (*Elvis*

Aron Presley and *A Golden Celebration*). But most reissues came out with little regard to their contents or quality, and when CDs took off, early CD reissues of Elvis' catalogue simply used whatever tapes were readily available.

Jørgensen and Semon wanted to take more care in their approach to Elvis' catalogue and had an ambitious project in mind. "When we said, 'The first thing we want to do is a five-CD box set of all of Elvis' '50s recordings, they looked at us as if we were absolutely insane," Ernst told me of the label's initial reaction to their idea. The heads of BMG (who owned RCA, and thus Elvis' catalogue) believed such a release would only be of limited interest; they projected sales of 20,000 copies.

But a good deal of effort was put into this set. The music encompassed the master take of every song Elvis released during the '50s, the classic period that featured what many considered his best work. Exciting rarities and previously unreleased tracks were included, such as the acetates of Elvis' first-ever-recordings, "My Happiness" and "That's When Your Heartaches Begin," and live recordings. There was also a full color booklet with an essay by Peter Guralnick and a sessionography.

When label executives saw the final product, they had to admit they were impressed. And they agreed that the set would probably sell more copies than they'd originally foreseen—maybe as many as 40,000. So when the set was released in June 1992, they were taken completely by surprise to find that a month later it had sold 100,000 copies. It would eventually sell more than half a million—excellent numbers for a five-CD package. The set was also nominated for a Grammy for Best Historical Album, though it lost to *The Complete Capitol Recordings Of The Nat "King" Cole Trio*.

The set received good reviews, and it was a terrific way to get all the '50s-era tracks in one collection. The set's success spawned two sequels, *From Nashville to Memphis: The Essential 60's Masters* (1993) and *Walk A Mile In My Shoes: The Essential 70's Masters*

(1995). The '60s set focused on Elvis' non-soundtrack, non-religious studio recordings; the '70s set presented singles, select studio recordings, and a CD of live songs.

Though all the sets had rarities and previously unreleased tracks, the majority of songs were previously available. It was how they were compiled that made all the difference. By choosing the best tracks to represent each decade, and presenting them in the best quality available, all three sets helped bring about a new appreciation of Elvis' musical accomplishments.

37 The "Message" Single

Elvis rarely made any political comments or sang "message" songs, generally saying, "I'm just an entertainer," when asked about his political views by reporters. But he took a chance with "In The Ghetto," which was undeniably a message song—and which became one of his most memorable hits.

"In The Ghetto" was written by Mac Davis, who met Elvis during the filming of *Live A Little, Love A Little* in 1968. Davis contributed the song "A Little Less Conversation" to the film's soundtrack and later wrote material for Elvis' Comeback Special, including the song "Memories," which reached No. 35 when it was released as a single in February 1969.

Davis had submitted a tape of material for Elvis' sessions at American Sound in 1969, two of which Elvis recorded, "Don't Cry Daddy" (a No. 6 hit) and "In The Ghetto." Davis had originally titled the song "The Vicious Circle," as the song begins with the birth of a boy into poverty who, because of his circumstances, becomes involved in crime and is killed; dramatically, at the time of

The First Elvis Musical

One month after Elvis' army hitch was up in 1960, a musical inspired by his military service opened on Broadway: *Bye Bye Birdie*.

"Birdie" is rock 'n' roll sensation Conrad Birdie, who's about to be inducted into the army. His manager, Albert, and Albert's secretary, Rosie, devise one last publicity stunt; having Conrad debut a new song, "One Last Kiss," on *The Ed Sullivan Show*, after which he'll bestow that kiss on one teenage fan. The lucky fan, chosen at random, is 15-year-old Kim MacAfee of Sweet Apple, Ohio. Complications arise from Kim's jealous boyfriend, Albert's jealous mother, and the adults of Sweet Apple who are scandalized by Conrad's behavior, but all is well by the show's end. Dick Gautier, later "Hymie the Robot" on *Get Smart*, played Conrad.

"Put on a Happy Face" is the show's best-known song, sung by Albert to cheer up one of Conrad's fans. Conrad himself parodies Elvis in the numbers "Honestly Sincere" and the breathy "One Last Kiss." "A Lot of Livin' to Do," sung by Conrad in anticipation of a big night out, is a song you could imagine Elvis actually singing (indeed, one of Elvis' own songs has a similar title).

Bye Bye Birdie became a film in 1963, with Jesse Pearson as Conrad and Ann-Margret in her breakthrough role as Kim MacAfee.

his death, another boy is being born into poverty, and so the cycle continues. Davis renamed the song when he heard black neighborhoods being referred to as "ghettos" on television. "I had always thought of ghettos being associated with Europe during World War II," he later said. "I had never thought of our slums as being ghettos."

The song was hardly radical, being essentially a plea for greater understanding, though it does end on a discouraging note; the song's protagonist isn't saved, and there's no hope that things will change. It was also along the same lines as the closing number from the Comeback Special, "If I Can Dream." But Elvis still hesitated to record the number, thinking it might be too outspoken. Finally, producer Chips Moman said if Elvis wasn't interested, he'd give it to another of his artists (among those who could've recorded the song was former football star Roosevelt Grier, whom Chips had just signed to his own American Group Productions record label). Faced with that prospect, Elvis agreed to record the song.

The song was recorded on January 20, 1969. Elvis and the musicians worked through 23 takes. Elvis' vocal never faltered: "One is provided with an incontrovertible glimpse of what the process might have been like for Elvis, if only he had been able to approach recording consistently as an art," Peter Guralnick wrote in his Elvis biography *Careless Love*.

The final version has one of Elvis' finest vocals. The empathy in his delivery immediately draws you in to the sad story, making you feel the desperation of the young man who can't get ahead and sorrow at society's indifference to his fate. Elvis' voice was especially emotive in songs of loss, and "In The Ghetto" is surely one of the most moving songs he ever recorded.

The song was the first number to be released from the American Sound sessions, issued as a single in April 1969, reaching No. 3 in the charts and selling more than 1 million copies. In 2007, Lisa Marie recorded "In The Ghetto" as a duet with her father, releasing the song as a charity single; it reached No. 1 on the iTunes sales chart.

38 Sweet Sweet Spirit

Elvis' first public performances were in church, his mother recalled him trying to sing along with the hymns when he was just two years old. As a teenager, he attended gospel performances in Memphis; his favorite group was the Statesmen, and he attended the same church as the Blackwood Brothers. Elvis sang hymns to warm up for recording sessions, at parties with friends, and to unwind after shows. He proudly stated to a reporter, "I know practically every religious song that's ever been written."

Elvis' first record of religious music was the four-song EP *Peace in the* Valley, released in April 1957. In addition to the title track, the EP also featured "Take My Hand, Precious Lord," "It Is No Secret (What God Can Do)," and "I Believe," the latter number recorded by one of Elvis' favorite singers, Roy Hamilton. The EP reached No. 39 on the singles chart and No. 3 on the EP chart, eventually selling more than 1 million copies. The four songs also appeared on *Elvis' Christmas Album*, released in October '57.

His first full album of religious material was *His Hand In Mine*, released in November 1960. He drew on songs he'd heard by the Statesmen and the Blackwood Brothers, as well as the Golden Gate Quartet, a group he'd discovered through Charlie Hodge (one of the Quartet's songs that Elvis recorded, "Swing Down Sweet Chariot," he also performed in the film *The Trouble With Girls*). Other highlights include the black gospel numbers "Milky White Way," "Working on the Building," and a song by a former member of the Jordanaires, "I'm Gonna Walk Dem Golden Stairs." *His Hand In Mine* reached No. 13 in the charts.

Another song recorded at the sessions, but not included on the album, was "Crying in the Chapel"; when it was released as a single in 1965, it reached No. 3 in the charts. This success led to interest in making another religious album, and *How Great Thou Art* was released in February 1967. Along with the Jordanaires and three female backing vocalists, Elvis also brought in the Imperials, a gospel group founded by former Statesman Jake Hess, to record with him; he even recorded a song written by the Imperials' piano player, Henry Slaughter, "If the Lord Wasn't Walking By My Side." Highlights include a bluesy version of "Where Could I Go But To The Lord," and the up-tempo "By and By," "Run On," and "So High." The standout was the title track, one of Elvis' most passionate performances, which would become an emotional high point of his concerts in the '70s. The album reached No. 18 in the charts, sold more than 2 million copies, and won a Grammy (Elvis' first) for Best Sacred Performance.

Elvis next recorded "You'll Never Walk Alone," from the musical *Carousel*, in September '67; the song was released as a single in 1968. Another religious number, "Who Am I?", recorded at the American Sound sessions in 1969 sessions, first appeared on a 1970 budget version of Elvis' Christmas album. Both songs, along with "Let Us Pray," which appeared in the film *Change of Habit*, were included in a 1971 collection of Elvis' inspirational songs, *You'll Never Walk Alone*. That same year, "Where Did They Go, Lord," was released as the B-side of the "Rags to Riches" single.

Elvis' third religious album was *He Touched Me*, released in April 1972. The album had a modern feel and sound in comparison with his earlier religious albums, due in part to the more modern material. "Seeing Is Believing" was co-written by Elvis' friend Red West and keyboardist/arranger Glen Spreen (who first worked with Elvis during the American Sound sessions), and "A Thing Called Love" was by Jerry Reed, who wrote "Guitar Man" and "U.S. Male." The Imperials returned to provide backing vocals, and the album also featured Elvis' version of the popular hymn, "Amazing Grace." The album didn't place high in charts, but did win a Grammy for Best Inspirational Performance.

Elvis received his final Grammy, for Best Inspirational Performance, for his rendition of "How Great Thou Art" from the 1974 album *Elvis As Recorded Live On Stage In Memphis*. Religious music was with him to the end; the album on his record player on the day he died was the latest release by J.D. Sumner and The Stamps, whose lead singer sang with Elvis in concert.

39 The Private Plane

It's not unusual for a rock star to own a plane. But not many own a plane that everyone knows the name of, as they do Elvis' plane—the *Lisa Marie*.

When he first began performing, Elvis' mother worried about him traveling by plane. Elvis himself became reluctant to travel by air when a small plane he was riding in stalled in mid-flight in 1956. So when he could, he traveled by other means. When he first performed in Hawaii in 1957, he journeyed to the islands by ship. And during his movie-making years in the '60s, he often traveled between Memphis and Los Angeles in a custom-designed bus.

When he returned to touring in the '70s, he would charter a plane, but by 1975 decided it made sense to buy one himself. He first tried to purchase a Boeing 707, but the deal fell through. He ultimately settled on a Convair 880 manufactured by San Diego–based General Dynamics in 1958 for Delta Airlines that had been taken out of service. Elvis purchased the plane on April 17, 1975, for $250,000 then spent more than $500,000 redesigning the interior, using the same firm that had customized Air Force One. The plane was delivered to Memphis on November 1, and Elvis took his first flight on November 27, traveling to Las Vegas for a two-week run of shows scheduled to begin December 1.

Elvis wanted to transform his plane into a "flying Graceland," and became very involved in choosing the interior color scheme (blue), and frequently traveled to Fort Worth, where the plane was being customized, to oversee the work. After refurbishments, the plane had a large lounge, a conference room, a guest room, and a master bedroom with a queen-sized bed. There was a quadrophonic 8-track stereo system, an air-to-ground phone system, and four

TVs hooked up to a videotape system. The bathrooms had a gold sink and faucets, and the belt buckles for the seat belts were also gold-plated. The seats were leather, suede, or tweed.

Embellishments on the outside of the plane include the aircraft's name, *Lisa Marie*, painted in fancy script on the plane's nose; on the tail is Elvis' personal logo, a gold lightning bolt with the letters "TCB" above it (for "Taking Care of Business—in a flash"). The plane's registration number was N880EP. Though Elvis occasionally took personal trips on the *Lisa Marie*, it was largely used when he was on tour. He was scheduled to fly on the *Lisa Marie* to Portland, Maine, on August 16, 1977, the day he died.

The *Lisa Marie* wasn't the only plane Elvis bought in 1975. He also bought a Grumman Gulfstream G-1 for his manager (who turned it down on the grounds that he couldn't afford to keep it) and an Aero Jet Commander, both of which were later sold. He also bought a Lockheed JetStar and ran into trouble when the people hired to refurbish the aircraft turned out to be con artists; an FBI investigation resulted and wasn't settled until after Elvis' death.

He also bought a Dessault-Falcon airplane in 1975, which he traded for a second Lockheed JetStar on July 13, 1976. The JetStar was renamed *Hound Dog II* and was mostly used by Parker, who would use it to fly in to different cities to do advance work when Elvis was on tour.

After Elvis' death, both planes were sold by Vernon in 1978. But after Graceland was opened to the public in 1982, efforts were made to reacquire them, and in 1984 both planes returned to Graceland, where they're still on display for visitors. Yes, you can climb up the steps and walk all the way through the *Lisa Marie*, imagining what it might have been like to hang out with Elvis in what he liked to refer to as "the pride of Elvis Presley Airways."

40 Who's That Girl?

It's one of the most famous images in rock 'n' roll: Elvis, seen backstage, cuddling with a female fan, both of them playfully sticking out their tongues to the point where they touch, tongue tip to tongue tip.

The picture was shot by Alfred Wertheimer during the summer of 1956. Wertheimer had been hired by RCA to take publicity pictures of their new star and had first photographed Elvis the weekend of March 17, 1956, when he appeared on *Stage Show* for the fifth time. In late June, Wertheimer joined Elvis again, shooting him while rehearsing and performing on *The Steve Allen Show*, then following him home to Memphis, photographing Elvis' show at Russwood Park on July 4.

In between the rehearsals and broadcast of *The Steve Allen Show*, Wertheimer also accompanied Elvis down to Richmond, Virginia, where he performed two shows at the Mosque Theatre on June 30. When Wertheimer met with Elvis at his hotel before the show, Elvis was accompanied by a young woman, Barbara "Bobbi" Owens, who'd "met" Elvis two days before when he was performing in Charleston, South Carolina, and Bobbi had called his hotel room on a dare. Her pluck got her an invitation to see the Richmond shows, Elvis sending a car to bring her from Charleston.

Wertheimer shot the two chatting in the hotel coffee shop and in the cab on the way to the theater. Before the show began, Wertheimer was coming down the backstage stairs when he came upon Elvis and Bobbi together in the stairwell. It was clearly an intimate moment, but Wertheimer couldn't resist taking a few pictures. He tried to be as unobtrusive as possible, but the couple

In this photo taken Sunday, January 8, 2012, Barbara Gray (center) signs a copy of the book Elvis at 21: New York to Memphis for Kimberly Roberts of Richmond (left) during a birthday celebration for Elvis Presley at the Virginia Museum of Fine Arts in Richmond, Virginia. The book features a photograph by Alfred Wertheimer of Gray and Presley kissing backstage at the old Richmond Mosque in 1956. To her left is Barbara's husband, Malcolm Gray. (AP Photo/ Richmond Times-Dispatch, Joe Mahoney)

were wrapped up in each other and didn't notice—or didn't care. Wertheimer took 48 shots; "Then my conscience said beat it. I left."

The picture of Elvis and Bobbi first appeared in the magazine *The Amazing Elvis Presley*, published in September 1956. It has since appeared in numerous other books and magazines, as well as on a wide array of items, such as art prints, posters, mugs, calendars, key chains and more.

But for years, it wasn't known who Bobbi was; Wertheimer hadn't bothered to get her name at the time, and usually referred to her as Elvis' "date for the day." "I didn't know anything about her but it seemed as if Elvis was a sailor and this was one of his ports," Wertheimer said. Bobbi had tried to talk to Wertheimer about the matter, but her claims were dismissed; Wertheimer had been approached by any number of women over the years who insisted they were the woman in the famous photograph.

Finally, in 2010, radio veteran Ron Brandon (who recorded Elvis' 1956 concert in Tupelo while working for WTUP radio), heard about Bobbi's story and put her in touch with journalist Alanna Nash, who's written a number of books about Elvis. With Nash and *Vanity Fair* magazine working as intermediaries, Bobbi, who now goes by her married name Barbara Gray, was able to speak with Wertheimer who was at last convinced that she was indeed the woman in the photographs. Not only did photographs of her in the 1950s match the appearance of the woman in Wertheimer's shots, she was also the right height; Wertheimer remembered the woman he'd photographed as being less than 5', and most of the women who approached him over the years were much taller.

Nash eventually wrote a story for *Vanity Fair*, "The Elvis Kiss Mystery—Solved!" that ran on the magazine's website on August 8, 2011. Wertheimer signed an affidavit acknowledging that Bobbi was the woman in his photographs, and she also received a financial settlement of $2,000. It's a fraction of what she could have earned over the years if she'd been properly compensated for use of the image, but she insisted to Nash that monetary gain was not her intention, "I just wanted to get my name on the damn picture."

Further reading: *Elvis '56: In the Beginning* and *Elvis at 21* both by Alfred Wertheimer.

41 The Islands of Aloha

Like Las Vegas, Hawaii was a place where Elvis both enjoyed some of his greatest career triumphs and escaped to relax with his family and friends.

Elvis' strong association with the islands may go back to his manager, who was stationed on Oahu as a private in the army from 1929 to 1931, a time when the island must have been especially idyllic before the rise of rampant tourism. Many visitors become entranced with Hawaii, and Parker brought Elvis to Hawaii for a number of work-related reasons, beginning with his first concerts there in 1957.

The trip was set up after Parker stated that Elvis had received 21,000 Christmas cards from Hawaii in 1956. Not wanting to fly, Elvis sailed to Honolulu on the USS *Matsonia*, arriving on November 9, 1957, and checking into the 14th floor of what was then the Hawaiian Village Hotel (later the Hilton Hawaiian Village). He made friends with local DJs Tom Moffatt and Rob Jacobs, after learning the two had arranged a promotional stunt, driving an Elvis impersonator around the island, wreaking havoc at a local football game when people thought it was the real Elvis being driven around the field.

Elvis performed two shows on November 10 at Honolulu Stadium, and Tom Moffatt was knocked out. "I'd never seen that kind of charisma with an audience before," Tom told me. "He closed the show with 'Hound Dog' and he jumped off the stage and was on his knees—wow! Anything after that was kind of anti-climactic. My favorite Elvis show is still that first one. Whatever he did with the audience, he had them in the palm of his hand. I'll never forget that show."

The following day, Elvis performed at Schofield Barracks, his last live show for more than two years. Parker kept in touch with Jacobs and Moffatt and had them set up a promotion collecting signatures from fans who wanted Elvis to come back to Hawaii. Parker had hoped Elvis' first post-army show would be in Hawaii, but it ended up being in Memphis on February 25, 1961. But a month later, Elvis was back on the islands, doing a benefit show at the Bloch Arena in Honolulu on March 25 to raise funds for a memorial for the USS *Arizona*, sunk in the attack on Pearl Harbor on December 7, 1941. The show raised more than $60,000, and it was Elvis' last live appearance for seven years.

Two days after the show, location shooting began for *Blue Hawaii*. When the film and soundtrack both proved to be big successes, Elvis was quickly sent back to the island in April 1962 to film *Girls! Girls! Girls!* Elvis plays another aspiring young man who works as a fisherman by day and a nightclub singer at night. But despite the location, the film's setting is never made clear, and there's a noticeable lack of Hawaiian-themed numbers; the film's most notable song was the decidedly un-Hawaiian "Return to Sender."

But Hawaii was front and center in *Paradise, Hawaiian Style*, filmed in 1965 and released the following year. Elvis plays a charter helicopter pilot juggling a different girlfriend on each island. A number of scenes were filmed at the Polynesian Cultural Center, on the north part of Oahu, still one of the island's premier tourist attractions; Elvis is seen riding a canoe in the Center's daily Canoe Pageant while singing "Drums of the Islands." But there was no tie-in single released for the film.

Elvis never made another movie in Hawaii, but he regularly returned to the islands on vacation. One fateful visit came in May 1968; while attending a karate tournament, Elvis and Priscilla met karate champion Mike Stone, the man Priscilla would leave Elvis for. He made two trips to Hawaii in 1969 and returned for his shows in November 1972 and the *Aloha From Hawaii* concerts in 1973.

The last vacation of Elvis' life was also in Hawaii, in March 1977. Elvis and his entourage first stayed at the Hilton then rented a home in Kailua. Over 20 years, Elvis was drawn to the islands by the lure of paradise that continues to draw visitors to Hawaii today.

Further reading: *Elvis in Hawaii* by Jerry Hopkins.

42 Visit Hawaii

There are many reasons to visit Hawaii, one of the world's most beautiful (and popular) tourist destinations. And Elvis fans in particular can have a lot of fun visiting Elvis-related sites on the islands.

Elvis first arrived in Hawaii in 1957 when his cruise ship, the USS *Matsonia*, docked in Honolulu Harbor. Every ship that pulled into the Harbor was greeted by the sight of the famous Aloha Tower, a 224' lighthouse (including the flag mast) that was Hawaii's tallest building when it opened in 1926. Today the building has been renamed the Aloha Tower Marketplace, and the complex has a variety of shops and restaurants. There's also an observation deck in the Tower open to the public.

On most of his visits to Honolulu, Elvis stayed at the Hilton Hawaiian Village, and the entry driveway still bears some similarities to how it looks in *Blue Hawaii*. Elvis stayed on the 14th floor of the Ocean Tower (now the Ali'i Tower).

There are a number of Elvis film sites around Waikiki. Stand on the beach in front of the Royal Hawaiian Hotel and look east toward Diamond Head; that's the panoramic view you see at the

Hawaiian Hijinks In *Lilo & Stitch*

Walt Disney's 2002 animated film *Lilo & Stitch* helped introduce Elvis to a new generation of kids growing up in the 21st century.

Lilo is a young girl living on the island of Kauai. She adopts a funny looking dog from the local pound, whom she names Stitch, not realizing he's actually an alien creature, the result of a genetic experiment being pursued by other aliens from a distant galaxy.

He's also quite rambunctious with a penchant for destroying things. In an effort to tame him, Lilo introduces him to Elvis' music in the hopes that Stitch will also become an Elvis fan. He does adopt some of Elvis' moves, donning a jumpsuit during a performance of the Elvis song "Devil in Disguise." Other Elvis songs featured in the film include "Heartbreak Hotel," "Hound Dog," and "Stuck On You."

After a few complications, all ends on a happy note, and Stitch is allowed to remain on Earth as a member of Lilo's family. The film got good reviews, largely due to its witty script, which made the movie just as much fun for adults as it was for kids. There were three straight-to-DVD sequels and a TV series. Among the *Lilo & Stitch* merchandise, you can find pins and other toys showing Stitch as Elvis complete with guitar and hair coif.

beginning of *Blue Hawaii*. Nearby Ala Moana Park is also seen in *Blue Hawaii*. The Ala Wai Yacht Harbor is easily recognizable as the marina you see in *Girls! Girls! Girls!* The Illikai Hotel is behind the Yacht Harbor and is another place where Elvis stayed.

There are other picturesque film locations outside of Honolulu. Scenes for *Blue Hawaii*, *Girls! Girls! Girls!*, and *Paradise Hawaiian Style* were all shot at Hanauma Bay, one of the best snorkeling spots on the island. Elvis and his *Blue Hawaii* co-star are also seen enjoying the spectacular views of Honolulu from Puu Ualakaa State Park. A number of scenes for *Paradise Hawaiian Style* were shot at the Polynesian Cultural Center in Laie, on the northeast side of the island. Elvis is seen riding in the Center's Canoe Pageant while singing "Drums of the Islands." The pageant and canoe rides are still offered at the Center today.

Thanks in part to Elvis' fundraising efforts, the USS *Arizona* Memorial at Pearl Harbor opened in 1962. And you'll certainly want to stop by the Neal Blaisdell Center to get your picture taken in front of the bronze statue commemorating the 1973 *Aloha From Hawaii* concert at the venue. During his last visit to Hawaii in March 1977, Elvis stayed in a rental home at Lanikai Beach in Kailua, on the east side of the island, though the house where he stayed has since been torn down.

Scenes from *Blue Hawaii* were also shot on the island of Kauai. The final third of the film takes place at the luxurious Coco Palms resort, which was sadly very badly damaged by Hurricane Iniki in 1992 and is no longer open. But you can still access the property on the movie tours offered by different companies (a number of movies have been shot on Kauai, including *Jurassic Park* and *South Pacific*). Scenes from *Blue Hawaii* were also filmed at Wailua River State Park and Lydgate State Park.

Though you won't see as many Elvis impersonators wandering around Honolulu like you do in Memphis or Las Vegas, you can still find a little Elvis in popular tourist locales. The main branch of Hilo Hattie's on Oahu unveiled a special selection of Elvis merchandise in 2012 (available online as well). The long-running *Society of Seven* show at the Outrigger Waikiki on the Beach features an Elvis in its variety show, and the *Legends in Concert Waikiki*, at the Royal Hawaiian Shopping Center, is another show with an Elvis well worth checking out.

Once you've experienced the aloha spirit of the islands, it'll be no surprise why Elvis returned there so many times for a little R&R.

43 The Award-Winning Documentary

Elvis On Tour, released in 1972, was not only the last Elvis movie released during his lifetime, it was also the only Elvis film to win an award.

The original plan had been for Elvis to release another live album recorded in Las Vegas in 1972, tentatively entitled *Standing Room Only*. It was then decided to film him on tour in the spring of '72 instead. Filmmakers Robert Abel and Pierre Adidge were asked to work on the project; the two had previously made a documentary about Joe Cocker, *Mad Dogs and Englishmen*, and were then working on *Let the Good Times Roll*, a concert film about '50s acts like Chuck Berry and Little Richard.

Neither man was particularly interested in working on the Elvis film, nor were they impressed with Elvis' Vegas act, which they saw in February '72. But they agreed to meet with him anyway and were soon won over by Elvis' own enthusiasm for the project.

Filming began on March 30 with a two-day shoot of pre-tour rehearsals. Abel then filmed the opening night of the tour, April 5 in Buffalo, New York, on videotape to have a visual reference of the show to help him plan future shoots. Formal shooting was then done on April 9 in Hampton Roads, Virginia; April 10 in Richmond, Virginia; April 14 in Greensboro, North Carolina; and April 18 in San Antonio, Texas.

Elvis also agreed to do an interview for the movie, with excerpts dropped in throughout the film providing a sort of narration. Parker was dead set against it, but Elvis' friend Jerry Schilling, who was also working on the film as an assistant editor, persuaded Elvis to agree. The 40-minute interview was shot in his old dressing room at MGM Studios in July '72. Unfortunately, only a small portion of the interview was used in the film; much of what was cut out was quite interesting, especially when Elvis critiqued the failure of his feature film career, admitting the scripts he was given literally made him sick: "At a certain stage I had no say-so in it… Hollywood's image of me was wrong, and I knew it, and I couldn't say anything about it, couldn't do anything about it." He also called the moment when he was made to sing to a hound dog on *The Steve Allen Show* in 1956 "about as funny as a crutch."

Aside from the pre-show rehearsals, and a brief look at Elvis' early years that features performances from *The Ed Sullivan Show* and a funny montage of kissing scenes from his movies, most of *Elvis On Tour* depicts just that: Elvis traveling on planes, en route to shows in his limo, pacing nervously backstage before a show, and in performance.

The crowds love him, packing the shows and screaming whenever he appears. But comparing the concert footage from this film with the footage shot during the making of *Elvis: That's The Way It Is*, it's clear that something has changed. It's not just his appearance (he's pale and puffy in contrast to the lean look of just two years before). In spite of the high kicks and karate chops, Elvis is somewhat lacking in both energy and vibrancy. There's a sense of his simply walking through his performance, striking poses, going through the ritual of dispensing of kisses and scarves to the fans, playing up style over substance. Abel himself noticed Elvis' diminishing energy through the short run of the tour, feeling that the opening night show had a freshness that was missing from the later performances, making him sorry that he hadn't formally filmed that opening night show.

It's still an invaluable record of Elvis in performance, of course, especially since so little official live footage of Elvis is available, which is surprising considering the number of shows he did throughout his career. And the film was a success when it was released in November '72; the following year it won a Golden

Globe for Best Feature Documentary. The film was released on DVD in 2010, though "Don't Be Cruel" was substituted for "Johnny B. Goode" during the film's opening sequence when copyright clearance for the latter song couldn't be obtained. The sharp-eyed will also notice future film director Martin Scorsese is credited as "Montage Supervisor."

44 The Debut Album

"Heartbreak Hotel" was still heading up the charts when Elvis' first album, *Elvis Presley*, was released in March 1956. The iconic cover has been much parodied over the years by artists as varied as the Clash, Pete Yorn, and k.d. lang, but it's still the original picture that has the greatest power: Elvis, on stage at the Fort Homer Hesterly Armory in Tampa, Florida, on July 31, 1955, throwing himself into the performance with such vigor you can practically hear the clarion call of his voice.

The album opens in an equally exciting fashion with a riveting cover of Carl Perkins' "Blue Suede Shoes," kicking off an eternal debate about which version is the definitive one (if you want a good workout when you're dancing, Elvis' version gets the nod). Overall, the album is a testament to Elvis' vocal diversity, presenting a good mix of rockers and slower tempo numbers. On the rocking side, Ray Charles' "I Got A Woman" was already part of Elvis' live show and would stay in the set through his very last concert 21 years later; he also tackles Little Richard's "Tutti Frutti" with gusto.

As far as ballads, RCA drew on some of the song masters they'd purchased from Sun: "I Love You Because," "Blue Moon," and "I'll Never Let You Go (Lil' Darlin')." Among the newer ballads was

"I'm Counting on You," by Don Robertson, who was disappointed when he heard the song had been given to Elvis, as he'd hoped his publisher would be able to place it with a bigger artist. Once the album took off, it was a different matter of course, and Robertson would go on to write a number of songs for Elvis.

Then there were the songs that fell somewhere in between, including two more from Sun ("Just Because" and "Trying to Get to You"). "I'm Gonna Sit Right Down and Cry (Over You)" and "One-Sided Love Affair" are teasingly playful, as if Elvis is just daring you to take him too seriously. "Money Honey" (originally recorded by Clyde McPhatter of the Drifters, one of Elvis' favorite singers) brings the album to a strong finish.

RCA was hoping to make some quick money out of this rock 'n' roll fad before it fizzled out. To their surprise and delight, *Elvis Presley* became their biggest seller to date (at least until the release of the follow up album, simply entitled *Elvis*). Coupled with the success of "Heartbreak Hotel," *Elvis Presley* helped establish Elvis as a major star.

45 The President Will See Mr. Presley

One the most unusual incidents in Elvis' life was when he decided, on the spur of the moment, to try to see President Richard Nixon— and remarkably found himself being ushered into the Oval Office within hours of making his request.

It all began with an argument. Upon concluding a fall tour in November 1970, Elvis went on a spending spree, buying several thousand dollars worth of guns, jewelry, and cars, as well as paying for the weddings of three friends and buying another friend a house.

President Richard Nixon meets Elvis Presley at the White House in Washington, D.C., on December 21, 1970. (AP Photo/Egil "Bud" Krogh/White House)

When his father and his wife confronted Elvis about his lavish spending on December 19, Elvis grew so angry, he left Memphis and flew to Washington, D.C. When he couldn't get in touch with a girlfriend who lived there, he flew to Dallas and then L.A. After spending a few hours sleeping at the home of his friend, Jerry Schilling, Elvis announced they were returning to DC, asking Jerry to call Graceland and request that Sonny West meet them there.

Elvis met Senator George Murphy on the plane and, after speaking with him, returned to his seat and began writing a letter to President Nixon. He told the president he wanted to help the country by reaching out to the counterculture ("The drug culture, the hippie elements, the SDS [Students for a Democratic Society],

Black Panthers, etc."). But his real intention, hinted at in the letter, was to acquire "Federal credentials" to help him do this work. He'd recently met voice-over actor Paul Frees (the voice of Boris Badenov in *Rocky & Bullwinkle*, and the Pillsbury Doughboy, among many others), who'd proudly shown him his Bureau of Narcotics and Dangerous Drugs (BNDD) badge that designated him as a Federal Agent. Elvis wanted such a badge for himself.

He arrived back in Washington on the morning of December 21 and dropped off his letter at the White House gates. While Jerry waited at the Hotel Washington, Elvis went to the BNDD offices, hoping he could secure a badge through them. His request was turned down. But he was then contacted by Jerry, who told Elvis he'd been called by deputy counsel Egil "Bud" Krogh about his letter. Krogh had invited them to the White House. On hearing this news, Elvis, Jerry, and Sonny, who'd just arrived from Memphis, all headed over.

Krogh had been an Elvis fan in the '50s and was intrigued by the idea of facilitating a meeting between Elvis and the president. He arranged for a 12:30 PM appointment during Nixon's "Open Hour," when brief meetings with the president were held. "If I had not been an Elvis fan, this would never have happened," Bud told me.

Elvis initially met the president on his own. He was flamboyantly dressed, especially in comparison to Nixon, wearing one of the two-piece suits he'd worn during his 1969 Vegas appearances, a championship belt given to him by the International Hotel, with a velvet jacket he'd worn in the *Elvis* special draped over his shoulders (mistakenly called a cape in other accounts).

The two initially made small talk, Elvis showing off his collection of police badges and giving Nixon photos of his wife and child (he'd wanted to present Nixon with a commemorative Colt .45, but wasn't allowed to bring the gun into the Oval Office). They then discussed the idea of Elvis getting involved in a government anti-drug program. This gave Elvis the perfect opportunity to ask for a BNDD badge. Nixon asked Krogh if it was possible to do, and when Krogh affirmed that it was, Nixon said, "I'd like to do that. See that he gets one." Elvis was so pleased he impulsively hugged Nixon, to the president's surprise.

Elvis then asked if the president could meet his friends, and Jerry and Sonny were brought in. Pictures were taken and Nixon gave everyone souvenirs with the presidential seal on them. Elvis received his badge in the afternoon and returned to Memphis the next day. It was a remarkable example of how Elvis could get whatever he wanted once he put his mind to it.

46 The TCB Band

In the '50s, Elvis' backing band was called the Blue Moon Boys. In the '70s, his backing group for live shows was the TCB Band ("TCB" stood for "Taking Care of Business").

The musicians for what would become the original lineup of the TCB Band came together when Elvis was preparing for his return to live performance in Las Vegas in 1969. He first approached people he'd worked with before, including Scotty Moore, D.J. Fontana, and the Jordanaires, all of whom turned him down because the fee they were offered was too low. He next asked the musicians he'd recently worked with at the American Sound sessions in early 1969 if they'd be interested. But they also turned him down, as no one was wanted to join a band that might end up going out on tour; there was more money in studio work.

Elvis ultimately decided to go in a completely new direction and approached a musician he had never worked with before: James Burton. Burton had been a guitarist in the *Louisiana Hayride* house band, the same radio program Elvis had appeared on (though the two hadn't appeared together), later playing with Ricky Nelson. During the '60s, he worked primarily as a studio musician (contributing some guitar to the soundtrack of *Viva Las Vegas*), and also in the house band of the TV rock program *Shindig* (who were called the "Shindogs").

Elvis called James at home, and the two talked for several hours; James ended up agreeing to be in the band and help Elvis put together the rest of the group. It was James who contacted bassist Jerry Scheff, another Shindog, who had also played bass on the soundtrack of *Double Trouble*. Jerry wasn't initially interested, but was won over by Elvis at the audition: "He was singing all the stuff he thought we would like, blues things, and stuff like that," he told me. "And I was blown away. I thought, *You know, what? I think I've got something to learn here.*"

James also contacted another studio veteran, guitarist John Wilkinson. (Elvis, who had first met John in 1956, gave him a phone call, as well.) And when pianist Glen Hardin, another Shindog, turned down James' offer, Elvis tapped Larry Muhoberac, another studio musician who'd played piano on a number of Elvis' movie soundtracks. Larry in turn contacted his friend, drummer Ronnie Tutt, then living in Texas. Ronnie hurried to L.A. to audition. Elvis was impressed with the way Ronnie was able to accent his body movements with the drums, so Ronnie was also hired.

After the first Vegas season, Muhoberac left and Glen Hardin joined. The core of the TCB Band was now in place: James Burton on lead guitar, John Wilkinson on rhythm guitar, Jerry Scheff on bass, Glen Hardin on piano, and Ronnie Tutt on drums. There were occasional changes in personnel, as one member or another took a break from the group, but these were the musicians who played with Elvis in concert the most. And all of them, except for Glen Hardin, played with Elvis on his final tour.

The TCB Band also recorded with Elvis. James Burton was at all of Elvis' studio sessions in the '70s, and the entire band (again excepting Glen Hardin) was on hand for Elvis' last studio sessions in 1976, held at Graceland. But they were primarily Elvis' live band, providing a solid musical foundation that Elvis could rely on. "He had a list of songs that he would just call upon at any moment," Ronnie Tutt told me, "in a rehearsal situation or even on the stage—he'd just start singing something, or he'd say 'Give me an E,' and somebody would hit the chord and off he'd go. He prided himself on the fact that we could all jump in and pretty much make a decent song out of it, even though we might not be sure of every little thing."

Jerry Scheff tells a similar story. "He'd start songs on stage that we'd never played before. Because he liked to play 'Stump the Band.' And he didn't stump us very often!" Elvis knew he could always count on the TCB Band.

47 Lucky in *Las Vegas*

Viva Las Vegas was Elvis' most commercially successful film. And a big reason for that success was the film's vibrant co-star: Ann-Margret.

Ann-Margret had previously starred in the film version of *Bye Bye Birdie*, based on the Broadway musical that satirized the Elvis phenomenon; the film's director, George Sidney, would also direct *Viva Las Vegas*. The film's promotional material drew on Ann-Margret's *Birdie* connection; a tagline used on one film poster read: "It's that 'Go-Go' guy and that 'Bye-Bye' gal in the fun capital of the world!" (Parker disagreed with the advertising approach, arguing that previous posters had never referred to Elvis as the "*Fun in Acapulco* boy" or "*Jailhouse Rock* boy").

Viva Las Vegas has a typically thin plotline. Elvis plays Lucky Johnson, a racecar driver who comes to Vegas in hopes of winning the Grand Prix. There he meets Rusty Martin (Ann-Margret), a swimming instructor at one of Vegas' hotels. Rusty initially spurns Lucky's attentions, shoving him off the high dive into the hotel's swimming pool. Unfortunately, the money in Lucky's pocket that he planned to use to buy a new car engine is sucked down the pool's drain, forcing him to work as a waiter at the hotel to pay his bill—and, more fortuitously, enables him to continue to court Rusty. Rusty eventually warms to Lucky, Rusty's father comes up with the cash for the engine, Lucky wins the race, and the couple marries.

In contrast to some of the songs in Elvis' recent movies ("Song of the Shrimp" in *Girls! Girls! Girls!*, "[There's] No Room to Rhumba in a Sports Car" in *Fun In Acapulco*), a more serious effort was made to get better material for *Viva Las Vegas*. The film opens with the brisk title song that plays over scenes of Las Vegas at night in all its neon glory; it's one of the best title songs of any Elvis movie, rivaling "Jailhouse Rock." "I Need Somebody to Lean On" is a lovely, sensitive number that Lucky sings when his relationship with Rusty is seemingly on the rocks. (Elvis recorded 20 takes to get it right.)

The most exciting parts of the film are undeniably the dance numbers. For the first time, Elvis had a female co-star who could match him move for move, and filmmakers took full advantage of it; when their first production number, "C'mon Everybody," proved to be successful, a second one was added, with the two dancing to "What'd I Say."

Ann-Margret had her own solo spot with the insinuating "Appreciation," performed during a talent show sequence. But during the filming Parker became increasingly alarmed, suspecting

Elvis Presley and actress Ann-Margret shown in a publicity photo for the 1964 film, Viva Las Vegas. (AP Photo)

Elvis' Girlfriends: Ann-Margret

When 22-year-old Ann-Margret first met Elvis on the set of *Viva Las Vegas* on July 9, 1963, she sensed they were going to have more than just a professional relationship. "I knew what was going to happen once we got to know each other," she wrote in her autobiography. "Elvis did, too. We both felt a current that went straight through us. It would become a force we couldn't control."

Ann-Margret Olsson was a Swedish-born actress who moved to the U.S. with her parents when she was five. After working as a dancer and singer, she began her recording career in 1961, and was quickly dubbed the "Female Elvis," even recording a cover of "Heartbreak Hotel."

The rapport Ann-Margret and Elvis enjoyed on-screen quickly led to an off-screen affair. Elvis was so taken with Ann-Margret, he'd send away his entourage in order to be alone with her; the two would then spend their time either riding around town on their motorcycles or taking in a quiet evening together at Elvis' home. But Ann-Margret wrote that she knew they couldn't marry because Elvis "had commitments, promises to keep," presumably referring to his relationship with Priscilla, who had just moved into Graceland three months before shooting on *Viva Las Vegas* began.

So the two parted after a year. They remained friendly, and Elvis made sure to send flowers to every one of Ann-Margret's openings in Las Vegas.

that the film's director was favoring Ann-Margret over Elvis. The two were originally scheduled to perform three duets in the film; at Parker's insistence, one duet ("You're the Boss") was cut and another ("Today, Tomorrow and Forever") was changed to a solo number for Elvis. Only "The Lady Loves Me" remained because it was essential to the plot; it's at the end of this jokey number that Rusty shoves Lucky into the swimming pool.

Of the remaining songs, "If You Think I Don't Need You" is light-hearted and pleasant; only a medley of "The Yellow Rose of Texas"/"The Eyes of Texas" is truly disposable (Lucky sings it in order to lure rowdy customers out of a casino). But instead of putting together an album, the decision was made to just release a single ("What'd I Say"/"Viva Las Vegas") in April 1964 and a four-track EP (*Viva Las Vegas*) in May 1964 in advance of the film's opening in June. Both releases fared poorly; "What'd I Say" reached No. 21, "Viva Las Vegas" reached No. 29, while the EP just barely cracked the Top 100, peaking at No. 92.

The film itself fared much better. The on-screen chemistry between Elvis and Ann-Margret is obvious (and also a reflection of the pair's off-screen chemistry). And if the film went over budget, it was nonetheless money well spent; *Viva Las Vegas* is a professional, high-quality film, in comparison with the cheap look of future releases like *Tickle Me* and *Harum Scarum*. It's the last truly successful Elvis film musical. And the title song is an anthem you hear everywhere in Las Vegas today.

48 First Performances

Elvis' first public performances were at church and school. Most of what is known about his other live performances up until 1954 is uncertain and contradictory.

His most well-known public performance as a child was on October 3, 1945, at the Mississippi-Alabama Fair in Tupelo. Oleta Grimes, a teacher at Elvis' school, had heard him sing and entered him in the children's talent contest held on that day. He sang "Old Shep," a Red Foley number about the death of a beloved dog—the kind of song for which the word "tearjerker" was created. Watching Elvis bravely sing the song *a capella*, without any musical accompaniment, must've brought a tear to more than one eye. Elvis won fifth place, the prize being free rides for the rest of the day, though

Only Available in America

One of the biggest mysteries of Elvis' career was why he never toured outside of the United States.

Elvis rarely left the U.S. at all. He performed five shows in Canada, all in 1957—two in Toronto on April 2, two in Ottawa on April 3, and one in Vancouver on August 31. His 1957 shows in Hawaii could also be considered "foreign" as Hawaii was not yet a state. He lived in Germany during his army service and visited Paris when he was on leave in 1959 and 1960. He also visited the Bahamas in October 1969. That was the extent of his non-U.S. travels.

The demand was certainly there for a world tour. From the time Elvis became a star in 1956, his manager received numerous offers from overseas promoters who were desperate to have Elvis tour abroad. The money Elvis was offered was substantial. But Parker never made a serious move to put together a foreign tour.

It's been assumed that Parker turned the offers down because, as an illegal alien, he was afraid to leave the U.S. Why he didn't get one of his many influential friends to quietly sort out his immigration status is another mystery, considering the hefty fees such a tour could've generated. There would also have been a psychological benefit, as well. Elvis loved rising to a challenge, which an overseas tour would have provided in abundance.

he recalled getting a "whipping" from his mother for going on a ride she felt was too dangerous.

Three months later, he got his first guitar for his birthday, and soon after he could be heard on local radio. Every Saturday, Tupelo station WELO broadcast the *WELO Jamboree*, an hour open to anyone who wanted to come down and perform. Elvis appeared on the program on more than one occasion, though the exact dates aren't known, sometimes backed by Mississippi Slim, who had his own show on WELO. (Elvis also went to school with Slim's brother, James Ausborn.)

When Elvis moved to Memphis, he regularly played guitar and sang for his friends at home and at parties. When he accompanied his friends Buzzy Forbess and Paul Dougher to the Memphis Home for Incurables to visit with the patients, he surprised them by bringing out his guitar and singing a few songs. It was the first time Buzzy had seen Elvis perform outside of their neighborhood.

Elvis' next confirmed public appearance was on April 9, 1953, at Humes High School's Annual Minstrel show, held in the school's auditorium. He was No. 16 on the bill, listed as "Guitarist—Elvis Prestly." Most of his classmates didn't even know he could perform, and his rendition of Teresa Brewer's "'Til I Waltz Again" went down well (in some accounts, he was even awarded an encore). The performance did much to boost his profile at school. "I was amazed how popular I became after that," he later said.

It was around this time that Elvis met Ronald Smith, who attended South Side High School. Ronald was a musician, as well, and the two performed together. In *Early Elvis: The Sun Years*, Ronald recalls playing with Elvis in Memphis and in Arkansas. The book lists other shows Elvis is said to have performed during this period, though some of the claims seem dubious, such as one woman's claim that Elvis did a 90-minute solo show at Memphis State College in 1954 that made the audience go "crazy." Elvis' other known shows that year have him doing no more than a few songs at a time and that his nerves were quite evident; he didn't become a confident performer for some time.

Ronald also played in the band Eddie Bond and the Stompers, who were the house band at Memphis club the Hi-Hat. Ronald suggested to Eddie that Elvis might be a good singer for the group, and Elvis was invited to perform with the band on May 15, 1954. Elvis sang two songs but wasn't hired. Bond later said it was because the club's owners hadn't liked Elvis' looks. But Elvis told his friends that Eddie told him he should stick to being a truck driver (he was then driving a truck for the Crown Electric company) "because you're never going to make it as a singer." "Man, that sonofabitch broke my heart," Elvis told his friend, DJ George Klein.

Two months later, Elvis had recorded his first single and was preparing to perform with Scotty Moore and Bill Black at the Bon Air club in Memphis on July 17. His future performances would be well documented. Certainly everyone who saw Elvis when he was first starting out as a performer can consider themselves very lucky.

49 The Unexpected Hit Single

The most surprising hit single of Elvis' career was "A Little Less Conversation," which was first released as a single in 1968 and peaked at a lowly No. 69. But when it was remixed by a DJ from the Netherlands and reissued in 2002, it became an international hit.

The song was co-written by Mac Davis and Billy Strange for the 1968 film *Live a Little, Love a Little*. Strange was writing background music for the film and passed the script on to Davis, who was then launching his career as a songwriter. Davis had written the song with Aretha Franklin in mind but thought it might work in a party sequence in Elvis' film. The song was also recorded for Elvis' Comeback Special but was ultimately cut from the show. Davis was disappointed the track hadn't fared better as a single, but working on the song had provided him with a valuable introduction to Elvis, whom he would write a number of songs for, most notably "In The Ghetto" and "Don't Cry Daddy."

Fast-forward 34 years. Dutch DJ Tom Holkenborg, whose professional name was "Junkie XL," was hired to provide a soundtrack for the advertising campaign Nike planned to air during that year's

World Cup tournament. Holkenborg thought the lyrics of "A Little Less Conversation," with their emphasis on "more action," were perfect for a sports event, and the song already had a lively beat. It marked the first time Elvis Presley Enterprises authorized a remix of an Elvis song. Holkenborg also agreed to modify his name, so when the single was released, it was credited to "JXL." "Changing my name for this single was about respecting Elvis and his fans," he explained.

The commercial proved to be a great success, and the single was released in June 2002. Unlike some remixes, the sound is more rock than electronic, and the song has an exciting crescendo in the bridge, not unlike what the Beatles did in their version of "Twist and Shout."

The single became a worldwide hit, topping the charts in more than 20 countries. In the U.S., it reached No. 50 in *Billboard*'s Hot 100 chart, topped the magazine's Sales chart, and reached No. 26 in the Adult Top 40 chart.

It was a tremendous success for Elvis; even reaching No. 50 was the highest charting release he'd had in the U.S. since 1981 when a new mix of "Guitar Man" had reached No. 28, making it his third highest charting posthumous hit on the pop charts. Because of its success around the world it was quickly added to the *ELVIS No. 1* hits collection and has since also appeared on compilations like *Good Rockin' Tonight*, a four-CD box set released in 2009 to commemorate what would have been his 75th birthday. It stands as an excellent example of how Elvis' songs can be given a modern spin without losing the original feeling that he brought to them.

50 All That Glitters

Though he didn't actually wear it that many times, the gold suit Elvis had designed in 1957 became one of his most famous outfits.

The suit was designed by Nudie Cohn, "Rodeo Tailor to the Stars." Nudie was born Nuta Kotlyarenko in 1902 in Kiev and emigrated to the U.S., growing up in Brooklyn. His first shop, Nudie's for the Ladies, was located in New York City and catered to strippers and showgirls. In the 1940s, he moved with his family to Los Angeles, where he began designing clothes with a Western look, and opened a new shop, Nudie's of Hollywood (when the shop later moved, it was renamed Nudie's Rodeo Tailors). He was soon designing clothes for a variety of country & western entertainers, finally capturing mainstream attention when he began designing outfits for Roy Rogers and Dale Evans. Nudie's clothes were known for their flamboyance; his website claims he was the first man to put rhinestones on clothing.

Elvis' manager gave Nudie a commission to design an especially extravagant outfit for Elvis, and he certainly succeeded. The shimmering gold outfit (generally said to be gold lame, though some accounts say it was gold leaf) had silver trim and rhinestones around the collar, cuffs, and pockets; a rhinestone "stripe" also ran down the outside pant leg. A single button held the jacket closed in front. There was a matching frilly shirt, a gold Western-style tie, and gold shoes. The cost of the outfit was said to be $10,000, but that turned out to be PR hyperbole; the actual cost was $2,500.

It was quite a glittering creation. But Elvis never really took to it. He first wore the suit for a show in Chicago on March 28, 1957, but after wearing it the next night at a show in St. Louis, he largely stuck to wearing the jacket with black dress pants. "After a while he came to be embarrassed by [the suit]," Elvis biographer Peter Guralnick wrote. "It was as if he were advertising the suit than the other way around."

But he wore the full suit for the cover of *50,000,000 Million Elvis Fans Can't Be Wrong: Elvis' Gold Records Vol. 2*, released in November 1959, which is where most people saw the outfit. The album's cover concept, which featured multiple images of Elvis wearing the suit, has been copied by other artists, included Rod Stewart, The Fall, and Bon Jovi.

Elvis never wore the full suit again after 1957. He last wore the jacket in public on March 25, 1961, at a performance in Honolulu. And when Bill Belew designed a similar-looking suit for Elvis to wear during his Comeback Special, he balked, telling the designer, "Billy, I have to be honest with you. I always hated that suit, and I will not wear it." Belew was surprised but eventually hit upon the solution Elvis had used, simply designing a gold jacket to be worn with black dress pants. "It was a way of rebelling against the Colonel," Belew told me, explaining Elvis' dislike of the suit. But it's nonetheless a fabulous outfit.

51 The Lost Album

Tomorrow Is A Long Time was one of Elvis' strongest albums of the 1960s. He strode confidently into the realm of country rock with lively covers of Chuck Berry's "Too Much Monkey Business," and Jerry Reed's "U.S. Male" and "Guitar Man," all of which featured the nimble fingerpicking of Reed himself. He displayed a powerful command of his vocal delivery on delicate numbers like "Indescribably Blue," "Love Letters," and the haunting "I'll Remember You," then shook things up with the gritty blues of "Down in the Alley" and "Hi-Heel Sneakers." And his performance on the title track, a Bob Dylan number, was superlative. Elvis' stock had dropped by the mid-'60s amidst a deluge of mediocre film songs like "Shake That Tambourine," "Queenie Wahine's Papaya," and "Yoga Is As Yoga Does." But *Tomorrow Is A Long Time* showed Elvis fully engaged as a contemporary artist once again, laying the groundwork for his future triumphs with the *Elvis* TV special and the American Sound sessions of early 1969.

Sounds pretty credible, doesn't it? But there's a catch. *Tomorrow Is A Long Time* is indeed one of Elvis' albums, but it didn't come out in the '60s—it came out in 1999. Its purpose was to cast a new light on Elvis' 1960s recordings.

From 1960 through 1968, Elvis released 26 albums. There were four studio albums, two religious albums, two greatest hits albums, a budget compilation, and the *Elvis* soundtrack. All the rest—16 albums' worth—were film soundtracks. Film work tied up Elvis to the point where he was rarely able to make the kind of records he wanted to. This led to the perception that as far as Elvis' music was concerned, the '60s was a veritable wasteland.

There's some truth in this assessment—no one cites "(There's) No Room to Rhumba in a Sports Car" or "Old MacDonald" as fine examples of Elvis at his best—but it's not the whole story. The songs that appeared on *Tomorrow Is A Long Time* were mostly used to pad out film soundtracks, but the strength of the material shows that they could have stood on their own.

Take "Tomorrow Is A Long Time," for instance. Bob Dylan evinced an anti-authoritarian attitude that Elvis would never have aspired to, but Dylan's love songs were certainly straight forward enough. By 1966, when Elvis recorded "Tomorrow...," Dylan was regarded as one of the premier songwriters of the era, who'd revolutionized the lyrical content of rock music. Releasing Elvis' exquisite rendition of a Dylan song as a single would've gone a long way toward re-establishing Elvis' credibility as a performing artist. Instead, it was left to languish, unnoticed, on the *Spinout* soundtrack.

Rock music went through great changes in the 1960s, and by the middle of the decade, Elvis was in danger of being left behind. And though he knew where he wanted to go musically, he didn't always have the will to overcome the obstacles to get there. "Guitar Man" was yet another track that nearly wasn't released because Jerry Reed refused to give up his publishing rights. A deal was eventually worked out. But Elvis didn't like having to fight hard to get good material and then have to fight even harder to get it released.

Yet all through the film years, first-rate, non-film songs were also being recorded. The box set *From Nashville to Memphis: The Essential 60's Masters I* makes the same point over its five CDs. If Elvis had been given more time to focus on recording non-soundtrack material, and if the songs had been as thoughtfully compiled on an album as they are on *Tomorrow Is A Long Time*, who knows how Elvis' recording career could have developed?

52 The First Post-Army Single

The big question on everyone's mind—including Elvis'—when he got out of the army was, could he pick up his career where he'd left off? With the release of his first post-army single, "Stuck On You"/"Fame and Fortune," it seemed that he could; the single quickly reached the top of the charts and sold more than 1 million copies.

There was a noticeable tension in the air when Elvis arrived for the session, held March 20, 1960, at RCA's studios in Nashville. Elvis spent the first hour at the studio chatting about his army experiences; recording began around 8:00 PM, with two songs destined for his first post-army album *Elvis Is Back*, "Make Me Know It" and "Soldier Boy."

It was midnight when he got to the songs that would make up the single. "Stuck On You" was a pleasant mid-tempo number, not too dissimilar to the pop swing of "All Shook Up." Gordon Stoker of Elvis' backing group the Jordanaires told me that Elvis didn't care for the song. "He didn't like it at all. He called it 'Stuck In You.'" This isn't evident from the recording; Elvis sounds fully engaged, especially when he hits the high notes during the song's bridge. He nailed the song in three takes.

He professed more interest in the B-side, "Fame and Fortune"— not surprisingly, as Elvis was always partial to ballads—and his confident delivery, in contrast to pre-army ballads he'd recorded like "I Was the One," showed how much he'd improved as a singer ("I Was the One" was co-written by Aaron Schroeder, who'd also co-written "Stuck On You"). The session finished with "A Mess of Blues," first released as the B-side of "It's Now or Never," and "It Feels So Right," which also appeared on *Elvis Is Back*.

"Stuck On You"/"Fame and Fortune" was then pressed and shipped in two days. RCA shipped one million copies to the stores without even waiting for any orders, packing the single in a generic record sleeve featuring two pictures of Elvis and celebratory text that read: "Elvis' 1ˢᵗ New Recording For His 50,000,000 Fans All Over the World."

Six days after the session, Elvis performed both numbers as part of his guest appearance on *The Frank Sinatra Timex Show: Welcome Home Elvis*, which was taped on March 26. Sharply attired in a tux, he has great fun during "Stuck On You," but there's a note of parody, as well. As he snaps his head from side to side, causing his top-heavy pompadour to bob precariously, snaps his fingers then lets his hand drop in a limp wrist, and teases his fans with exaggerated body movements, it's clear he's not taking the proceedings too seriously.

It was different with "Fame and Fortune," of course, which Elvis actually performed first on the show. The fans scream a bit at the beginning (prompting a brief chuckle from Elvis), but the quiet nature of the song quickly subdues them, and Elvis sings with heartfelt sincerity.

By the time the special aired on May 12, "Fame and Fortune" had reached No. 1. The single offered a clear indication of the direction Elvis' musical career would take; more pop and less rock. And for the moment, that was enough to satisfy his fans.

Recording in Memphis: The Jungle Room Sessions

Bringing his career full circle, Elvis' last recording sessions were also his last sessions in Memphis.

After 1973, Elvis became increasingly reluctant to return to the recording studio. There were no recording sessions at all in 1974 (the first time that had happened since 1959), and just a three-day session in 1975. In desperation, RCA arranged for Elvis to record at his home in 1976 with equipment set up in the downstairs den—the room later dubbed the "Jungle Room"—and a recording truck parked out back.

The first session was held February 2–8. Some nights went well; on the 2nd and 5th Elvis managed to record three songs. But on the 3rd and 7th he recorded just one song. And on the night of the 8th, he didn't come down from his bedroom at all, and the musicians were sent home.

The session's highlight was obviously "Hurt," which Elvis knew from Roy Hamilton's 1955 version. After the opening chord, the song begins with an agonized cry, as if drawn out from the depth of Elvis' soul; the song would provide an emotional climax in his live shows for the rest of his life. It was quickly rushed out as a single the next month, reaching No. 28.

Elvis' poignant rendition of "Danny Boy" was another highlight. Nearly all the songs recorded at these sessions reflected the same downbeat, at times maudlin, mood, something readily seen in the song titles: "Bitter They Are, Harder They Fall," "Love Coming Down," and "I'll Never Fall in Love Again." The exception is the upbeat "For the Heart" by Dennis Linde, who also wrote "Burning Love." The sudden jolt of energy reveals what's missing from the other songs; Elvis isn't interested in putting out more than minimal effort.

Part of the problem is the musical backing layered over the songs when they were later released (10 of the 12 songs recorded during the sessions would appear on Elvis' next album, *From Elvis Presley Boulevard, Memphis, Tennessee*, which peaked at No. 41). Listen to the same songs without the string overdubs, available on the Follow That Dream edition of the album, and the performances are all much stronger.

Elvis was aware his records didn't sound as good as they could. Drummer Ronnie Tutt told me how one time Elvis called him upstairs to his room, played Ronnie some of his own records, then had him listen to records by other current recording artists. "The sound difference was amazing," Ronnie recalled. "It filled the room, it was big, it was gigantic, it was the way things are supposed to be mixed. And he said, 'Why don't my records sound like that?' He didn't know enough musically to be able to ask more pointedly about it, but he knew his records just didn't have that impact, and that drive, and that kick."

The second Jungle Room session was held October 29 and 30. On the first night, Elvis managed to record another sad song of heartbreak

Elvis' Red Period

Graceland came in for a major makeover in 1974. Elvis' girlfriend, Linda Thompson, worked with interior designer William Eubanks to revamp the TV Room and the Pool Room downstairs, while Elvis found the Tiki-style furniture you see in the Jungle Room. Guests coming through the front door found new chandeliers in the entrance hall and the dining room. There were new mirrors in the wall moldings, as well as colorful stained-glass panels.

But the most eye-catching change was Elvis' decision to add red to the rooms on the first floor—a lot of red. A thick, red shag carpet covered the floor, going all the way up the main staircase. Red drapes hung from the walls. There was red Louis XIV furniture trimmed in gold and offset by white throw pillows and white "fake fur" rugs. The red color scheme was also used in the upstairs room.

It was a look typical of the over-the-top style of the 1970s. When Graceland was opened to the public in 1982, the downstairs rooms were redone in the more sedate blue-and-white color scheme that was used in the '60s. But stories about Graceland's "red era" have piqued curiosity, resulting in occasional special exhibits of furnishings from the period.

("It's Easy For You"), a frisky song about a new romance ("Way Down"), and Johnny Ace's posthumous hit "Pledging My Love."

But the sessions were also continually delayed with the musicians sitting downstairs waiting for Elvis to appear. Bassist Jerry Scheff recalled that Elvis brought the musicians up to his room one by one, dressing them up in flamboyant outfits from his personal wardrobe. "And when we started to record, with everybody all dressed up, we couldn't record," Jerry told me. "Every time we'd start to record a song, if one of us looked over at Elvis or if he looked over at us, we'd start laughing."

On the 30th, Elvis didn't come downstairs at all, so the band recorded a backing track for Jim Reeves' "He'll Have to Go." Elvis overdubbed his vocal later; it was the last studio recording he ever made.

"Moody Blue," recorded at the February '76 session, was released as a single in December that year (reaching No. 31), with "Way Down" following in June '77 (peaking at No. 18, Elvis' first Top 20 hit in two years). Both sides of the single appeared on the *Moody Blue* album, also released in June, along with the remaining studio tracks from the Jungle Room sessions and two live songs. It was the last album released during Elvis' lifetime; sales after his death would take it all the way to No. 3.

54 *Elvis* Album

If RCA was pleased at the success of the *Elvis Presley* album, they were positively thrilled at the success of the *Elvis* album released just seven months later in October 1956. *Elvis Presley* sold 300,000 copies at the time of its release; *Elvis* generated sales of 500,000 copies.

Like *Elvis Presley*, *Elvis* opens with a rocker, a cover of Little Richard's "Rip It Up." A keen Little Richard fan, he also recorded two more of his tunes, "Long Tall Sally" and "Ready Teddy" (and he'd do a fabulously kinetic version of the latter song during his September 9 appearance on *The Ed Sullivan Show*). Bookending the album was a bright rendition of "How Do You Think I Feel," which Elvis knew from Jimmie Rodgers Snow's version (and which he'd previously tried recording at Sun).

But most of the record was taken at a slower tempo. "When My Blue Moon Turns to Gold Again" is light pop, pure and simple. So is "Paralyzed," another pleasant number from the pen of Otis Blackwood, writer of "Don't Be Cruel" and "All Shook Up." "Anyplace is Paradise" was also a jaunty slice of pop but with a touch of blues swing.

The blues really come to the fore with "So Glad You're Mine," by Arthur "Big Boy" Crudup, who'd written the very first song Elvis released, "That's All Right." It's a terrific performance, far more sensual vocally than his other material; just listen to how he delivers the words "Ooo-wee!" He's equally heartfelt on "Love Me," the second Jerry Leiber/Mike Stoller number he covered (the first was "Hound Dog"). The legendary songwriting team had written the number as "a parody of a corny hillbilly ballad" Leiber explained, but Elvis played it straight and turned in a very affecting performance.

On the softer side, "First in Line" and "How's the World Treating You" were both lovely ballads, but they have some stiff competition here with "Old Shep." This was the song that Elvis had sung as a 10 year old at the Mississippi-Alabama Fair and Dairy Show in Tupelo. Elvis doesn't sound like he would have as a child of course, but the song's emotional pull is undoubtedly still the same as when he first sang it.

As with all of Elvis' best albums, *Elvis* is a testament to his diversity as a singer. Blues, ballads, pop—Elvis loved to tackle it all. It also laid the groundwork for what was to come. The release of *Elvis* brought the heady year of 1956 to a fitting conclusion, capping a year of success that was unparalleled in the music business.

55 The First Color Movie

The film *Loving You* had a lot of "firsts" for Elvis. It was the first time Elvis received star billing in a movie (he was officially only a supporting player in his first film, *Love Me Tender*). It was his first film in color and the first to feature his newly dyed black hair (and he'd continue to dye his hair black for the rest of his life). It was the first movie to have a song by Jerry Leiber and Mike Stoller (the title track, a romantic ballad). It featured the first outfit he wore that could truly be considered iconic. And it marked the first time his life story was fictionalized in a movie.

Elvis plays Deke Rivers, a truck driver discovered by an ambitious press agent who arranges for Deke to join the group of country musicians she works with. Deke's hot new style of music becomes an instant sensation but also attracts controversy. There are further complications due to a love triangle between Deke, Glenda (Lizabeth Scott), the press agent, and Susan (Dolores Hart), a young singer in the group, that becomes a quadrangle when Tex (Wendell Corey), Glenda's ex-husband and leader of the band, decides he'd like to win Glenda back again.

With Elvis playing a singer, most of the songs appear in performance sequences. In a neat twist, one "performance" is an impromptu rendition of "Mean Woman Blues" that Deke performs in a café after a local tough guy challenges Deke to show what he can do. Deke agrees, hoping to stave off a fight, but when fisticuffs break out anyway, Deke handily KO's the tough guy so that he lands sprawling across a jukebox.

"Got A Lot O' Livin' To Do" appears in the film's climactic concert sequence and is particularly joyous, with Elvis cutting some sharp dance moves; his parents, who visited Elvis in California during the film shoot, can be seen in the audience, clapping along, Gladys never taking her eyes off her son. The concert sequences are especially exciting, due in no small part to director/screenwriter Hal Kanter spending time with Elvis before shooting began and witnessing first hand the hysteria he provoked in live performance. Kanter was determined to get some of that thrill into the movie.

Elvis also wore a terrific costume during the sequence where he performs "Teddy Bear." It was the first outfit Nudie Cohn ever designed for Elvis: a shiny white western-style shirt with burgundy

Elvis Presley poses with house guest, Venetia Stevenson, a Hollywood starlet who had recently been dubbed "World's Most Photogenic Girl" in a photography magazine contest. Elvis and his guest were spotted leaving through the rear door of a downtown Memphis theater early on August 9, 1957, where they attended a private showing of his latest movie, Loving You. (AP Photo)

The Lost Film

On October 20, 1955, Elvis performed two shows in Cleveland put together by Cleveland DJ Bill Randle, which were also filmed for a movie short with the working title *The Pied Piper of Cleveland: A Day in the Life of a Famous Disc Jockey*. Elvis shared the bill with Pat Boone and Bill Haley and His Comets.

And no one's seen the film since.

Bill Randle had met Elvis the previous February when Elvis played his first show in Cleveland. Randle had passed on the name of a contact who helped Elvis secure an audition with the television show *Arthur Godfrey's Talent Scouts* in March. Elvis failed the audition, but Randle kept his eye on the rising performer. And when he set up the October shows, he made sure Elvis was on the bill.

The afternoon show was held at Brooklyn High School, the evening show at St. Michael's Hall. The film's director, Arthur Cohen, had refused to shoot Elvis, describing his performance as "pitiful," but Randle gave camera operator Jack Barnett extra money, and Elvis was filmed. But the film was only shown once in Cleveland and never received wide distribution due to legal difficulties. Randle sold the rights to Universal/Polygram in 1993, but the footage has yet to be released. It would be exciting if it was, as it would be the earliest known sound footage of Elvis.

trim, matching burgundy trousers with white trim around the pockets and outside leg seam, accented by a white scarf. Kanter also used something he had observed at one of Elvis' shows in this scene. He'd seen a pair of twins clapping their hands to the music in a unique way, one twin using her left hand to hit the right hand of the other twin. During "Teddy Bear," there's a shot of the audience with a pair of twins doing the same thing.

"Teddy Bear" was released as a single in June 1957, and the *Loving You* soundtrack was released the following month. Both records topped the charts. The movie had its premiere at the Strand Theater in Memphis on July 9, but Elvis didn't attend; he waited until a midnight screening of the film was held on July 10, taking his parents and his new girlfriend, Anita Wood. The film got some good reviews; as *Variety* noted, "Elvis shows improvement as an actor." While *Love Me Tender* gave Elvis a chance to get his feet wet as an actor, *Loving You* was the first movie to show what he could really do.

56 Recording in Memphis: The Memphis Recording Service Demo Sessions

The very first records Elvis recorded were personal demos, and they revealed a lot about his influences.

Elvis variously told reporters that when he walked into what was then called the Memphis Recording Service in the summer of 1953, he wanted to make a record "to surprise my mother" or "to hear what I sounded like." It was probably no accident that he chose to do so at the Memphis Recording Service because the studio and Sam Phillips had been the recent subject of an article in the *Memphis Press–Scimitar*.

Anyone could make a cheap two-sided acetate at the Memphis Recording Service for $3.98 (plus tax). At that first session, Elvis chose to record two songs his friends had heard him perform at their casual gatherings. "My Happiness" was a hit in 1948 for Jon and Sondra Steele. It's a pretty song, and Elvis' version is gentle and delicate as he accompanies himself on acoustic guitar; one can easily imagine his girlfriends giving a little sigh as they watched him perform. He also performed "That's When Your Heartaches Begin," which he knew from the Ink Spots' version of the song that was released in 1941. It's less confident than "My Happiness," and during the spoken word recitation Elvis comes to an abrupt stop. But his plaintive vocals nonetheless made an impression; before he left the studio, Phillips' assistant Marion Keisker made sure to write down his name and telephone number.

Elvis returned to the studio on January 4, 1954, which cost $8.25. He recorded two more ballads, "I'll Never Stand in Your Way" by Joni James and "It Wouldn't Be the Same Without You." The songs were similar in style and sound to the two he'd previously recorded—the same yearning vocals and simple acoustic guitar strumming. Elvis always had a fondness for ballads, especially because they gave him a chance to show how expressive a vocalist he could be. They also give an indication of the kind of songs Elvis was drawn to at the time and the kind of singer he aspired to be.

The first people outside of Elvis' family to hear the records were the patrons of Charlie's Record Shop, a store Elvis visited regularly. The shop had a jukebox, and the owner agreed to put Elvis' records on it, giving him a thrill every time someone happened to give them a spin. All four songs have since been officially released, and you can most readily find them on the *Sunrise* (1999) compilation.

57 Last Performances

Elvis' last tour was a 10-day jaunt during June 1977. He opened at Southwest Missouri State University in Springfield, Missouri, on June 17 then played shows in Kansas City, Missouri; Omaha, Nebraska; Lincoln, Nebraska; Rapid City, South Dakota; Sioux Falls, South Dakota; Des Moines, Iowa; Madison, Wisconsin; Cincinnati, Ohio; and he closed on June 26 with a show at the Market Square Arena in Indianapolis, Indiana.

It was Elvis' fifth tour of the year, all of which were of about similar length. No tour ran longer than two weeks. During the second tour of the year, which began March 23 in Arizona and should've ended April 3 in Florida, the final four dates were canceled when Elvis became ill; he returned to Memphis on April 1 and checked into Baptist Memorial Hospital for five days. But most tours ran smoothly.

There was some excitement during the final tour. When Elvis arrived in Madison on June 24, he noticed a fight about to break out at a local gas station. He demanded that his limo stop so that he could assist and leapt from the car, striking a karate pose. The would-be attackers stopped in their tracks when they realized who he was, and the fight ended before it started. When the police arrived, he continued hanging out, posing for pictures with anyone who was interested.

The next day in Cincinnati, frustrated when the hotel's air conditioning wasn't working properly, he took matters into his own hands, not even waiting for a car; he simply took off down the street to find a new hotel. And two of the shows were filmed during the tour for his upcoming TV special.

His manager's birthday happened to be June 26, 1977. Before the show, Elvis received a special plaque in honor of RCA pressing the two billionth Elvis Presley record while manufacturing Elvis' latest album, *Moody Blue*. It was an impressive accomplishment for a performer who continued to set records throughout his career.

For the show, Elvis wore a white jumpsuit with a huge Mexican sundial on the front and back. The quality of Elvis' performance had varied over the tour, as it had for the past few years. "His voice was there," Jerry Scheff told me, "it just depended on how much energy he had." But for this show he was in good form. The 19-song set was a mix of old hits with a few lesser-known numbers: "See See Rider," a medley of "I Got A Woman" and "Amen," "Love Me," "Fairytale," "You Gave Me A Mountain," "Jailhouse Rock," "It's Now Or Never," "Little Sister," a medley of "Teddy Bear" and "Don't Be Cruel," "Please Release Me," "I Can't Stop Loving You,"

"Bridge Over Troubled Water," "Early Morning Rain," "What'd I Say," "Johnny B. Goode," "I Really Don't Want To Know," "Hurt," "Hound Dog," and the standard closer, "Can't Help Falling In Love."

Elvis' performances of the dramatic numbers like "You Gave Me A Mountain," "Bridge Over Troubled Water," and "Hurt" were especially passionate, while the *Indianapolis Star* picked "It's Now or Never" as the evening's best song. "At 42, Elvis is still carrying around some excess baggage on his mid-section, but it didn't stop him from giving a performance in true Presley style," the paper wrote. "Elvis' older numbers seemed to draw more applause, although just about everything he did created mass hysteria, especially his leg jerks.... The packed arena was indication enough that Elvis is still as popular as ever."

So Elvis' live performing career came to a close on a high note. Of course, Elvis didn't know it was his last show. After a seven-week break, he was preparing to go out on another short tour, a 12-date run set to begin on August 17 in Portland, Maine, and conclude with two homecoming shows in Memphis on August 27 and 28.

58 The Last TV Special

Elvis In Concert was Elvis' last TV special, airing just over seven weeks after his death on CBS on October 3, 1977.

The special was announced on June 1. The reason why Parker set up such a show, which would involve filming Elvis on tour at a time when he was obviously not at his best, isn't clear. According to Peter Guralnick's *Careless Love*, Parker variously told people that it was Elvis who wanted to do the special, or that Parker wanted to give him a challenge, or that he'd asked CBS for so much money ($750,000) he thought they'd refuse.

The special was filmed over two nights on Elvis' final tour, June 19 in Omaha, Nebraska, and June 21 in Rapid City, South Dakota. Omaha was the third date of the tour, and the show was not considered to be especially good. Elvis realized this himself, telling the special's producers, "I know I was terrible." He was determined to do better in Rapid City, and he did; most of the songs in the special are drawn from this performance.

No one knows how the special would have turned out if Elvis hadn't died. The producers hadn't expected to end up with footage of Elvis' last performances. But there was still concern over his appearance; although he was in relatively good voice, he moved sluggishly and seemed tired, his eyes drooping. So the show was padded with a lot of footage of fans talking about Elvis.

In fact, the show's first eight minutes consist of such footage before Elvis takes the stage to perform the standard opener, "See See Rider," from Rapid City. "That's All Right" and an edited version of "Are You Lonesome Tonight?," also from Rapid City, follow; the "Teddy Bear"/"Don't Be Cruel" medley is from Omaha. After more fan comments come "You Gave Me a Mountain" and "Jailhouse Rock," both from Rapid City. There are still more fan comments, then comes "How Great Thou Art" from Omaha, and "I Really Don't Want to Know," "Hurt," "Hound Dog," and "My Way," all from Rapid City. The final number, "Can't Help Falling in Love," is from Omaha. Then there are two statements from Vernon—one filmed during the tour and one filmed after Elvis' death—with a clearly distraught Vernon thanking the fans for their support.

A soundtrack album was also released in October, featuring more songs from the two shows; it reached No. 5, while the single "My Way," released the following month, reached No. 22. The album has since been released on CD. But the show itself has never been officially released on either video or DVD, mostly because of concerns about Elvis' appearance. Even those who knew Elvis were surprised at how much they had overlooked. When Myrna Smith, one of the Sweet Inspirations, talked to her future husband, Jerry Schilling, on the phone after the Rapid City show, she assured him that Elvis looked "really good." Yet four months later, when she watched the show on television, she burst into tears at the sight of her former boss: "We were all wearing blinders," she admitted.

But some footage from the special has been released over the years. Footage of "Are You Lonesome Tonight?" and "My Way" from Rapid City appears in the 1981 documentary *This Is Elvis*. "Lonesome" was used to illustrate Elvis' decline, as he stumbles over his words during the middle spoken-word section. Footage of "Love Me" from the Omaha show was substituted for "Lonesome" in the film's video release. Elvis' performance of "Unchained Melody," from Rapid City, also appears on the *Elvis: The Great Performances* DVD box set.

But Elvis Presley Enterprises has always been concerned with presenting Elvis in the most positive light, so an official release of the complete special seems unlikely. The only place to find it for now is on the collector's circuit, which seems a shame. The lavish bootleg set *The Final Curtain*, which has six CDs, six DVDs, and a 400-page book, shows that fans certainly have an interest in this period.

59 Elvis Is Dead. Or Is He?

There's not just a controversy about how Elvis died. There are also those who don't believe Elvis Presley died at all—at least not on August 16, 1977.

The most widely circulated rumor posits that Elvis faked his death in order to escape from the pressures of show business. Various kinds of "proof" have been offered to back up this assertion, such as the spelling of his middle name being "Aaron" on his tombstone, while it was "Aron" on his birth certificate. It's also been said that Elvis' life insurance policy with Lloyd's of London was never claimed after his death; since he was alive, to do so would have been insurance fraud. But in fact, Elvis has no such policy. Elvis was also said to have been a government agent and went into hiding as part of the Witness Protection Program.

Then there's the phenomenon of Elvis sightings. Over the years, numerous people claimed to have seen Elvis after his death, generally in some out-of-the-way place. The tabloid *Weekly World News*, in a story headlined: I'VE SEEN ELVIS IN THE FLESH, reported that Elvis had been spotted at a Burger King in Kalamazoo, Michigan. The Ottawa-based Elvis Sightings Society claims there have been so many Elvis sightings in the city, a street was even renamed Elvis Lives Lane.

Author Gail Brewer-Giorgio explored this idea in her book *Orion: The Living Superstar of Song*, first published in 1978. The story of "Orion" paralleled Elvis', from the twin who dies at birth, to the mother who dies while Orion is in the service, to his lavish mansion "Dixie-Land," to his increasing use of drugs. But Orion manages to escape his prison of fame by the book's end, staging his own death then driving away, an anonymous man once again, as a tribute song to Orion plays over the car radio.

Brewer-Giorgio then turned to Elvis' own life, writing a series of books about the possibility that Elvis hadn't died: *The Most Incredible Elvis Presley Story Ever Told* (1988); *Is Elvis Alive?* (1988), which came with a cassette tape purporting to have a recording of Elvis' voice; *The Elvis Files: Was His Death Faked?* (1990); *The Elvis Cover-Up* (1997); and *Elvis Undercover: Is He Alive and Coming Back?* (1999).

The Elvis Files was also released as a DVD, hosted by actor Bill Bixby, who co-starred with Elvis in *Clambake* and *Speedway* and also hosted the similarly themed *The Elvis Conspiracy* (1992). There's no shortage of other films asserting that Elvis might still walk among us, though not all of them (e.g., *Elvis Is Alive*, 1999; *Elvis Found Alive*, 2012) take the subject that seriously. The 2002 cult film *Bubba Ho-tep* imagines Elvis living in a nursing home in East Texas, befriending a fellow resident who claims to be John F. Kennedy.

And there are naturally thousands of websites discussing the subject. Do a Google search on the phrase "Elvis is alive," and you'll get 148,000 results (the same search on Bing generates 119,000 results). So you can while away the hours exploring numerous different theories. Who knows; maybe "the truth is out there."

60 Imitation Elvis

If you weren't lucky enough to see Elvis perform live, the closest you can ever come to seeing him perform is watching his films, his TV appearances, and the live concert films. But for some fans, that's not enough. They go out to see Elvis impersonators.

Elvis impersonator Matt Lewis performs during the Legends in Concert show at the Imperial Palace hotel-casino in Las Vegas on Friday, June 29, 2007. Lewis is known as one of the best in the business and was voted as such by USA Today *in 2005.* (AP Photo/Jae C. Hong)

There are tribute acts for numerous rock acts, but Elvis impersonators are strangely controversial. Some fans feel impersonators diminish Elvis' legacy, though in fact there have been Elvis impersonators since Elvis rose to fame in the 1950s; one could say the musical (later film) *Bye Bye Birdie* was based around an Elvis impersonator, since the plot was clearly inspired by Elvis being drafted at the height of his fame. The comedian Andy Kaufman further popularized the idea of imitating Elvis by adding a great Elvis impersonation to his act (just check him out on YouTube).

Other fans feel impersonators are demeaning. It's certainly true that some mean to parody Elvis with their impersonation. Others just impersonate Elvis for fun and lack the higher-end costumes, props, and music that the professionals utilize. And most of the impersonators choose to emulate the '70s Elvis, the jumpsuit period, the Elvis era that is most frequently ridiculed by critics, meaning that simply being a '70s Elvis opens up the impersonator to criticism.

Elvis himself didn't seem particularly bothered by impersonators. He's said to have enjoyed watching Andy Kaufman's impersonations of him; given his own sense of humor, he was

The Real Life Orion

The story of Jimmy Ellis is certainly one of the strangest tales of an Elvis imitator.

Ellis was born James Hughes Bell on February 26, 1945, in Pascagoula, Mississippi, and was later adopted by a family named Ellis. His recording career began in 1964, and it was quickly noticed that he sounded uncannily like Elvis. In 1972, Shelby Singleton, then the owner of Sun Records, released the single "That's All Right"/"Blue Moon of Kentucky" by Ellis, though it wasn't credited to him. Nor were his performances on later Sun releases, like Jerry Lee Lewis' *Duets* album, and *Trio+*, which featured Lewis, Carl Perkins, and Charlie Rich.

Singleton then unveiled his mystery singer as "Orion," inspired by the character in Gail Brewer-Giorgio's book, with Ellis wearing a bejeweled mask to maintain an air of mystery. Ellis had previously released the album *Ellis Sings Elvis* under his own name, but now he became Orion full time.

But after an initial burst of popularity, Orion's star began to wane, especially after Ellis dramatically removed his mask during a show. The mystery gone, Orion's star faded further. But Ellis continued performing and recording, both under his own name and Orion's, even donning his mask again.

Sadly, Ellis' life came to sudden end on December 12, 1998, when he and his fiancée were murdered during a robbery at one of the convenience stores Ellis owned. The following year, Germany's Bear Family Records released the Orion box set *Who Was That Masked Man?*

likely a fan of Kaufman's off-the-wall comedy. And a month before his death, on July 19, 1977, he wrote a letter to an impersonator named David Ferrari that read in part, "I really do appreciate you as a fan, and mimicry is a sincere form of being a fan.... This is a great compliment to me that you would work so hard on this act like mine." Although he did suggest that Ferrari shouldn't just stick to impersonation, "Do develop your own special talents and abilities though, David."

After Elvis' death, Elvis impersonation became increasingly popular. You can find impersonators of every age, nor are they limited by gender or race. There are female Elvis impersonators, and performers like "El Vez," who bills himself as "The Mexican Elvis," and uses his show to comment on social issues (such as reworking the song "In The Ghetto" to "In The Barrio"). In 2007, after decades of not including Elvis impersonators in official events, Elvis Presley Enterprises adopted an "if you can't beat them, join them" attitude and now hosts a yearly "Ultimate Elvis Tribute Artist Contest"—the phrase "tribute artist" is seen as a more respectful term than "impersonator."

Many impersonator events are organized as contests. Elvis Week in Memphis naturally attracts a lot of impersonators, and casinos and clubs across the country usually have an impersonator show scheduled around the time of Elvis' birthday or the anniversary of his death.

The words "Elvis impersonator" (or "tribute artist") do conjure up the stereotype of a crazy Elvis fan in an outlandish costume—probably a jumpsuit. But those who like impersonators don't feel that way. They not only enjoy the camaraderie of hanging out with other Elvis fans while watching a performer sing the songs of artist they love; they also see Elvis impersonators as vitally important in helping to keep Elvis' legacy alive.

61 Big in the Big Apple

Though he made several notable television appearances in New York City, Elvis didn't play the Big Apple until 1972.

Elvis had first ventured to New York on March 23, 1955, when he auditioned for the TV show *Arthur Godfrey's Talent Scouts*. He failed to generate any interest, and the rejection stung. New York was a sophisticated city, and Elvis and his crew were regarded as country hicks. He never felt entirely comfortable in the city—one reason he didn't play any shows there.

But by 1972, he'd taken his Vegas show on the road, selling out arenas around the country. Now New York might be ready for him. And it was—when his first three shows booked at Madison Square Garden sold out, a fourth was quickly added, which also sold out. Elvis' four shows on June 9 (one show), June 10 (two shows), and June 11 (one show) marked the first time an artist had sold out four consecutive performances at the venue. A total of 80,000 tickets were sold.

Before the first show on the 9th, a short press conference was held. Elvis provided jokey answers for most questions, though he answered a few seriously. Asked why he didn't record more hard rock songs, he admitted it was hard to find a good one; asked what he attributed his longevity to he first joked, "Vitamin E," then apologized: "I was only kidding…. I enjoy the business. I like what I'm doing." But he brushed off questions about his views on the Vietnam War and the women's liberation movement, demurring, "I'm just an entertainer."

Recognizing that the shows were a major event, RCA recorded both concerts on June 10 and announced they'd have an album ready for release the following week, just eight days later. So rushed was the production that *Elvis As Recorded Live at Madison Square*

Garden (which featured the June 10 evening show) didn't even use a photo from the show on the cover. A photo from his April 16 performance in Jacksonville, Florida, was used instead, as the pre-printed jackets were prepared before Elvis had even stepped on stage at Madison Square Garden.

It was an important release for another reason; it marked the first time a complete Elvis show had been officially released, and it was the first time a live album had been drawn from a single show. So it was not only an excellent souvenir for those who had attended the shows, it also allowed other fans to experience an Elvis concert in its entirety—as well as providing a great incentive to see Elvis live themselves, if they hadn't already.

The show also reveals how Elvis understood the importance of pacing. He opened the show with his very first single, "That's All Right." It was the last tour that featured "That's All Right" as the first song; from August 6 on, "Also Sprach Zarathustra" would always segue into "See See Rider." Elvis then performed more recent material: "Proud Mary," "Never Been to Spain," and "You Don't Have to Say You Love Me," building up to the drama of "You've Lost That Lovin' Feeling." He then sang Tony Joe White's "Polk Salad Annie," a down-home slice of Southern swamp rock that Elvis always had fun with.

Elvis next gave a nod to his '50s hits: "Love Me," "All Shook Up," "Heartbreak Hotel," a medley of "Teddy Bear" and "Don't Be Cruel," and "Love Me Tender." Then came an unusual choice, "The Impossible Dream," from the musical *Man of La Mancha*. It was the first song from a musical that Elvis ever performed (aside from songs from his own films). After a race through "Hound Dog" came his last big hit, "Suspicious Minds." The remaining songs alternated quieter numbers with big, dramatic performances: "For the Good Times," "An American Trilogy," "Funny How Time Slips Away," "I Can't Stop Loving You." Then the standard closer, "Can't Help Falling in Love."

The shows received rave reviews; *The New York Times* called Elvis "a champion, the only one in his class." When the double album hit the streets, it reached No. 11 and sold more than 2 million copies. The June 10 afternoon show was released in 1997 as *An Afternoon in the Garden*. Today, both shows are available on the *Prince From Another Planet* set, its title taken from *The New York Times'* review.

62 The Set Closer

The songs Elvis performed live changed throughout his career. Some songs came and went, but there were other numbers that remained staples of his set. One was "Hound Dog," which his fans always enjoyed seeing him perform live. And from July 31, 1969, on, there was another song that made its debut in the closing slot, and it would hold that spot all the way through Elvis' very last show on June 26, 1977: "Can't Help Falling in Love."

The song first appeared in *Blue Hawaii*. Elvis sings the song at the birthday party of his girlfriend's grandmother, first accompanied by the sound of a music box, which makes it sound even more charming.

The song was written by Hugo Peretti, Luigi Creatore, and George David Weiss, who'd previously written the title track for the Elvis film *Wild in the Country*. The writers had been told by Elvis' publishers that the scene needed a song with a "European flavor," and Peretti and Weiss drew suitable inspiration from the melody of the 1784 French song "Plaisir d'Amour" ("Pleasure of Love"), written by French classical composer Jean-Paul-Égide Martini. While they were working on the melody, Creatore suddenly came up with the line "I can't help falling in love with you." Peretti and Weiss instantly felt that should be the song's title, and the number was completed the following day.

The original song, based on a poem by Jean-Pierre Claris de Florian, was about heartbreak; the Peretti/Creatore/Weiss number was an ode to everlasting love. According to Weiss, it was because of Elvis that the song appeared in *Blue Hawaii*. Although it had been dismissed as a "dumb ballad," after hearing the demo Elvis had announced, "I wanna do that one in my movie." "They thought he was nuts," Weiss recalled.

Elvis recorded the song on March 23, 1961, patiently working his way through 29 takes. It's easy to see why Elvis would be drawn for the song. He'd always liked ballads, and this one was written just for him; instead of covering a standard, he now had the chance to create one himself. It's a lovely, restrained performance; not a dramatic showstopper, but delivered with sweet, heartfelt sincerity. The song was released as a single at the end of November (a different version from the one that appeared in the movie, without the music box intro), reaching No. 2 and selling more than 1 million copies.

Elvis first performed it for an audience in both stand-up concerts taped for the *Elvis* Comeback Special, on June 29, 1968. Just over a year later, it became the closing song during his first Las Vegas season, and it remained the closing song for every subsequent show. It's a song that highlights Elvis' diversity as a singer—something he always loved doing for audiences. But it was also a bittersweet experience for fans to hear in concert because once that distinctive piano introduction struck up, they knew it was the end of another show.

63 Deck the Halls

Christmas was one of Elvis' favorite holidays. So it was no surprise that he released a number of Christmas records during his lifetime.

The first was the appropriately titled *Elvis' Christmas Album*, released in October 1957. The album featured four songs that had previously appeared on the *Peace in the Valley* EP, released in April 1957 and eight new songs. There were two traditional carols ("O Little Town of Bethlehem" and "Silent Night"), and eight modern numbers, the best of which are "Blue Christmas" and "Santa Claus is Back in Town." "Blue Christmas" had been recorded by other acts, but Elvis gave it a light, bluesy touch and made it his own. "Santa Claus Is Back In Town" was written especially for him by Jerry Leiber and Mike Stoller, a wailing R&B number that ruffled the feathers of those who felt it might be a tad too raunchy for a Christmas song.

But that paled to the fuss that erupted over his rendition of "White Christmas," performed in a light blues arrangement inspired by The Drifters' 1954 version of the song. The song's composer, Irving Berlin, had made no remarks about The Drifters' version, but he didn't hesitate to take on Elvis, calling Elvis' performance a "profane parody" of his Christmas classic, and he actually went so far as to call radio stations and ask them not to play it, or any other song on the album.

Berlin's actions did put a dent in sales, but the album (which also featured "I'll Be Home for Christmas," "Santa Bring My Baby Back [To Me]," and a hiccupping version of "Here Comes Santa Claus") went to No. 1 anyway. Elvis' next Christmas release was the heartfelt song, "If Every Day Could Be Like Christmas" (written by his friend Red West), released as a single in November

1966 with "How Would You Like to Be" (from *It Happened at the World's Fair*) on the flip side; it failed to chart.

Elvis recorded his second Christmas album in 1971 during a weeklong session in Nashville when he recorded more than 30 songs. It was another mix of traditional carols ("O Come All Ye Faithful," "The First Noel") and modern numbers ("On a Snowy Christmas Night," "Winter Wonderland," "It Won't Seem Like Christmas [Without You]," "I'll Be Home on Christmas Day," "If I Get Home on Christmas Day," "Silver Bells," and another Red West number, "Holly Leaves and Christmas Trees"). The performances are more laidback compared to the previous holiday album, but there's another bluesy classic in "Merry Christmas Baby," a sort of sequel to "Santa Claus is Back in Town," which runs close to six minutes and has a nice swampy guitar line from James Burton.

The song "The Wonderful World of Christmas" was adapted for the record's title, *Elvis Sings The Wonderful World of Christmas*, and the album was released in October 1971, hitting No. 1 on *Billboard's* Christmas Albums chart.

Elvis' Christmas songs have since been repackaged in various configurations, and you'll want to be sure to get one of the sets that features all of the Christmas songs. Those that do include *White Christmas* (2000), *Christmas Peace* (2003), and *Elvis Christmas* (2006). The collector's edition of the 1994 set *If Every Day Was Like Christmas* doesn't have the songs from the *Peace in the Valley* EP, but it does have a few previously unreleased tracks and comes in a sleeve that features a pop-up model of Graceland all decked out for the holidays.

64 The Collector's Label

"Follow That Dream" isn't just the title of an Elvis film. It's also the name given to Elvis' own collector's label, which makes rare recordings officially available to the fans.

The Follow That Dream label was established in 1999 by Ernst Jørgensen, who's overseen all of Elvis Presley's record releases for RCA since 1991. As he explained in an interview, the bootlegging of Elvis' material had escalated dramatically in the early '90s in Europe, with many bootlegs being sold through Elvis fan clubs. If an official collector's label was set up, fan clubs could continue to make money by selling those releases. Those not affiliated with fan clubs would also have access to rare recordings that were released legitimately. Thus it was a great way to beat the bootleggers at their own game.

The first FTD release was *Burbank '68: The NBC-TV 'Comeback Special,'* released in July 1999, which featured rehearsals, live songs, and alternative versions of songs from the *Elvis* special. Early releases presented home recordings, studio outtakes, and live performances. There were around 200 shows in RCA's vaults, a legacy of Elvis' manager deciding to record many of Elvis' '70s performances. The live CDs are some of FTD's biggest sellers.

FTD then began expanding its range of releases. In 2001, they began issuing what's called the "Classic Albums" series; each release contains a complete original album and a second CD of bonus tracks (many of them unreleased), packaged in a 7" gatefold sleeve with an accompanying booklet. Elvis' soundtrack albums and greatest hits collections have also been released in one- and two-CD sets.

The first release of FTD's book/CD packages occurred in 2001. *That's The Way It Was* featured pictures and information from the filming of the documentary *Elvis: That's The Way It Is*, along with a CD of live performances. The books have become increasingly elaborate; the 2012 set *A Boy From Tupelo: The Complete 1953-55 Recordings*, had a book that ran more than 500 pages and included three CDs. In 2009, the resurgence of interest in vinyl led to vinyl FTD reissues of Elvis' albums.

Whatever era of Elvis most interests you, you'll certainly find an FTD release with rare material from that period. FTD is primarily a mail-order label, and the easiest way to buy releases is through EPE's website, www.shopelvis.com. Releases are also available at Graceland's shops.

65 Elvis Week

Every Elvis fan should visit Memphis, and Graceland, at least once in their lives. But for the full-on fan experience, you should attend Elvis Week in August.

Elvis Week is a celebration of Elvis' life and work, and it had a very organic beginning. One year after his death on August 15, 1978, members of the Elvis Country Fan Club gathered outside of Graceland's gates spontaneously. Graceland wasn't even open to the public yet, and there were no officially organized events. But Elvis' fans wanted to go somewhere where they could share their thoughts and feelings about him with other fans, and Graceland was the obvious choice. Eventually, the gatherings became more organized.

Today, the Elvis Country Fan Club organizes and sponsors the Candlelight Service on the night of August 15. Fans gather outside Graceland's gates for a short ceremony featuring songs and brief comments. Then fans walk up Graceland's driveway to the Meditation Garden, bearing candles. Some leave tributes at the gravesite. Attendance is such that the fans continue to walk up to the Meditation Garden throughout the night and into the morning.

As more fans began to arrive prior to August 15 and stayed for a few days afterwards, more events began to be organized. What's now called "Elvis Week" grew to the point where it currently runs about a week; Elvis Week 2013 ran from August 10 to 17. Elvis Presley Enterprises puts on a number of events: there are special movie screenings, panel discussions with people who knew or worked with Elvis, musical performances, and the Ultimate Elvis Tribute Artist Contest. Special events are also set up for specific anniversaries; Elvis Week 2013 had a screening of a re-edited version of Elvis' *Aloha From Hawaii*, as well as a listening party of the 1973 Stax Studio recordings, as it was the 40th anniversary for both events.

There are numerous other events held during Elvis Week. One of the best (not least because it's free) is DJ George Klein's Elvis Memorial Service held at the University of Memphis on August 16, which features a variety of speakers. Klein also hosts an Elvis Mafia Reunion at Alfred's on Beale Street earlier in the week. Elvis' nurse Marian Cocke hosts the Elvis Presley Memorial Dinner, which raises money for charity and also features various speakers. A number of other Elvis fan clubs put on events around Memphis, usually benefiting some charity. There are also non-EPE-sponsored performances around town featuring musicians who played with Elvis or by Elvis impersonators. And hotels will set aside rooms for sales of Elvis merchandise.

Some fans have felt Elvis Week has become too commercial, less about remembering Elvis and more about making money. It's true that ticket prices can add up. But you can still find events that are free or inexpensive. Throughout Elvis Week at Graceland, there are free performances at Graceland Crossing (across the street from the mansion). There are also free walk-ups to the Meditation Garden in the morning and evening, a good time to marvel at all the impressive floral arrangements that have been sent in by fans around the world. You can find Elvis Tribute Artists performing on Beale Street, a great place for people watching in itself. Bars and restaurants are full of Elvis fans during Elvis Week—strike up a conversation and ask them for suggestions. Scan the local paper and drop by the Memphis Convention and Visitor's Bureau at 47 Union Avenue (www.memphistravel.com) for more ideas.

Here are two other things to keep in mind. Memphis in August is hot. Very hot. Temperatures are generally in the 90s, with humidity at 90 percent—or more. This doesn't deter Elvis fans, though, and you'll find crowds everywhere. So if you plan to tour Graceland or Sun Studio during your trip, schedule your visit early in the week. Arriving early is a good rule of thumb in general during Elvis Week in order to beat the crowds.

There's also a smaller scale Birthday Celebration held in January, around the days of Elvis' birth. There's a free ceremony held at Graceland on January 8, complete with birthday cake, with a few other gatherings and music events also scheduled.

For information on Elvis Week and the Birthday Celebration, go to Elvis' official website, www.elvis.com.

66 Visit Las Vegas

There's certainly an "Elvis vibe" in the air when you visit Memphis, particularly during Elvis Week and Birthday Week. But there can be an Elvis vibe in Las Vegas all year round.

Part of that is due to the impersonators in town. The *Legends In Concert* show has been running in Las Vegas for more than 30 years now, and while the show has moved to different hotels during those years (at time of writing it was being performed at the Flamingo), you can always count on there being an Elvis in the cast. The Flamingo was also used as a location for the film *Viva Las Vegas*.

Peter "Big Elvis" Vallee is an impersonator who's been working in Vegas for many years and at time of writing is doing free shows at Harrah's Las Vegas (www.bigelvislasvegas.com). There are a number of other tribute shows running in Vegas, but they change regularly, so you need to verify that the event is still running. At time of writing, *Tribute Royalty* was running at Planet Hollywood; *Million Dollar Quartet*, about the Sun Records era, was running at Harrah's; and *The King Starring Trent Carlini* was running at the LVH.

The LVH is the renamed Las Vegas Hilton, formerly the International, where Elvis performed, and it's one of the few places associated with Elvis in the city that's still around. In recent years, it's also been home to the Las Vegas Elvis Festival, a four-day event held in the summer (www.lasvegaselvisfestival.com). The hotel also has a commemorative Elvis statue in the lobby.

Jesse Garon has been designated the "Official Elvis of Las Vegas" by Vegas mayor Oscar B. Goodman (www.vegaselvis.com). He'll pick you up from the airport in a '50s pink Cadillac (formerly owned by Lucille Ball), take you for an hour's spin on Las Vegas Boulevard (known as "The Strip"), or preside over your wedding at some picturesque spot, like the "Welcome to Las Vegas" sign. There are many other opportunities to have an Elvis at your wedding in Las Vegas. Two places worth checking out are the Viva Las Vegas Wedding Chapel, which offers a wide variety of theme weddings (www.vivalasvegasweddings.com), and the Graceland Wedding Chapel (www.gracelandchapel.com). While visiting the Graceland Wedding Chapel, I was told that it also has an Elvis connection; the

The Entrance Music

For most of the 1970s, when Elvis walked out on stage at the start of his shows, he was accompanied by the glorious strains of "Einleitung, oder Sonnenaufgang" ("Introduction, or Sunrise") from Richard Strauss' tone poem *Also Sprach Zarathustra* ("Thus Spake Zarathustra")—better known to most people as the theme from Stanley Kubrick's 1968 science fiction masterpiece, *2001: A Space Odyssey.*

The idea to use the theme came from Corky Guercio, the wife of Joe Guercio, the conductor of the International Hotel's orchestra, who also toured with Elvis. Corky had told her husband the majestic music made her think of Elvis, and her husband agreed, suggesting to Elvis that they open the shows with it. Elvis also liked the idea. As Guercio observed, "[Elvis] didn't want to be just a guy walking out there, he wanted to be a god."

"Sunrise" was first used during a run of shows Elvis did in November 1970, and by the next year it was the standard opener, initially segueing into "That's All Right," but later changed to "See See Rider." The number became increasingly grandiose over time. "We set it up to the point where you got to the last chord, and the timpanist played the final set of eight notes and it would build to such a frenzy that it was orgasm time," Guercio said. "It was like the ultimate orgasm." "Sunrise" provided the perfect way open Elvis' shows with a touch of drama.

original owner was a friend of Elvis' and asked permission to use the name "Graceland." If you're already married, you can arrange to have Elvis at a "renewal of vows" ceremony.

The New Frontier Hotel where Elvis first performed in 1956 is gone, as is the Aladdin where he married Priscilla in 1967 (Planet Hollywood now stands on the site). The Sahara, where he stayed while *Viva Las Vegas* was being filmed, is being remodeled and will open under a new name. That leaves the Tropicana, another location setting for *Viva Las Vegas*, although the hotel has been remodeled since Elvis' day.

The Elvis-a-Rama museum is now sadly closed. But a new home has been found for *The King's Ransom* exhibit (www.thekingsransom.com). Previously at the Imperial Palace on the Strip, *The King's Ransom* is now located in Binion's Gambling Hall & Hotel on Fremont Street (the area they call "Downtown" in Vegas). The exhibit was put together by collectors Bud Glass and Russ Howe, and it features a wide range of fascinating items: stage outfits, personal items, and one of Elvis' cars. It's definitely worth checking out, and by the way, while you're at Binion's, you can also have your photo taken with $1 million, for free.

You'll also find Elvis impersonators working the Strip or on Fremont Street, posing for photos with tourists for tips or passing out brochures for area attractions. So don't be surprised if you have quite a few Elvis sightings during your stay. And in the casinos you'll find Elvis slot machines, although you may have to wait to use one; they're very popular.

67 The Chart Toppers That Didn't Happen

"(Marie's The Name) His Latest Flame"/"Little Sister," released in August 1961, was Elvis' most successful double-sided single of the decade. But did he cheat himself out of having two No. 1 hits by placing them both on the same record?

Both the A- and the B-sides of a number of Elvis' singles hit the charts over the years. "Hound Dog"/"Don't Be Cruel" was the most successful, with both sides considered to have topped the charts. "His Latest Flame" and "Little Sister" didn't get quite that high; the former reached No. 4, while the latter peaked at No. 5. It's possible that each song helped to cancel out the other's success.

Both songs were written by the songwriting team of Doc Pomus and Mort Shuman, who wrote a number of songs that Elvis recorded (one of the best being "Viva Las Vegas"). "His Latest Flame" was written with Bobby Vee in mind, and "Little Sister" was earmarked for Bobby Darin, but the composers felt that neither artist recorded a satisfactory version of the songs. So Del Shannon ended up being the first to officially release "His Latest Flame" when it appeared on his first album, *Runaway With Del Shannon*, which came out right before Elvis' version was released as a single.

Elvis ended up recording the songs after Pomus and Shuman had been contacted by Elvis' publishers, who asked if they had any material available for an upcoming session. The songwriters readily offered these two songs, which Elvis recorded at a June 25, 1961, session in RCA's Nashville studios. He also recorded a third Pomus/Shuman number, "Kiss Me Quick," at the session.

"His Latest Flame" has an invigorating Bo Diddley–style rhythm and tells the bittersweet story of a man who learns that the woman who pledged her love to him yesterday has now taken up with his best friend. But instead of saying anything, he swallows his pride and wishes his friend the best of luck. The musical arrangement gets increasingly complicated as the song progresses, with a jangly piano and claves giving the number an energetic boost during the bridge.

"Little Sister" is a good deal sassier, with a nice guitar lead by Hank Garland that neatly straddles the line between blues and pop. There's another woman-done-me-wrong theme—the song is addressed to the younger sister of a woman who's another two-timer—but Elvis' vocal is so breezy it's hard to believe he cares what the older sister is doing anymore, as long as he can score a date with the younger one. This is something common to both songs—a somewhat downbeat lyric paired with a sprightly melody, making them sound more optimistic.

Both songs were also clearly the strongest songs recorded at the session, making it a shame that "His Latest Flame" and "Little Sister" weren't each released as a single in their own right. So instead of getting two No. 1s, Elvis had to settle for having two Top 5 hits with the songs—in the U.S., anyway. Interestingly, in the UK, both sides of the single did top the charts.

68 Recording in Memphis: Stax

Elvis recorded in two of Memphis' most important studios—Sun and American Sound. In 1973, he recorded at another legendary studio: Stax.

Stax began in 1957 as a Memphis record label called Satellite Records and was owned by Jim Stewart. Jim's sister, Estelle Axton, later became involved in the company. In 1960, the company moved into a former movie house on East McLemore Avenue that had enough room for both a recording studio and a record shop. The company was also renamed "Stax," taken from the first two letters of Jim and Estelle's last names. Stax became the home of Memphis soul—artists including Isaac Hayes, Otis Redding, and Booker T. & the M.G.'s all recorded for the label.

When Elvis was told by RCA that he needed to get back into the studio, Stax was a good choice. It was not far from Graceland, and Elvis knew the neighborhood; as a teenager, Elvis had attended the First Assembly of God Church just down the road. His previous Memphis sessions had resulted in classic recordings and hit records; it was hoped the same magic could be created at Stax.

But the first set of sessions got off to a bad start. Elvis was due to arrive at the studio at 8:00 PM on July 20, 1973, but didn't turn up until 11:00 PM. The musicians who'd previously worked with him at American Sound and in Nashville were surprised at how Elvis had changed. He'd put on weight, and his lack of interest was evident. "He looked like he was miserable, both in health and in life," drummer Jerry Carrigan told me. "It was just awful to see." Elvis had brought his karate instructor Kang Rhee to the session, and their "clowning around with guns and stuff" made keyboardist Bobby Wood nervous. Elvis also had a large entourage with him, which proved to be a distraction.

Elvis ended up spending so much time fooling around the first evening, he didn't end up recording anything. He did record four tracks on the 21st, then less on each subsequent day; three on the 22nd, two on the 23rd, and one on the 24th. Difficulties with the studio's equipment delayed recording, and when he learned on the 24th that his personal microphone had been stolen, he got up and went home. The sessions were over.

None of the material recorded at the sessions fared well; of the two singles released, "I Got a Thing About You Baby," a pleasant piece of country pop released in January 1974, peaked at No. 39. The album *Raised On Rock/For Ol' Times Sake*, released in October 1973, only reached No. 50.

The songs recorded at the next Stax sessions, December 10–16, 1973, didn't fare much better on the pop charts, though the material was noticeably stronger. RCA also sent in their own equipment to avoid the problems they'd had with Stax's studio equipment.

The sessions got off to a good start with the spiritual infusion of "I Got a Feeling in My Body" by Dennis Linde, who'd also written Elvis' last big hit, "Burning Love." Elvis recorded 18 songs during the seven days of the sessions, some of the highlights being a rousing cover of Chuck Berry's "Promised Land," a poignant version of Danny O'Keefe's "Good Time Charlie's Got the Blues," Jerry Reed's "Talk About the Good Times," another spiritually-themed number, and "My Boy," an emotional number about the trauma of divorce, which Elvis had been performing in his live show. The songs appeared on the albums *Good Times* (1974) and *Promised Land* (1975), and though their performance on the pop charts wasn't impressive (the albums reached No. 90 and No. 47, respectively), they did very well on the country chart, reaching No. 5 and No. 1, respectively.

The Stax sessions were the last major sessions of Elvis' career. And it was clear that Elvis was becoming increasingly unhappy with his situation. Elvis himself admitted as much to bassist Norbert Putnam during the December sessions, telling him how he wanted to tour overseas and that he was thinking of ending his managerial relationship with Parker. He then got up and said, "Well, I guess it's time to go back to being Elvis"—admitting that his image had become something of a burden.

69 "Hound Dog" Two: The Steve Allen Show

In Elvis' appearance on *The Steve Allen Show*, host Allen tried to defuse the controversy that had erupted over Elvis' gyrating performance on *The Milton Berle Show*. Elvis went along with his plans, but he later admitted he wasn't very happy about it.

By the time Elvis appeared on the Berle show on June 5, he was already booked to appear on Allen's show, which would air July 1. He was now guaranteed to attract attention, but would he prove too hot to handle? Allen mulled it over, admitting that he had yet to come to a final decision about whether Elvis would appear but stating, "If he does appear, you can rest assured that I will not allow him to do anything that will offend anyone."

In the end, it was decided Elvis would perform on the show; the ratings bonanza was too great to pass up. But Allen decided to turn concerns about Elvis' appearance back on the critics by having Elvis wear a tuxedo and tails. Elvis also performed his first number, "I Want You, I Need You, I Love You," on a fancy-looking set with stately columns and a chandelier, emphasizing Allen's satiric approach to putting rock 'n' roll in a "classy" setting.

But Elvis didn't seem to get the joke; he appeared uncomfortable and awkward in his formal wear, and in his opening remarks with Allen he sounded very half-hearted. And things didn't get any better. For his second song, "Hound Dog," Allen wheeled out—what else?—a basset hound wearing a top hat for Elvis to sing to. The poor dog didn't look any happier than Elvis did about the proceedings, which were over quickly because Elvis performed a shortened version of the song, putting his arm around the dog and giving her a kiss at the end.

Then he had a sketch to get through, a parody of country shows like the *Grand Ole Opry*, called "Range Roundup," and featuring Elvis as "Tumbleweed" Presley, singing a song in which he rhymed "galoots" with "blue suede boots."

The fans weren't happy at seeing their idol trussed up and were quick to respond, turning up at RCA's New York offices with picket signs that read, "We want the GYRATIN' Elvis." But there was an unexpected payoff. For the first time, *The Steve Allen Show* beat *The Ed Sullivan Show* in the ratings, and as a result Sullivan finally agreed to book Elvis for the program.

But Elvis was still smarting from his appearance when he arrived back in Memphis on July 4. When he took the stage that night at Russwood Park, he made a point of telling the frenzied crowd, "You know, those people in New York are not gonna change me none. I'm going to show you what the *real* Elvis is like tonight!"

70 The Best Elvis Biographies

If you want to learn more about Elvis' life and career, the best place to start is by reading Peter Guralnick's two-volume biography of Elvis: *Last Train to Memphis: The Rise of Elvis Presley* and *Careless Love: The Unmaking of Elvis Presley.*

"When I started out writing about music, the only reason I did it was to tell people about this music that I thought was so great," Peter told me. Before digging into Elvis, Peter had written a number of books on American roots music, including *Searching for Robert Johnson* and a series of books with short essays on musicians and producers: *Feel Like Going Home: Portraits in Blues, Country, and Rock 'n' Roll*; *Lost Highway: Journeys and Arrivals of American Musicians*; and *Sweet Soul Music: Rhythm and Blues and the Southern Dream of Freedom.*

So when Peter began his work on Elvis in 1988, he already had contacts with a number of people who had worked with Elvis, such as Sam Phillips and Scotty Moore. And though he originally planned to write just one volume, he came to feel that the story had a natural break between the period before Elvis went into the army and the period after Elvis came out of the army.

"I was in the middle of writing what turned into the first volume in '92, and I realized all of a sudden that these were two different stories," he explained. "And that it was as if a curtain came down; this is the end of act one, at Elvis' mother's death, and the other story was an entirely different one. And I felt that it was an important enough story that it ought to be told, at sufficient length." Hence, *Last Train to Memphis*, published in 1994, ends on the day Elvis leaves for Germany. *Careless Love*, published in

1999, picks up the story from when Elvis arrives in Germany and continues through to his death.

Peter spoke to just about all of Elvis' main friends and associates (with the notable exception of his manager). And he never takes his eye off the fact that what makes Elvis important is his work, not the legend that has grown up around him. As he put it in the introduction of *Last Train to Memphis*, "I wanted to rescue Elvis Presley from the dreary bondage of myth, from the oppressive aftershock of cultural significance."

The Wrath of Goldman

Albert Goldman's *Elvis* was published in 1981. It was the first biography to tell Elvis' full life story in one volume, and it quickly soared up the bestseller charts. But it also provoked outrage among Elvis fans for what they felt were mean-spirited depictions of their idol—as in the book's opening chapters when a latter-day Elvis is described as lying on his bed "propped up like a big fat woman recovering from some operation on her reproductive organs."

It hadn't started out that way. As Lamar Fike, the Memphis Mafia member who was Goldman's main source, told writer Alanna Nash, "At first, [Goldman] liked Elvis. But later, he started disliking him. And by the end of the book, I think he hated him." Still, it wasn't a totally negative portrayal. Goldman writes favorably about some of Elvis' work, calling "That's All Right" "his first great moment in the ring," and saying of the Comeback Special's soundtrack, "No Elvis Presley album either before or since has ever delivered so much musical energy, excitement, or imaginative stimulation."

But Goldman was also quite critical of Elvis' behavior and what he saw as his failures as an artist. In his later book, *Elvis: The Last 24 Hours* (1991), which posits that Elvis committed suicide, he denounces Elvis as "a profoundly specious character, a false messiah.... Ultimately, his talent was not for art but for artifice." Goldman's words angered many—but may well have played a role in spurring on the hundreds of subsequent Elvis authors who have wanted to challenge his views in their own books.

Last Train to Memphis is especially evocative of the era, which not only saw Elvis Presley's burst into stardom, but also the rise of the modern-day record industry when rock music became the dominant musical genre. The books also hold the reader's interest because of Peter's determination to tell the story "from the inside out," as he puts it, letting the story unfold naturally without pre-conceptions and the benefit of hindsight.

As a result, the books are also free of judgment or sensational-ism. Peter does discuss controversial subjects, such as Elvis' drug use, but in a straight-forward, even-handed fashion. "What I've tried to do is to be as fair to all of the characters as I can be," he explained. "And it's really irrelevant what my personal feelings are. What I'm trying to do is to explore what the relationships of each of the people is to the others, and to give each person his or her due in terms of the world which I'm portraying. I think the biggest thing, though, is to have respect for your subject. I think if you have respect for your subject, you may make mistakes, but you won't trample all over the truth."

Both books were widely acclaimed on publication, each becoming *New York Times* bestsellers and winning prestigious honors, including the Ralph J. Gleason Music Book Award. They're now generally considered to be the definitive biographies on Elvis and an excellent starting point for immersing yourself in his world. Elvis fans will also be interested to learn that Peter's next book also has a strong connection to Elvis; it's a biography of Sam Phillips.

71 The Hit Makers: Jerry Leiber and Mike Stoller

The songwriting partnership of Jerry Leiber and Mike Stoller wrote a number of Elvis' best-known songs, as well as a host of classic records for other artists.

Jerome Leiber, born April 25, 1933, and Mike Stoller, born March 13, 1933, met in Los Angeles when they were 17. Jerry was a lyricist, and Mike a composer; by 1952 they had their first hit record, "Hard Times," by Charles Brown. Other hits followed, including "Kansas City" and "Hound Dog."

Leiber and Stoller weren't particularly overwhelmed by Elvis' cover of "Hound Dog," preferring the bluesy delivery of the artist who'd originally recorded the number, Big Mama Thornton (though they liked to joke they became quite fond of Elvis' version once it became a million seller). Elvis also recorded Leiber and Stoller's "Love Me" in 1956, and two of their songs for *Loving You* ("Hot Dog" and the film's title track) in 1957. They finally met Elvis during the sessions for *Jailhouse Rock* in April and May 1957 and came away impressed with his musical knowledge.

"We thought we were the only two white kids who knew anything about the blues," Mike told biographer Peter Guralnick, "but he knew all kinds of stuff." "He knew all of our records," Jerry marveled. "And he was a workhorse in the studio—he didn't pull any diva numbers." The two ended up producing the *Jailhouse Rock* sessions, and Mike even appeared in the movie as a piano player.

Elvis enjoyed working with Jerry and Mike and asked if they'd write "a real pretty ballad" for him. The two promptly came up with "Don't," making a demo for Elvis and giving it to him. It was then that they learned what a tightly controlled world Elvis lived in;

they were scolded for bringing a song directly to Elvis instead of to the publishers. And on one occasion when Mike was hanging out at Elvis' hotel, he was told by Parker he had to leave. One of Elvis' entourage later explained to him, "The Colonel doesn't want Elvis to develop a friendship with anyone but us."

Parker nonetheless called on the two when he needed another track for Elvis' first Christmas album, and they wrote "Santa Claus is Back in Town" on the spot. And they were back in the studio with Elvis in January 1958 when he recorded songs for *King Creole*, which included three Leiber and Stoller numbers.

But when the two pitched an idea of their own for Elvis, they were quickly shot down. Jerry had been approached by a New York agent who had the idea of making a musical based on the novel *Walk on the Wild Side*, which would star Elvis and have a score by Leiber and Stoller. They excitedly pitched the idea to Elvis' publishers but were sternly told not to interfere in his career again.

The final break came when Parker wanted the pair back in the studio with Elvis to oversee his last studio session before entering the army. Parker had sent Jerry a contract in advance of the session, and Jerry was surprised to open the envelope and find a blank sheet of paper with a space for his signature. When he questioned Parker about it, he was told, "Don't worry, we'll fill it in later." Neither Jerry nor Mike wanted to sign a contract under those terms, and they never worked with Elvis again.

It's not clear if Elvis ever knew the reasons the two men he referred to as his "good-luck charms" weren't with him in the studio any more. They only wrote one more song for Elvis—at the request of the song's co-writer, Doc Pomus, "She's Not You" was released as a single in 1962. And Elvis did record other Leiber and Stoller numbers originally recorded by other artists: "Bossa Nova Baby" (for *Fun In Acapulco)*, the title song of *Girls! Girls! Girls!*, "Little Egypt" (for *Roustabout)*, and "Saved," which appeared in the '68 Comeback Special.

The last Leiber and Stoller number Elvis recorded was "Three Corn Patches" in 1973—not one of their better songs. "Hound Dog," "Jailhouse Rock," and "Trouble" provide a much better legacy of the excellent work Elvis created with the help of his good-luck charms.

Further reading: *Hound Dog: The Leiber & Stoller Autobiography* by Jerry Leiber, Mike Stoller, and David Ritz.

72 The Backing Singers

Elvis first met members of the Jordanaires after a show at the Ellis Auditorium in Memphis on October 31, 1954. He told Hoyt Hawkins, the vocal quartet's baritone singer, that he'd sure like to have the group back him on his own records someday. Hawkins politely agreed that the group would like to do so very much—little suspecting that in 1956 the quartet would indeed begin working with Elvis and go on to make records with him for the next 12 years.

The roots of the Jordanaires go back to the original edition of the Foggy River Boys formed in the early '40s in Springfield, Missouri (the second version of the group, formed in 1954, featured Charlie Hodge, who would meet Elvis during his army days and join his entourage). There were various personnel and name changes over the next few years; the group finally adopted the name the Jordanaires in 1948. The next year, they joined the *Grand Ole Opry*, and in the 1950s they became recording artists, releasing their own records and finding work backing other artists (they were backing Eddy Arnold at the October '54 show Elvis saw).

But initially, only the group's tenor, Gordon Stoker, was booked to record with Elvis, at the January '56 session where

"Heartbreak Hotel" was recorded and the April '56 session where "I Want You, I Need You, I Love You," was recorded. Stoker was part of an ad hoc group of backing vocalists that included Ben and Brock Speer of the Speer Family gospel group. Elvis wasn't happy with the sound, and Gordon was quick to point out that the entire quartet hadn't been booked—only he had. Elvis listened, and the next time he returned to the studio in July to record "Hound Dog" and "Don't Be Cruel," he made sure the entire group (Gordon Stoker, Hoyt Hawkins, Hugh Jarrett, and Neal Matthews at the time) was present. "We had a lot of movement in our singing, and we had a lot of rhythm," Gordon explained to me. "And that rhythm in our singing is really what Elvis liked."

The quartet was also at Elvis' side for his live shows and television performances, and they also appeared in Elvis' movies. When he got out of the service, the Jordanaires were waiting for him in the studio, appeared with him on Frank Sinatra's TV special, and performed at Elvis' only live shows in 1961 before he devoted himself to making movies. But you hear their bright vocals on every soundtrack from *G.I. Blues* to *Speedway*.

Working with Elvis also helped boost the Jordanaires' own career. "Because we were so popular with Elvis, everybody in the world wanted us to work on their records," Gordon told me. "Elvis opened the door for a lot of musicians and a lot of background singers. As a matter of fact, there was no one making a big fat living doing background singing until Elvis came along."

The Jordanaires' last session with Elvis was a September 22, 1970, session in Nashville. Elvis rushed through four songs, anxious to get back to Los Angeles, a sharp contrast to the concentration he'd exhibited when first working with the Jordanaires in 1956. But Gordon looks back on the time that the Jordanaires spent with Elvis in a positive light. "We had a lot of fun with everything we did with him," he told me. "He made the best out of every situation."

The Jordanaires were asked to join Elvis' band when he returned to live performance in the summer of 1969, but they turned down the offer because the fee was too low. "We could make more money here in Nashville," Gordon explained. "But we hated to quit 'cause we loved him dearly and we hated to quit him. And Elvis to a certain extent resented that. He said in an interview, 'They make so much money in Nashville you can't get 'em out of Nashville.' But later we saw him and he said, 'I understand you had to do what you had to do. You had families, and you had to do what you thought was best.' I'm so glad that he did agree with us later. 'Cause I didn't want him peeved at us. He was a real sweet-natured guy."

73 The First Film

Elvis' movie career got off to an unusual (and in retrospect, disappointing) start with the Western drama *Love Me Tender*, released in 1956. He didn't star in the film, and it was one of only two movies where he dies at the end. More importantly, it was hardly a prestige release; it was very much a B-picture, and as such it was not the best vehicle for launching a charismatic star like Elvis in the first dazzling year of his national fame.

But it's nonetheless important as Elvis' debut film. Two months after his first appearance on *Stage Show*, in March 1956, Elvis came to Los Angeles to make a screen test for producer Hal Wallis. Wallis readily agreed to sign him but couldn't initially find a good picture for him. Elvis' contract allowed him to make films with other studios, so Parker set up a deal with 20th Century Fox, and Elvis was signed to make a picture then called *The Reno Brothers*, which began shooting on August 22, 1956.

The film was set in Texas in 1865, with Elvis as the youngest Reno brother, Clint, welcoming home his three elder brothers, returning from the Civil War, having fought on the Confederate side. Complications immediately arise; Clint and his mother (Mildred Dunnock) had been under the mistaken impression that the eldest brother, Vance (Richard Egan), had been killed, and Clint had married Vance's fiancée, Cathy (Debra Paget), as a result.

Another twist comes with the arrival of Federal troops in search of money the Reno brothers and some of their fellow soldiers had robbed from a Union train, not realizing at the time that the war was over. Other members of the gang use Clint's jealousy to persuade him that Vance is trying to run off with all the money as well as Cathy. Clint shoots Vance but not badly; another of the gang shoots Clint, who dies in Cathy's arms.

Elvis had not wanted to sing in his movies, and *The Reno Brothers* was originally a straight dramatic film. But songs were added to the film anyway, mostly upbeat and enjoyable numbers. In a party sequence, Elvis performs "Let Me" and "Poor Boy," throwing in a bit of bump and grind that was certainly anachronistic for the 1860s. The folksy "We're Gonna Move" was used in a scene where the Reno family relaxes after dinner. Then comes the song that provides the film's recurring musical theme, "Love Me Tender," a ballad based on the melody of the Civil War–era tune "Aura Lee." Once the song was earmarked for a single, it was decided the film's title should be changed to match it; *The Reno Brothers* was dropped and the film became *Love Me Tender*.

Elvis plays Clint as a naïve innocent, though he gets some dramatic scenes to sink his teeth into, as well. His rage when he suspects his wife of two-timing him is frightening, and the emotional struggle during his final confrontation with Vance is believable and poignant. Elvis admitted to being nervous about making his first movie, and the cast was also apprehensive. But when Elvis proved to be a hard worker, determined to do his best, eager to learn,

Elvis' Other Co-Stars

A lot of interesting actors appeared in Elvis' movies; some well known, others then rising performers.

Barbara Eden makes a pre–*I Dream of Jeannie* appearance in *Flaming Star*. Tough guy Charles Bronson is Elvis' boxing coach in *Kid Galahad*; Elvis was later a fan of Bronson's action films in the '70s. TV's future Batgirl, Yvonne Craig, appears in both *It Happened at the World's Fair* and *Kissin' Cousins*. Ursula Andress, the first-ever Bond Girl (she played Honey Ryder in the first 007 film, *Dr. No*) is one of Elvis' romantic interests in *Fun In Acapulco*.

Double Indemnity star Barbara Stanwyck played a carnival owner in *Roustabout*. Another veteran actor, Jackie Coogan, who co-starred with Charlie Chaplin in *The Kid* in 1921 and was later Uncle Fester on TV's *The Addams Family*, plays a police sergeant in *Girl Happy*. Harry Morgan, Sgt. Friday's sidekick in *Dragnet*, works alongside Elvis on a riverboat in *Frankie and Johnny*. His zaniest co-star was Elsa Lanchester, the original Bride of Frankenstein (in the film of the same name), who sings "Yoga Is As Yoga Does" with Elvis in *Easy Come, Easy Go*.

A singing star of an earlier era, Rudy Vallee, runs an ad agency in *Live a Little, Love a Little*. And *The Trouble With Girls* not only has cameos from John Carradine and Vincent Price, but it also features Dabney Coleman, future star of *9 to 5* and *Tootsie*.

and open to taking suggestions and advice, he became liked and respected by all.

When word spread that Elvis would die in the movie, there was an outcry from fans, who picketed the Paramount Theatre in New York where the film would premiere. To soothe them, footage of Elvis singing the title song was superimposed over the film's final scene; Clint might lie buried in the family graveyard, but there was Elvis, up on the screen still singing.

By the time *Love Me Tender* opened on November 15, the title song had given Elvis another No. 1. The reviews were mixed, though they didn't hurt the box office; the film recouped its budget in the first week of release. Some critics went out of their way to criticize Elvis' performance, though in truth it was the material that was weak, not Elvis. But it set an unfortunate precedent—with Elvis in the cast, even a less-than-stellar movie could make a profit.

74 The Last Hit Single

"Burning Love" was Elvis' last major hit during his lifetime. It reached No. 2 in the charts and sold more than 1 million copies. And, ironically, it was a song Elvis didn't like and hadn't wanted to record in the first place.

Elvis recorded the song during a three-day session, March 27–29, 1972, held at RCA's studios in Hollywood. Songwriter Dennis Linde had written the song for his wife, and it had previously been recorded by Arthur Alexander. Elvis' producer, Felton Jarvis, had heard the song and liked it, thinking it would be perfect for Elvis.

Yet Elvis evinced little interest in the song. But Jarvis and Elvis' friends in the studio were all convinced that it could be a hit, and after much persuasion, Elvis finally agreed to record it. Even so, he rushed through the song, recording six takes "in almost throwaway style," as Peter Guralnick wrote, "and everyone could see that Elvis' heart wasn't really in it."

That's hard to believe if you hear the finished version. The song kicks off with a lively guitar line played by Linde himself, and the excitement rises during the chorus when the backing vocalists join in. The pace never slackens, and the subtle gospel feel of the chorus is undoubtedly due to the fact that the backing vocalists are the gospel quartet the Stamps. The song also has a terrific fade out, as Elvis sings about being a "hunka-hunka burning love." It's a fun and vibrant performance.

"Burning Love" was released as a single in August 1972. Elvis had already been performing it live; he added it to the set list for his April 1972 tour, in part because footage for the documentary *Elvis On Tour* was being shot at the same time, and "Burning Love" was one of the new songs in his set (his April 18 performance in San Antonio appears in the final film).

But Elvis' unhappiness with "Burning Love" remained. He didn't perform it during his landmark shows at Madison Square Garden in June 1972, nor did he perform it during his usual August/September season in Las Vegas.

But it was back in the set by November, perhaps because by then the song was a hit. And he performed it in his *Aloha From Hawaii* shows, giving it some national exposure. But considering what a big hit it was for Elvis—it was the first Top 10 hit he'd had since "The Wonder of You" in 1970—he didn't perform it as much as you'd expect. Still, four live versions of the song ended up being released: the *Elvis On Tour* version, the versions in the two *Aloha From Hawaii* shows, and a version from the June 6, 1975, show in Dallas that appeared on the 1980 box set *Elvis Aron Presley*.

And the success of the "Burning Love" single was squandered when it was made the title track of a lackluster budget album called *Burning Love and Hits From His Movies*, released in October 1972. The movie songs were in no way "hits," and all had been previously released. But as a budget release, Presley's manager would get a higher cut of the profits (a 50-50 split for budget albums). So the opportunity to build a good album around "Burning Love" that could have enhanced Elvis' career was scuppered for the sake of generating more income. The strong sales of both *Elvis As Recorded at Madison Square Garden* (released in June 1972) and "Burning Love" had Elvis' career on an upswing. But the chance to build on that momentum was not taken. And "Burning Love" would be the last Top 10 hit single of Elvis' lifetime.

75 Rockin' on the *Hayride*

Elvis made his live radio debut on the *Grand Ole Opry*. But the first, and only, radio program where he became a regular performer was the *Louisiana Hayride*.

The *Louisiana Hayride* was a live country music show broadcast on Saturday nights from the Municipal Auditorium in Shreveport, Louisiana. The program had a less conservative booking policy than the *Grand Ole Opry*, booking rising performers like Hank Williams, Kitty Wells, Slim Whitman, and Jim Reeves to name a few—hence its nickname, "the Cradle of the Stars."

Even before Elvis had appeared on the *Grand Ole Opry*, Sam Phillips had been approached by the *Louisiana Hayride* about having him appear on the program. Sam knew Elvis' musical style would be a good fit for the *Hayride*. But he didn't want to miss the chance to get some national exposure first, so he told the *Hayride*'s booker, Pappy Covington, that Elvis wouldn't be available until after his *Opry* appearance (which at that point wasn't even confirmed yet). And just two days after Elvis was on the *Grand Ole Opry*, Sam called Covington, and Elvis' first appearance on the *Hayride* was set for October 16, 1954.

Recordings survive of a number of Elvis' *Hayride* appearances, including that first one. Elvis was nervous, and Scotty stumbles a bit on his solo in "That's All Right" during the first spot. But they all showed a good deal more confidence during the second spot, and Elvis was immediately signed as a *Hayride* regular.

The money wasn't much—Elvis received $18 per appearance, Scotty and Bill just $12. But the exposure was invaluable, and the *Hayride* booking office was also able to set up other gigs for them. Allowances could also be made if Elvis was on tour and unavailable on Saturday nights.

One thing that's especially interesting about the *Hayride* recordings is that you get to hear Elvis perform a few songs he never recorded in the studio: "Hearts of Stone," "Tweedle Dee," and

A young Elvis Presley on the stage of the Louisiana Hayride in Shreveport, Louisiana. The image was taken by Shreveport photojournalists Jack Barham and Langston. (AP Photo)

"Maybellene." Ernst Jørgensen, who has produced Elvis releases since the 1980s, feels there's more *Hayride* material to be found. "We know that Elvis did the following songs, and these would all be priceless: 'Sittin' On Top Of The World,' 'Lovey Dovey,' 'Rock Around The Clock,' 'Pledging My Love,' 'Only You,' and 'Sixteen Tons.' But I'd be happy finding live versions of 'Mystery Train' and 'Milkcow Blues Boogie,' as well." The *Hayride* also led to a change in Elvis' band when D.J. Fontana, who played drums in the *Hayride*'s house band, was taken on as Elvis' regular drummer.

By 1956, Elvis' schedule was too busy to accommodate the *Hayride*, and on April 2 of that year, Parker bought out the remainder of Elvis' contract with the program. As part of the deal, Elvis had to make one more appearance with proceeds donated to charity. The show was held on December 15, 1956, and broadcast from the Louisiana Fairgrounds. The show had captured Elvis all along the way as his rise to fame progressed, and he would prove to be the *Hayride*'s biggest star.

There's no one set that has all of Elvis' *Hayride* recordings. *A Boy From Tupelo* (2012) has all known recordings through 1955, but it doesn't have the December 1956 live show. *The Complete Louisiana Hayride Archives 1954–1956* (2011) does have the December '56 live show, but it doesn't have the March '55 performances included on *A Boy From Tupelo*. *Elvis At The Hayride* (2006), a companion release to Frank Page's book *Elvis: The Louisiana Hayride Years*, doesn't have the March '55 performances or the complete December '56 performance, but it is cheaper than either of the other releases.

Further reading: *Elvis: The Louisiana Hayride Years 1954–1956* by Frank Page and Joey Kent; *Louisiana Hayride Years: Making Musical History in Country's Golden Age* by Horace Logan and Bill Sloan; *Louisiana Hayride: Radio and Roots Music Along the Red River* by Tracey E.W. Laird.

76 Live, Not Necessarily In Person

Yes, it's true—20 years after his death, Elvis actually started appearing in concert again.

No, it wasn't that the "Elvis is alive" rumors turned out to be true after all. It was really Elvis' film image that was going on tour. The twist was that live musicians were part of the show, too.

The concert idea was the brainchild of Todd Morgan, who was EPE's Director of Media and Creative Development (Morgan died in 2008). Morgan was planning a reunion event for the 1997 Elvis Week and decided it would be more interesting as a concert. Footage of Elvis in performance (primarily from *Elvis: That's The Way It Is*, *Elvis On Tour*, and *Elvis: Aloha From Hawaii via Satellite*) would be projected onto a large screen with his vocal track isolated; the live music would then be provided by musicians and singers accompanying Elvis as he sang. Best of all, the live performers would be people who'd actually performed with Elvis.

The musicians were initially dubious about the idea, not sure how it would come off, and were surprised to discover how tricky it was to actually do. "You had to pay attention to the count offs, because obviously the tape [with Elvis' vocal] is going to play with or without you," pianist Glen Hardin told me. "But once we got the hang of it, it became very easy." Bassist Jerry Scheff told me that it was simply a matter of watching Elvis as he moved, like they'd always done during the hundreds of hours they'd spent on stage with him during the '70s; only this time, they were watching Elvis on the TV monitors that had been set up around the stage.

The 1997 show, billed as "Elvis In Concert" and held on August 16 at the Mid-South Coliseum in Memphis, had a large

The Spoken Word Album

Having Fun With Elvis On Stage was one of the oddest Elvis albums he ever officially released.

The album was the idea of Elvis' manager. Parker had deduced that RCA had no rights to any spoken-word recordings Elvis might release, so he decided to issue one himself on his own Boxcar Records label. But instead of having Elvis reading poetry, Parker's idea of a "spoken word" release was to cobble together Elvis' stage chat during his live shows.

It wasn't as strange an idea as it seems. Elvis was prone to off-the-wall observations and bizarre non-sequiturs in his stage patter, and when he first returned to live performance, he often shared stories of how his career began. A careful edit could've shaped the material into a narrative arc, breaking up the career history with the occasional joke. But no such care was taken. Instead, the album rambles on for 37 minutes, the quotes thrown together in a seemingly random fashion that makes no sense. Why, for example, include the many drawn out "We-l-l-l-s" Elvis would make before launching into a song?

The album was first released in August 1974 and sold at Elvis' concerts. RCA later released it in October of that year. It only reached No. 130 on the pop charts but surprisingly reached No. 9 on *Billboard*'s Country Albums chart. It remains one of the few official Elvis records that has never been reissued on CD.

cast: the core of the TCB Band (James Burton, Jerry Scheff, Glen D. Hardin, and Ronnie Tutt), the Sweet Inspirations, the Imperials, J.D. Sumner and the Stamps, Voice (whom Elvis had hired to be his own personal gospel group in the '70s), the Jordanaires, soloist Millie Kirkham, the ever-faithful Charlie Hodge, and Scotty Moore and D.J. Fontana. Even the comics who'd opened Elvis' shows in the '70s, Jackie Kahane and Sammy Shore, were on hand, as well as Elvis' conductor at the Las Vegas Hilton, Joe Guercio. Additional backing was provided by the Memphis Symphony Orchestra.

I was lucky enough to be there that night, and it was quite exciting; none of these performers had ever been all together for a show before. Having live musicians helped make the performance feel like a real concert, and the crowd response was such that it felt like Elvis was really there, too, and not just on film. As an extra treat that night, a newly created video of "Don't Cry Daddy" was played, featuring both Elvis and Lisa Marie singing the song. It brought down the house.

The next year, a smaller-scale version of the show went on the road, and over the years, the production (sometimes renamed "Elvis: The Concert" or "Elvis Presley In Concert") has toured the U.S. and around the world: Canada, Britain, Europe, Australia, New Zealand, Japan, Singapore, Thailand, and Brazil. The events in Memphis during Elvis Week are the most elaborate with bigger casts. It's not just the closest you can get to seeing Elvis perform in concert; it's also an opportunity to see those who have played with Elvis. And since "Elvis In Concert" began, a number of those performers have died: Myrna Smith (the Sweet Inspirations), John Wilkinson (guitarist in the TCB Band), and Gordon Stoker (the Jordanaires). Others, like Scotty Moore, no longer play live.

In 1998, the show also received an award that Elvis would never have expected to get: a designation from Guinness World Records as "The first live tour headlined by a performer who is no longer living." It's certainly an entertaining show that's well worth seeing if you get the chance. The show is also available on CD and DVD (*Elvis Lives: The 25th Anniversary Concert*).

77 The Signature Song

A "signature song" is usually associated with just one artist. But "My Way" is an exception; it's a signature song for Frank Sinatra, who first recorded it, but it's also strongly identified with Elvis.

The song was written by Paul Anka, who took the melody of a French pop song called "Comme d'habitude" ("As Usual") he heard on the radio while vacationing in France. Anka was intrigued by the melody and purchased the rights to the song, intending to write English lyrics for it (interestingly, the song originally had English lyrics and was called "For Me").

Anka had always wanted to write a song for Frank Sinatra, and when Sinatra told him he was thinking of retiring, Anka pulled out "Comme d'habitude" and crafted a set of lyrics for the song. They referenced Sinatra's upcoming retirement ("...the end is near") as well as the way Sinatra spoke ("Ate it up and spit it out"). "Everything in that song *is* him," Anka wrote in his autobiography. He further described the song as being about, "Someone at the end of their career defiantly watching a home movie of their life."

Sinatra's version came out in 1969 and reached No. 27 in the charts, helping to put off his retirement for a few years (he did announce his retirement in 1971 but returned to performing in 1973). Elvis was not surprisingly drawn to the dramatic possibilities of the song and told Anka that he intended to record it himself. Anka tried to dissuade him, telling him, "Elvis, it's not really your kind of song." But Elvis was insistent, telling Anka, "Those words, they mean so much to me."

Elvis first recorded the song in June 1971, but for some reason, this studio version was not released at the time (it was later included on the 1995 box set *Walk A Mile in My Shoes*). Because it wasn't released, this version is unfinished; Elvis' vocal is somewhat restrained (he doesn't go all out on his final note for example) and a final version would undoubtedly have had a lush orchestral backing overdubbed onto the track.

So the song was put aside. But Elvis returned to it for his *Aloha From Hawaii* concerts. The new arrangement fully plumbs the song's drama, starting out with Elvis singing solely accompanied by the piano, and building over four minutes to a grand crescendo with Elvis' band, the orchestra, and backing singers all supporting him as he rises to the song's final notes in triumph. It was the kind of showy ending Elvis liked to bring to a lot of songs he did in concert in the '70s.

"My Way" remained a staple of Elvis' live act; the last time he performed the song in concert was on June 25, 1977, in Cincinnati, Ohio, his next-to-last show (and a live version of the song from his June 21, 1977, concert in Rapid City, South Dakota, was released posthumously as a single and reached No. 22). But Anka continued to have mixed feelings about Elvis' performance of the song, saying in his autobiography, "In the end, that song and those words has resonance for him but not in the way I intended. Basically, given Elvis' pathetic state at the end [of his life], it was in the opposite sense that the words had had for Sinatra. There was nothing defiant or heroic about Elvis at that point."

And it's true that in listening to performances from Elvis' later years, there's a decided poignancy in hearing him sing about facing that final curtain when his own life seemed increasingly encumbered by problems. But Anka's comment overlooks the point that it was surely the song's defiance and heroism that attracted Elvis' attention in the first place. And when he performed it, it's clear that he didn't see it as a song that underscored the problems in his life but as an affirmation; that after all he had gone through, and how far he had come, he still wanted to rise to the challenge and come out swinging.

78 Elvis and Race

Since he was a Southerner, it was often assumed that Elvis was also a racist, that he "stole" his music from the African American community, and looked down on black people as his inferiors.

Elvis was influenced by the blues, gospel, and R&B—and also by country, folk, pop, and even opera. Drawing on the music he grew up with and reworking it into something new and fresh was key to his success. This musical melding is also what created rock 'n' roll, which brought R&B and country together. What Elvis did in covering the blues of Arthur Crudup's "That's All Right" was no different from Chuck Berry being inspired by the country song "Ida Red," popularized by Bob Wills & His Texas Playboys and reworking it into Berry's first big hit, "Maybellene." In neither case were Elvis' or Chuck's versions of the songs copies of the originals; they stand as independent works.

And Elvis readily acknowledged his influences. Asked about rock 'n' roll by a reporter in Charlotte, North Carolina, in June 1956, he said, "The colored folks been singing it and playing it just like I'm doin' now, man, for more years than I know...and nobody paid it no mind 'til I goosed it up. I got it from them." He was a big admirer of numerous black artists—Jackie Wilson, Fats Domino, James Brown—and never hesitated to tell them so when he got the chance. When Elvis met one of his of his big idols, Roy Hamilton, during his sessions at American Sound in 1969, he gave Roy a song that Elvis was meant to record, "Angelica," telling Roy that he would do a better job with the song.

A more serious charge of racism was leveled against Elvis in an article in the April 1957 issue of the African American interest magazine *Sepia*, which alleged that he made the statement, "The only thing Negroes can do for me is to buy my records and shine my shoes." No corroborating source was ever given for the quote. After the article appeared, Louie Robinson, the associate editor of *Jet*, another African American weekly magazine, went to Los Angeles where Elvis was working on *Jailhouse Rock*, to ask him about the comment. "I never said anything like that, and people who know me know I wouldn't have said it," he told Robinson, who decided to take Elvis at his word, interviewing different black people who knew Elvis in Tupelo, Memphis, and L.A. In Tupelo, Dr. W.A. Zuber remembered the young Elvis attending black church services: "People around here say he's one of the nicest boys they ever knew. He just doesn't impress me as the type of person who would say a thing like that." Other interviewees Robinson spoke to agreed with Zuber's views.

Elvis also took the opportunity to again acknowledge the black roots of his music, telling *Jet*, "A lot of people seem to think I started this business, but rock 'n' roll was here a long time before I came along. Nobody can sing that kind of music like colored people. Let's face it; I can't sing it like Fats Domino can. I know that. But I always liked that kind of music." When Robinson's article ran in *Jet*'s August 1957 issue, he concluded, "To Elvis, people are people, regardless of race, color, or creed."

Over the years, black performers who knew Elvis have defended him. "There's no way Elvis was a racist," James Brown said. And Estelle Brown spoke for all of the Sweet Inspirations (Elvis' backing singers for his live shows from 1969 till his death) when she said, "Elvis was not a racist. I can tell you that, we can all tell you that, and we're black, ain't we? We should know." As late as 1970, the promoter for Elvis' shows in Houston told Elvis he couldn't have "those black girls" perform with him. Elvis replied that if the Sweets couldn't perform, than neither would he. The Sweets stayed on the bill.

79 Elvis and the Fab Four

The only contemporaneous rock act who brought about the kind of seismic musical and cultural shift that Elvis did was the Beatles. But while the Beatles greatly admired Elvis (as John Lennon once stated, "Before Elvis, there was nothing"), Elvis' feelings about the Fab Four were more ambivalent.

The Beatles had Elvis songs in their live act in their early days and on British radio, though they never made a studio recording of any Elvis number. Elvis was the ultimate rock star as well as the standard to which all other rock performers aspired. When the Beatles' manager, Brian Epstein, was trying to secure a record deal for the band, he would insist that the Beatles would one day be "bigger than Elvis."

When the Beatles finally arrived in America in February 1964, Elvis had to feel some jealousy. The Beatles were set to appear on *The Ed Sullivan Show* and had the No. 1 album and single in the country. In contrast, Elvis had spent the last few years cranking out movies he was less and less interested in, and his records were no longer soaring up the charts the way they once had. But Parker saw an opportunity to get a little publicity for his client, and half an hour before the Beatles made their debut *Ed Sullivan* appearance on February 9, 1964, a telegram was delivered to their dressing room that read: "Congratulations on your appearance on *The Ed Sullivan Show* and your visit to America. We hope your engagement will be a successful one and your visit pleasant. Give our best to Mr. Sullivan. Sincerely, Elvis & The Colonel." It was, as Sullivan noted in his opening remarks, a "very, very nice" gesture. But Elvis himself never made any public comment about the group's appearances on the show.

The Beatles hoped to meet up with Elvis during their first American tour that summer, but the closest they came was when Paul McCartney spoke with Elvis over the phone. The meeting would have to wait until next summer, when the Beatles toured America in August 1965 (there was even a suggestion that the band might make an appearance in Elvis' latest film, *Paradise, Hawaiian Style*, but the plans fell through).

A meeting was arranged for August 27 at Elvis' Los Angeles home. Some accounts say Elvis wasn't interested in the Beatles, saying, "Hell, I don't want to meet those sons of bitches!" but others insist there was no jealousy. For their part, the Beatles were nervous and shared a joint in their car on the way over. But when finally face-to-face with Elvis, they were so flummoxed that for a moment no one spoke. At last Elvis declared, "If you guys are gonna sit there starin' at me all night, I'm going to bed!" which broke the ice and everyone relaxed. The rest of the evening was spent chatting and playing pool; there are conflicting accounts about whether the Beatles jammed with Elvis. Unfortunately, aside from a few photos of the Beatles leaving Elvis' house, there are no other pictures of the two acts together.

Elvis never spoke of the meeting publicly. But when he returned to live performance in Las Vegas in 1969, he included a medley of "Yesterday" and "Hey Jude" in the show (and a studio version of the latter song appeared on the 1972 album *Elvis Now*). He also praised the band's music in interviews at the time, pointing to "I Saw Her Standing There" as a song he particularly liked. And he later added the Beatles' "Something," to his set list, while "Little Sister" would often segue into the Beatles' "Get Back." Yet when he met with President Nixon in December 1970, he attacked the group for being "kind of anti-American." Clearly, he still felt a little threatened.

Both George Harrison and Ringo Starr saw Elvis in concert in the '70s, and George confessed to a friend he was still nervous around his idol. Elvis never saw the Beatles, or solo Beatles, perform live. Though the Beatles and Elvis liked each others' work, there would always remain some distance between them.

80 Sam Phillips' Assistant: Marion Keisker

Though there's some question as to who first recorded Elvis at the Memphis Recording Service in 1953, there's no doubt at all about who first spoke to him when he walked through the door: Marion Keisker.

Marion was born in Memphis on September 23, 1917, and had been on Memphis radio since 1929 when she was 12 years old, starting out as a regular on the children's show *Wynken, Blynken & Nod* on WREC. She married in 1939 and moved to Illinois, but she returned to Memphis in 1943 after her divorce. In 1946, she was back at WREC, hosting a talk show under the name Kitty Kelly. It was while working at WREC that she met and, she admitted, fell in love with Sam Phillips. "He was a beautiful young man," she told Peter Guralnick. "Beautiful beyond belief, but still had that country touch, that country rawness."

When Sam decided to go into business for himself, Marion became his assistant, though because there was little money coming in, she continued working at WREC. The two built the studio together, and when the studio opened she became the office manager; while Sam worked with the musicians, she kept the studio logs and dealt with pressing plants and record distributors.

Marion was sitting behind the desk when Elvis arrived for the first time at the Memphis Recording Service in the summer of 1953. While he waited to record his acetate, he asked Marion if she knew of anyone looking for a singer. As Marion recalled the conversation in numerous interviews, she asked Elvis, "What kind of a singer are you?" "I sing all kinds," Elvis replied. "Who do you sound like?" Marion asked, trying to get a fix on what kind of singer he might be. "I don't sound like nobody," he told her. "What do you sing, hillbilly?" Marion asked. "I sing hillbilly," Elvis conceded. "Well," Marion said, "who do you sound like in hillbilly?" Elvis again gave his enigmatic response: "I don't sound like nobody."

It was Marion who thought to write down Elvis' name and phone number after his session; she misspelled his last name as "Pressley" but added the words, "Good ballad singer. Hold." After making his second acetate at the studio, Elvis occasionally came by and chatted with Marion, who began to feel protective toward the shy young man. It was her continual recommendations to Sam that he give Elvis a call that led to Sam finally bringing in Elvis for a session in June 1954—which led to Elvis' first professional session the following month.

Marion continued working for Sam until 1957. She was right by Elvis' side as his career took off, taking him to his newspaper interviews, riding with him to Nashville when he made his *Grand Ole Opry* appearance, helping to get his Sun releases to the radio stations that would play them. Elvis was grateful for her support, and even after signing with RCA, he continued to drop by the studio to talk.

In 1955, Marion left WREC and joined the staff of WHER, the first radio station with an all-female staff, co-founded by Sam (the station's slogan was "1000 Beautiful Watts"). But Marion and Sam had a falling out in 1957, and Marion left Memphis to join the Air Force. She wouldn't see Elvis again until she attended Elvis' farewell press conference in Friedberg, Germany, on March 1, 1960. As he came into the room, Marion said, "Hi, hon." "Marion!" Elvis exclaimed on seeing her. "In Germany! And an officer! What do I do? Kiss you or salute you?" "In that order!" she jokingly responded. Elvis later came to her assistance when he saw her being reprimanded by a captain, who accused her of staging the incident. "Captain, you don't understand," Elvis told him. "You wouldn't even be having this [press conference] today if it wasn't for this lady." "That was a very significant thing for me," Marion told Peter Guralnick. "That was the first and only time that Elvis indicated publicly that he recognized the role that I had played."

Marion died of cancer in Memphis at age 72 on December 29, 1989.

81 The World's First Supergroup

What started out as a laid-back jam session at Sun Studio on the afternoon of December 4, 1956, quickly began burning bright with such star power that Sam Phillips contacted a reporter to come in and document the first, and only, performance of the "Million Dollar Quartet."

Elvis had been driving around Memphis with his friend Cliff Gleaves, and a girlfriend, Marilyn Evans, when he passed the studio and spotted a fleet of Cadillacs parked outside. Guessing that there was a session going on, he promptly parked and walked in to find Sun Records' newest star, Carl Perkins, working on some songs with a little help from a brash young piano player that Sam Phillips had just signed, Jerry Lee Lewis.

Carl Perkins' career had taken off in early 1956 with his first single for Sun, "Blue Suede Shoes" (which Elvis had also recorded for his first album). Though he was backing Perkins on this session, Jerry Lee Lewis had just released his own single on Sun, "Crazy Arms," and next year his career would explode with the release of

"Whole Lot of Shakin' Goin' On" and "Great Balls of Fire." As the session was winding down, a jam session naturally sprang up between the musicians.

Recognizing that something extraordinary was happening, Sam Phillips quickly began to roll tape. "Who knows?" he said to musician and songwriter Jack Clement, who was also hanging out at the studio, "We may never have these people together again." He also put in a call to Johnny Cash to come over. Cash had started his career at Sun in 1955 with the release of the single "Cry! Cry! Cry!" and his most recent release was "Train of Love." (Cash recalls the session a bit differently; he's said he was already in the studio). And Sam didn't forget to invite the press, telephoning Bob Johnson of the *Memphis Press–Scimitar*, who promptly came over with a photographer as well as UPI reporter Leo Soroka.

The session offers a rare look at what Elvis was like when he was out of the public eye, and the end result was typical of the kind of impromptu sing-a-longs he loved to do with his friends while strumming a guitar or playing the piano. There was plenty of gospel music—lively renditions of "When the Saints Go Marchin' In," "Just A Little Talk With Jesus," and "Down By The Riverside"—and, in a nod to the season, instrumental versions of "Jingle Bells" and "White Christmas." Most of the songs are incomplete, as the musicians easily switch from one song to another. In one illuminating sequence, Elvis recalls the experience of watching Billy Ward and His Dominoes covering "Don't Be Cruel" when he caught the act in Vegas. He'd been quite impressed with the singer in the band, not knowing at the time it was Jackie Wilson, who would later become a friend, demonstrating how Jackie had slowed down the song and made it "Much better than any record of mine.... I went back four nights straight and heard that guy do that. Man, he sung the hell out of the song, and I was under the table looking at him!"

The *Press–Scimitar* photographer took the only shot of Sun Records' biggest stars all together: Elvis at the piano, Carl with his guitar, Jerry Lee and Johnny on either side. "I never had a better time than yesterday afternoon," Bob Johnson wrote in the article that ran the next day. "That quartet could sell a million." Sam quickly sent around Johnson's article to local DJs, heralding his "Million Dollar Quartet."

Portions of the session first appeared on the album *The Million Dollar Quartet*, released in England in 1981. Various permutations of the session have subsequently been released; at time of writing, the most comprehensive version is the 50th anniversary edition of the session, *The Complete Million Dollar Quartet*, released in 2006. The session also provided the basis for the musical *Million Dollar Quartet*, co-written by Colin Escott (who has written extensively about Sun Records and Elvis) and Floyd Mutrux. The show premiered in 2006, later ran on Broadway, and can now be seen in various touring productions.

82 A Night at the *Opry*

Elvis' first major radio appearance after his first single was released was on the *Grand Ole Opry* in Nashville. It didn't pay off for him like he hoped, but it gave him the greatest exposure he'd ever had up to that point.

The *Grand Ole Opry* was a weekly country music show broadcast live on Nashville-based radio station WSM (and it's still on the air today). Sam Phillips first approached Jim Denny, the manager of the *Opry*, at the end of August 1954 when "Blue Moon of Kentucky" reached No. 3 on *Billboard*'s Country & Western Territorial Best Seller chart. Denny wasn't especially a fan of the record but eventually agreed to let Elvis appear on October 2.

Elvis: The TV Series

There have been numerous cinematic depictions of Elvis. In my view, the best came in the underrated 1990 TV series called *Elvis*.

The show had the stamp of approval from Elvis Presley Enterprises, as Priscilla Presley was one of the show's producers. Longtime Elvis friend Jerry Schilling was also a producer, as was Rick Husky, whom Jerry had brought in to work with Elvis in the '70s when Elvis was considering a return to movie making.

Rick also conceived the series, which covered Elvis' pre-fame years. Elvis, played by Michael St. Gerard (who starred in the 1988 version of John Waters' *Hairspray*), is seen cutting records at Sun, playing the *Grand Ole Opry*, and still torn between his day job and his desire to pursue a career in music. Millie Perkins, who co-starred with Elvis in *Wild in the Country*, played Gladys. Elvis' singing voice was provided by country singer Ronnie McDowell, something he's done in more than one film.

The mood of the series was laid-back and thoughtful, and though incidents in Elvis' career were fictionalized for the show, the plotlines basically paralleled his real life story. The show premiered on February 6, 1990. Unfortunately, ratings were not good, and the last episode aired on May 19, 1990. Thirteen episodes were shot, but only 10 initially aired. All episodes were later aired when the show was reshown on cable under the title *Elvis: The Early Years*. But so far, there has been no DVD release of the program.

Elvis was nervous about the performance and even more nervous when he first ran into Bill Monroe, who originally recorded "Blue Moon of Kentucky," as a number of country fans had taken exception to Elvis' rocked-up version. But Monroe was generous to the young singer, telling him that he had in fact just recut "Blue Moon of Kentucky" himself, drawing on Elvis' arrangement.

Elvis performed "Blue Moon of Kentucky" on the show that night, but the audience was underwhelmed, giving him what was described as a "polite but somewhat tepid reception." Elvis and his musicians then made a second appearance on the *Midnight*

Jamboree radio show broadcast from the Ernest Tubb Record Shop in Nashville.

It's been said that Jim Denny was especially critical of Elvis' performance, telling him he should stick to driving a truck. Sam Phillips denied this, saying, "He didn't give me any great accolades, he just grabbed me by my skinny arm and said, 'This boy is not bad'…he was a damn tough man, but he did me a favor."

It was also said that Elvis was so disappointed about the lukewarm response he'd received and Denny's criticism that he cried all the way home the next day. But Marion Keisker disputed the story, sarcastically wondering where the witness who'd supposedly seen Elvis crying had been. "There was only Sam and Elvis and me in the car. We were in good spirits. I'd like to see where that other person was sitting."

Though Elvis was never asked to appear on the program again, Sam didn't consider his appearance a failure. Though the *Louisiana Hayride* had already been asking about having Elvis appear on their show, Sam wasn't about to miss the chance to get Elvis on the biggest country radio program in the nation. Jim Denny had given them some grudging praise, they'd made some new contacts, and, most importantly, introduced Elvis to a whole new audience.

83 The Hometown Album

Though Elvis performed a number of shows in Memphis, there's only one official recording of him playing in his hometown: the 1974 album *Elvis: Recorded Live On Stage In Memphis*.

After 1954, Elvis rarely performed live in Memphis; it was as if he left the city to work and came home to relax. In 1955 and 1956 he played a total of four shows in Memphis. In 1961, he played two benefit shows at the Ellis Auditorium in Memphis then, amazingly, he didn't play another Memphis show until 1974. When the four shows scheduled for March 16 and 17 at the Mid-South Coliseum sold out, a fifth was added on March 20, and it was also decided to record the show.

When it was first released, *Elvis: Recorded Live On Stage In Memphis* only had 14 songs (including two medleys). In 2004, the Follow That Dream label released the entire concert, as did RCA/Legacy in 2014.

Of the 30 different songs, 13 were numbers he'd performed in the '50s, though a number of them were performed as medleys, not entire songs; one medley featured "Long Tall Sally," "Whole Lotta Shakin' Goin' On," "Your Mama Don't Dance," "Flip, Flop and Fly," "Jailhouse Rock," and "Hound Dog." This was in part to take care of all the rock 'n' roll hits that people wanted to hear but that Elvis was less interested in performing.

"Even from the very beginning in Las Vegas, all the old rock stuff he would combine them into medleys so we could get through 'em fast," bassist Jerry Scheff told me. "He wanted to be respected for his voice, he wanted to sing stuff like 'The Impossible Dream,' and all those songs where he could really get emotional in them and also show off his range. He wanted to be respected as a vocalist, and I'm sure that he thought he was too old to do the rock 'n' roll thing anymore. That's my opinion."

While he raced through "Jailhouse Rock" and "Hound Dog," he took more time with a bluesy "Trying to Get to You" and Arthur Crudup's "My Baby Left Me." And there were certainly other numbers that highlighted the power of his voice, like "Steamroller Blues" and a medley where "Blueberry Hill" segued unexpectedly into "I Can't Stop Loving You." It was also the first time a Memphis audience got to hear "An American Trilogy," a showstopper in Elvis' live show made even more dramatic when a large American flag was unfurled to cheers and applause.

Elvis had J.D. Sumner sing the intro of "Why Me Lord" before taking over the lead himself, then going into "How Great Thou Art," a stirring performance that won Elvis his third Grammy for Best Inspirational Performance. He threw another religious number into the set as well, when "I Got a Woman" segued into an extended "Amen," obviously delighted when Sumner reached way down deep to hit the low notes. "Polk Salad Annie" and "Suspicious Minds" were also highlights, and the show opened and closed with "See See Rider" and "Can't Help Falling In Love," respectively. Before singing the final number, Elvis announced, "It's always been said that a person cannot return to their hometown, but you have disproven that theory completely. You really made it worthwhile." It had been a good homecoming.

Elvis: Recorded Live On Stage In Memphis was released in July and reached No. 33 in the charts. It was his lowest-charting live album and the last live album released during his lifetime, though live tracks would continue to fill out some of his subsequent studio albums. And he performed two more times in Memphis at the Mid-South Coliseum, on June 10, 1975, and July 5, 1976. There were plans for him to perform in the city in 1977; the tour that was to have begun August 17 in Portland, Maine, had been scheduled to end with two days of shows in Memphis on August 27 and 28.

84 The Best of the Rest of Elvis' Movies

Some of Elvis' movies have been discussed in a number of previous entries; now we'll start rounding up the rest of them.

Elvis wasn't happy with how his film career turned out, and it was certainly ill-managed. It's astonishing that Tom Parker never demanded script and song approval for a star of Elvis' caliber. It's also surprising that Parker had Elvis focus on making movies at the expense of making music in the 1960s; in the '50s, he'd been able to do both.

The stereotypical view of Elvis' films is that the '50s films were good and the '60s films were not. But some of the '60s films (like *Blue Hawaii*) can stand on their own, while a number of the rest aren't necessarily bad, they're just not quite good enough. Stronger scripts and better music could have worked wonders; the Beatles' *Help!* has as thin a plot as Elvis' *Harum Scarum* (and both feature villains from the exotic East), but the superior comedy and great songs in the Beatles film made it more fun—and commercially successful.

Here's what you could call the "best of the rest:"

Drawing on his real-life army service, in *G.I. Blues* (1960) Elvis plays a soldier stationed in Germany with Juliet Prowse as his love interest in this romantic comedy. It's the first film to neuter the "rebel Elvis" of the '50s, but the performances are good and the songs are better than average.

Certainly the most literate of Elvis' movies, *Wild in the Country*'s (1961) script was by noted writer Clifford Odets. Elvis is an aspiring writer caught between a good girl (Millie Perkins), a bad girl (Tuesday Weld), and an older woman (Hope Lange). This attack on the hypocrisy of small-town morals shows where Elvis' dramatic film career could've gone.

Follow That Dream (1962) has Elvis as part of an ad hoc family that decides to homestead on public land. It's a failed attempt at social satire, but it does show Elvis' skill at comedy.

Fun in Acapulco (1963) is the first of Elvis' films to veer sharply toward kitsch—what else can you say about a scene where he's dressed up as a matador and singing "The Bullfighter Was a Lady"? Elvis plays a singer at a Mexican hotel, and while some of the songs are silly, "Bossa Nova Baby" is a definite highlight.

Kissin' Cousins (1964) is too kitschy for some; indeed, it's almost a parody of an Elvis movie. Elvis plays lookalike cousins, the Air Force cousin trying to persuade the country cousin to let the family's land be used as a military base. Elvis didn't like the blond wig he had to wear as the country cousin, but it's still fun seeing two Elvi.

Roustabout (1964) lets rebel Elvis return—briefly—in a black leather jacket and riding a motorcycle. He plays a singer who gets a job as a handyman at a carnival, a loner who realizes he's found a new "family" among his fellow workers. The musical highlight is "Little Egypt."

Live a Little, Love a Little (1968) is interesting because of its offbeat storyline. Elvis plays a photographer whose life is disrupted by an eccentric woman (Michele Carey) who gets him fired from his job, then moves all of his possessions into her home. There's a bizarre dream sequence (Carey's dog sings to him), and, daringly, it's implied that the couple actually sleep together.

The awkwardly titled *The Trouble with Girls (and How to Get Into It)* (1969) has Elvis as the head of a Chautauqua troupe (a travelling educational show). He doesn't actually have much trouble; he handily wins over a union rep (Marlyn Mason) and finds time to solve a murder. Elvis is more of a co-star than a leading man in this ensemble piece, and if the film drags at times, it's nonetheless engaging.

Change of Habit (1969) is Elvis' last feature film. He plays a doctor working at a free clinic in the ghetto; Mary Tyler Moore is one of three female volunteers who show up to offer assistance. What Elvis doesn't know is that the three women are nuns, sent out to work in the world as ordinary citizens before taking their final vows. The drama is kept on a superficial level, but there is an intriguing ending. We never learn who Moore chooses in the end—Elvis, or the Lord?

Juliet Prowse beguiled both Frank Sinatra and Elvis Presley. Here she plays opposite Presley in G.I. Blues *in Hollywood on July 6, 1960. Scenes like this developed into dates, which Juliet successfully managed to juggle between dates with Sinatra.* (AP Photo)

85 The Rest of Elvis' Movies

As the 1960s progressed, Elvis became increasingly unhappy with the films he was making, showing his displeasure by putting on weight and recording the soundtracks with an obvious lack of enthusiasm. "He hated most of the film songs," Gordon Stoker of Elvis' backing group, the Jordanaires, told me. Elvis fans will of course want to see every movie he made, but none of these films would rank in the Top 10:

Flaming Star (1960) gave Elvis a chance at straight drama (he only sings once in the movie) as the mixed race son of a white man and a Native American woman in the 1880s American west. It's an obvious plea for racial tolerance, and the second movie in which Elvis dies at the end, but the film tends to drag.

Kid Galahad (1962) is the second remake of a movie first released in 1937 then remade in 1941. It's surprisingly dull for a boxing film. Aside from the opening song, "King of the Whole Wide World," there isn't much to listen to, either.

It's the setting—the 1962 Seattle World's Fair—that's important in *It Happened at the World's Fair* (1963), not the plot. Elvis is a crop-dusting pilot whose plane is impounded. What "happens" at the Fair is that while he and his partner try to raise cash to get it back, Elvis ends up looking after a Chinese farmer's niece and falls in love with a nurse. The sole decent song, "One Broken Heart For Sale," lasts barely a minute and a half.

Girl Happy (1965) is a predictable romantic comedy with Elvis as a musician who's been asked to keep his eye on a night-club owner's daughter as she parties in Fort Lauderdale. To no one's astonishment, they fall in love by the film's end. It was hoped the song "Do the Clam" might result in a new dance craze. It didn't.

Tickle Me (1965) (the most embarrassing film title of any Elvis movie) has Elvis working at an all-female dude ranch/health spa, padded out with a subplot involving hidden treasure in a nearby ghost town. The soundtrack recycled tracks Elvis had previously released, meaning not a single new song was recorded for the film.

In *Harum Scarum* (1965) Elvis is an actor kidnapped by a Middle Eastern tribe who want him to sacrifice a rival king. Even Parker was embarrassed by the storyline, suggesting a talking camel be added to the plot to make it more obvious that this wasn't a film to take seriously.

Frankie and Johnny (1966) is a period piece with Elvis as a singer on a riverboat, torn between two women. The original song

The Anti-Hits Album

Thousands, perhaps hundreds of thousands, of Elvis bootlegs have been released. One of the most humorous was the compilation *Elvis' Greatest Shit!!*, first released in 1980 (and now an unauthorized CD).

The album is more of a pirate release than a bootleg. Strictly speaking, a "bootleg" features previously unreleased material, while a "pirate" has previously released material, but is not a record that's been officially sanctioned by the record company. Most of the songs on *Elvis' Greatest Shit!!* were previously released, and all but one of them are songs from his movies.

Even in the context of the films, the movie songs were often silly. "(There's) No Room to Rhumba in a Sports Car" and "The Walls Have Ears" lament disruptions to Elvis' plans for romance. "He's Your Uncle, Not Your Dad" stresses the patriotic duty of paying taxes. "Yoga Is As Yoga Does" rhymes "serious" with "posterious." Elvis particularly hated "Dominic" (from *Stay Away, Joe*) about an impotent bull, and he begged his producer not to release it on a record.

The cover art is equally satiric. The front cover has a mock-up of a *National Enquirer* cover, picturing Elvis in his coffin (the real *Enquirer* had run the same picture), and the record label is purported to be "Dog Vomit" records. The cover also brags the songs are "The Very Best Of The Very Worst." Elvis, who disliked most of the movie songs he had to record, would have probably agreed.

is changed so that Frankie (Donna Douglas) doesn't gun down Johnny (Elvis) out of jealousy, in order to supply the requisite happy ending.

Spinout (1966) is Elvis' second time around as a racecar driver, and his second time around with co-star Shelley Fabares. The best songs on the soundtrack album are those that aren't in the movie, including "Tomorrow is a Long Time."

Easy Come, Easy Go (1967) has Elvis as a former navy diver searching for sunken treasure. He also meets the counter culture (in a yoga class), and the one-time rebel comes off like a first-class square.

Double Trouble (1967) is set in London when the film begins, but Elvis (playing a singer) doesn't get much chance to swing there. After the opening scenes, he moves on to the Continent, pursued by an obsessed fan and, more ludicrously, diamond smugglers.

Clambake (1967) is a modern-day variation of *The Prince and the Pauper*, with the well-off Elvis changing places with a water skiing instructor. Again, the best songs on the soundtrack album are those that don't appear in the film (like "Guitar Man").

Elvis plays a Native American for a second time in *Stay Away, Joe* (1968), trying to give his father (a scenery-chewing Burgess Meredith) a start in the cattle business. What could've been a pungent satire quickly degenerates into slapstick nonsense.

Speedway (1968) has two good moments—when Elvis (playing a racecar driver for the third time) sings "Let Yourself Go," and when Nancy Sinatra (an IRS agent), sings "Your Groovy Self." But overall, there's too much dead time in this unimaginative reworking of *It Happened at the World's Fair*: good guy Elvis gets in trouble due to an incompetent buddy.

With his love of action movies, a "Spaghetti Western" would seem an obvious choice for Elvis. But *Charro!* (1969) has a decided lack of suspense, despite some intense moments (Elvis is branded in one scene). A lost opportunity.

86 Dr. Feelgood

After "Colonel" Tom Parker, Dr. George Nichopoulos is probably the most notorious figure in Elvis' life.

Elvis met the man he called "Dr. Nick" on February 26, 1967. Elvis had been spending a lot of time at a ranch he owned not far from Graceland, and he had developed saddle sores from too much horseback riding. A girlfriend of George Klein, one of Elvis' friends, recommended calling Dr. Nick, a doctor at the clinic where she worked. Dr. Nick arrived that day, and he and Elvis quickly became friends.

Dr. Nick next treated Elvis in January 1969 when Elvis was suffering from laryngitis, which interrupted his sessions at American Sound. After prescribing medicine for Elvis, he was perturbed to find out that Elvis had taken it all at once when it should have lasted an entire week. It was an early clue to his famous patient's incautious approach to taking medication.

Dr. Nick began treating Elvis more regularly when the singer returned to live performance. Dr. Nick would be on hand at the beginning and end of Elvis' Vegas seasons and went with him on tour. His travels strained the relationships he had at his practice and with his family, but he continued to remain "on call" for Elvis, sometimes going out to Graceland no matter what hour he was called because Elvis simply wanted someone to talk to.

In 1973, Elvis' abuse of medication began causing serious problems. During a hospital stay in October that year, Dr. Nick was surprised to learn that Elvis had become addicted to Demerol; Elvis hadn't mentioned that another doctor was administering the drug to him via injections. While he was being treated in the hospital, Dr. Nick and Joe Esposito made a search of Graceland, finding huge jars of medication: Dexedrine, an amphetamine, and Placidyl and Seconal, used to treat insomnia, none of which Dr. Nick had ever prescribed for Elvis. He also learned from Joe that Elvis was seeing numerous other doctors at the time and getting prescription drugs from them, making the potential of dangerous drug interactions a real possibility.

It was then that Dr. Nick made a fateful decision. "Either I could confront Elvis and tell him to find another doctor, or I could continue to treat him, knowing I would probably never have complete knowledge of or control over what, if any, additional medications he might take," he wrote in his autobiography. He elected to stay and try to help Elvis.

He first tried to limit Elvis' drug use. He wouldn't allow Elvis to take his medications himself; either Dr. Nick or a nurse would dispense them directly to Elvis. He also made placebos, enlisting Elvis' entourage to empty capsules and fill them with artificial sweetener; Dr. Nick was even able to convince Knoll, the manufacturers of the painkiller Dilaudid, to make lookalike pills without any active ingredients.

But Elvis was a difficult patient. If he couldn't get what he wanted, he'd simply go to another doctor. Dr. Nick would make other suggestions regarding diet and exercise; Elvis would make some changes in his lifestyle, but soon end up falling back into his old routine. "It's hard to convince somebody what's right and wrong or what they need to do," Dr. Nick told the *Observer* in 2002. "It's hard when you've got somebody that thinks they have all the answers, and no matter what you throw at 'em, they've got answers for you."

After Elvis' death, Dr. Nick's relationship with him began giving him legal difficulties. In 1979, the Tennessee Board of Medical Examiners charged him with 14 counts of overprescribing drugs to Elvis and 13 other patients (including Jerry Lee Lewis). He was found guilty in January 1980; his license was suspended for three months, and he also received three years' probation. He then faced criminal prosecution on similar grounds and was acquitted of all changes in November 1980. But in 1992, the Medical Board again charged him with overprescribing, and Dr. Nick ended up losing his medical license in July 1995. He appealed, to no avail.

In 2009, Dr. Nick published a book telling his side of the story to help offset his legal bills. He also turns up in Memphis as a guest during Elvis Week.

Further reading: *The King and Dr. Nick* by George Nichopoulos, M.D.

87 The Seeker

Elvis was raised a Christian. But in his adult life, he became curious about other religions and spiritual philosophies.

Elvis' spiritual awakening began on April 30, 1964, when Larry Geller walked into his life. Larry worked as a hairdresser and arrived at Elvis' Bel Air home to fix his hair for a photo shoot the following day. When Elvis casually asked him about his interests, Larry replied that he was interested in metaphysical questions about the meaning of life. Intrigued, Elvis asked Larry what he felt the purpose of life was. As Larry recalled in his 1980 book *The Truth About Elvis*, he said, "We're here to find out why we're here. That's our purpose. And when we find out, and go out fulfilling it, then we know our mission."

To his astonishment, Elvis became tremendously excited, telling Larry he thought about similar things himself but had no one to talk to about them. Larry was happy to oblige, bringing Elvis books like *The Impersonal Life* by Joseph Benner (which would become a particular favorite of Elvis'), *Autobiography of a Yogi* by Paramahansa Yogananda, *Beyond The Himalayas* by Murdo MacDonald-Bayne, and *The Prophet* by Kahlil Gibran, among others, which the two would discuss for hours while Larry worked on Elvis' hair.

In retrospect, it's not as unusual a direction for Elvis to pursue as it might seem at first glance. By 1964, Elvis realized his career was in a rut. He was unhappy with the movies he was making, not to mention their accompanying soundtracks. His supremacy on the record charts was being challenged by a new crop of musicians led by the Beatles, who were generating the kind of acclaim Elvis used to enjoy. He'd put a lot of effort into getting Priscilla's parents to agree she could move to Memphis to be with him, but his continued involvement with other women indicated he wasn't yet certain he'd made the right choice.

Elvis spoke to Larry about the void he felt in his life, despite all he had achieved. If his success hadn't made him happy, what good was success? As he delved into his reading, his entourage became dismayed. He wasn't interested in his usual activities, like watching football with the guys, and if he hosted a party, he preferred to spend the time reading aloud from one of his spiritual books.

In 1965, he began visiting the Self-Realization Fellowship's retreat on Lake Shrine in the Pacific Palisades (the Fellowship is an organization founded by Paramahansa Yogananda in 1920), which promoted meditation. He later spent time with Fellowship's president, Sri Daya Mata, at the Fellowship's headquarters on Mt. Washington, outside of Los Angeles. He amused Daya Mata by asking if there was a "shortcut" to enlightenment and also told her he wanted to become a teacher for the organization. Daya Mata told him she felt it was not what he was best suited for but assured him, "The inner peace you seek can be yours no matter what your work."

Elvis also had Jewish roots, as his great-great-grandmother on his mother's side was Jewish. He sometimes wore necklaces that had either the Jewish "Chai" symbol (meaning "living") or a Star of David, in addition to a necklace with a crucifix; when asked why he wore symbols of two different religions, he jokingly replied he didn't want to be kept out of heaven on a technicality. He later had watches designed that featured both a Star of David and a cross in the center that he would give to his friends.

Parker felt threatened by Larry's influence over Elvis, saying Elvis was "on a religious kick." "It's no damn kick," Elvis told his friends. "It's my life, and my life is no kick." But when Elvis fell in his bathroom and hit his head prior to filming *Clambake* in March 1967, Parker jumped in and said Elvis was being distracted by the ideas in his religious books. Elvis was no longer allowed to be alone with Larry, who was eased out of the group—for a time. By the mid-1970s, Larry was back, bringing Elvis books and continuing their discussions. And after Elvis' death, Larry fixed his hair one more time before Elvis was buried.

Further reading: *The Truth About Elvis* and *If I Can Dream: Elvis' Own Story* by Larry Geller.

88 Tell 'Em Phillips Sent You

When Elvis was making his first records, Dewey Phillips was the top DJ in Memphis. As such, he was well placed to give Elvis' career an early boost.

Dewey was born on May 13, 1926, and began his career in radio in his early twenties. While working in the record department of W.T. Grant's in downtown Memphis, he got the idea of spinning records to attract customers, adding his own idiosyncratic patter. He succeeded in attracting attention and parlayed this success into a 15-minute spot on WHBQ radio in 1949. According to one story, while hanging around the station, he distracted the on-air DJ by setting a trash can in the hallway on fire, and, when the DJ rushed to put out the flames, Dewey commandeered the microphone himself.

Eventually, Dewey was on the air six nights a week from 9:00 PM to midnight. He called his show *Red, Hot and Blue*. Dewey was one of the first white DJs to play a steady diet of black music, especially rhythm & blues. But his show was also eclectic; "Teens listened to Dewey because they never knew what sounds would be coming out of their speakers," Elvis historian Bill Burk wrote. Sister Rosetta Tharpe, Frank Sinatra, Ike Turner, B.B. King, Little Richard, Jimmy Reed, the Johnny Burnette Trio—"Daddy-O-Dewey" served up a musical smorgasbord. This made the show highly regarded by not just Memphis' African American community; there was also a growing white audience.

His commentary and presentation was another drawing card. If he didn't like a record, he'd simply take it off the turntable before it had finished playing. He'd play records at the wrong speed. He reworked ad copy to his own unique specifications, as in this plug for Falstaff beer: "If you can't drink, freeze it and eat it. If you can't do that, open up a cotton-picking rib and pour it in!" Naturally, he had his own catchphrases—"Tell 'em Phillips set you!" was often punctuated with a brash "Dee-gaw!"

Sam Phillips was no relation, but he eagerly sought out Dewey; here was a man who shared his own musical interests. The two men even set up a record label, The Phillips, but they only managed to put out one single, "Boogie in the Park" by Joe Hill Louis, before it fell apart. The men nonetheless maintained a friendship, and Dewey would regularly give his friend a plug on the air, giving the command "Call Sam!" throughout his show.

Sam gave Dewey a copy of Elvis' first record, "That's All Right," before it was even released. On the night Dewey aired the

Elvis' First Airplay

Memphis DJ Dewey Phillips is said to have given Elvis his first airplay when Sam Phillips gave him an acetate of "That's All Right." But on what date did that happen? And was Dewey really the first person to play an Elvis record on the air?

Both *Last Train To Memphis* (by Peter Guralnick) and *Elvis Day By Day* (by Guralnick and Ernst Jørgensen) say Dewey played "That's All Right" on July 8, 1954. But in Bill Burk's *Early Elvis: The Sun Years*, Fred Cook, a DJ at WREC, claims Marion Keisker came to him on July 7 with a copy of "That's All Right"/"Blue Moon of Kentucky." Fred played part of one side (he couldn't remember which) on the air that day, but quickly took it off, as he didn't like it. The problem with Fred's story is that Sam Phillips had only made one-sided acetates of "That's All Right" at that point.

Although Guralnick and Jørgensen state in *Elvis Day By Day* that there's no way to confirm when Dewey Phillips first played "That's All Right," Jørgensen makes that leap in his 2012 book, *A Boy From Tupelo*, saying that Dewey played "That's All Right" on July 6. In any case, Dewey was the first person to play an Elvis record all the way through.

record, Sam brought Elvis into the studio for an interview. Elvis was nervous, telling Dewey, "Mr. Phillips, I don't know nothing about being interviewed." "Just don't say nothing dirty," Dewey replied. He then continued chatting to Elvis, not telling him that he'd turned the microphone on, to help him relax. Dewey said Elvis broke out in a "cold sweat" when he learned he had been on the air without realizing it.

In 1957, Dewey moved to television, hosting the locally broadcast show *Phillips' Pop Shop*, which aired in the afternoon. In 1958, the show was moved to midnight, to make way for Dick Clark's *American Bandstand,* and renamed *Night Beat.* But it was taken off the air when a co-host fondled a life-size cut-out of Jayne Mansfield on the set. Dewey lost his job at WHBQ the same year. His life began a downward slide; he separated from his wife, work became hard to find, and his abuse of alcohol and drugs (painkillers and amphetamines) steadily increased. He moved back in with his mother and was found in his bed, dead of a heart attack, on September 28, 1968.

Dewey and Elvis had a falling out in 1957 when Dewey stole an acetate of "Teddy Bear" while visiting Elvis in L.A. during the making of *Loving You* and played the record on the air before it was released. They later made up, but the friendship was never the same. Elvis was still saddened by Dewey's death and went to the funeral. Dewey's estranged wife told Elvis she was glad to see him and that Dewey would have wanted him there. "Mrs. Dorothy," Elvis told her, "Dewey was my friend."

Further reading: *Dewey and Elvis: The Life and Times of a Rock 'n' Roll Deejay* by Louis Canton.

89 Everybody Was Kung Fu Fighting

Karate wasn't a mere hobby for Elvis. It was a discipline he studied for most of his life. It also had a big influence on his performing style.

Elvis discovered karate while in the army. He first trained with Shotokan stylist Juergen Seydel when he was stationed in Germany. He took his training very seriously; when on leave in Paris in January 1960, he made sure he was able to continue his training by working with Tetsuji Murakami. Elvis was way ahead of the curve; interest in the martial arts had yet to cross over into the mainstream.

Soon after he left the army, Elvis met Ed Parker at a Kenpo karate demonstration at the Beverly Hills Hotel on May 12, 1960;

he became lifelong friends with the man who modernized Kenpo into American Kenpo Karate. Elvis also received his first-degree black belt the same year, from Chito-ryu stylist Hank Slomansky. During the '60s, he was able to make some use of the moves he learned in karate in the fight scenes in his movies. During their association, Ed Parker would award Elvis a seventh-degree black belt.

Ironically, karate also played a role in the dissolution of his marriage. While attending one of Ed Parker's tournaments in Hawaii in 1968, Elvis and Priscilla met Ed's friend, karate champion Mike Stone. Wanting to share her husband's interests, Priscilla began studying karate with Parker, and later had an affair with Stone, whom she would eventually leave Elvis for.

When Elvis returned to live performance, he'd frequently work some karate moves into the more energetic numbers. Drummer Ronnie Tutt even took up karate himself so he could better accent Elvis' moves on his drums when Elvis decided to show off a karate routine during shows.

Ed Parker also recommended that Elvis train with Kang Rhee, a Tae Kwon Do expert who developed the PaSaRyu style of karate. Elvis first went to Master Rhee's studio on March 29, 1971, and received a fourth-degree black belt from him that day. Elvis was given the nickname "Master Tiger" while studying with Rhee. In 1974, Rhee awarded Elvis an eighth-degree black belt. At time of writing, Rhee still operated a karate school in Memphis.

By the '70s, karate had become popular in the United States due to the success of Bruce Lee's film *Enter The Dragon* and David Carradine's TV series *Kung Fu*. As a result, Elvis became interested in making a karate-influenced film himself. He first spoke about making a feature film, an action movie, saying, "I want to be the baddest motherfucker there is." Rick Husky, a friend of Jerry Schilling's who worked in television, wrote out a 30-page treatment of just such a film, casting Elvis as a former CIA agent called back into action to track down the drug dealer who murdered his friend. But the idea never got any further than Husky's treatment.

Elvis then considered making a documentary with Ed Parker, which would feature martial arts experts from around the world and Elvis as narrator. He envisioned a dramatic ending for the film in which he'd be seen standing on a hilltop, performing "The Lord's Prayer" in Native American sign language. A business plan was drawn up, Jerry Schilling was made the film's executive producer, a film office was established in Los Angeles, and preliminary footage was shot. In September 1974, Elvis was filmed going through karate routines at the Tennessee Karate Institute in Memphis, a business Elvis had partially funded that was run by his friend, Red West. On December 20, 1974, a rough cut of the footage was screened for potential investors. But the film was shut down just four days later, the reason given being as Elvis' health problems. Footage from the project was later released on *The New Gladiators* DVD in 2002 (retitled as simply *Gladiators* when reissued with new footage in 2009).

It's a shame one of Elvis' karate films didn't come to fruition. Such a film would've given him the perfect avenue to demonstrate his love of, and skill in, the martial arts.

90 Discover the Music That Made the Man

Everyone knows that Elvis is the King of Rock 'n' Roll. But it's often overlooked that his versatility as a singer drew on all of his influences, not just the big bold beat of rock. And one of the best ways to gain a greater appreciation of his music is to explore the wide range of music he listened to while growing up.

Religious music was certainly the bedrock of Elvis' musical foundation. He heard the music in church and loved joining in the singing. In Memphis, he not only heard music at his own church, the First Assembly of God, he'd also slip into African American churches to hear the livelier gospel music at their services. Memphis-based gospel quartet the Blackwood Brothers also attended the First Assembly of God church, and Elvis saw them there and at the All-Night Gospel Singings held at the Ellis Auditorium, where he also saw groups like the Speer Family, the Sunshine Boys, and the Statesmen. The Statesmen were particular favorites of Elvis, not only for their singing but also for the less-than-secular body movements made by bass singer Jim "Big Chief" Wetherington, which Elvis took special note of.

Country music was another important cornerstone in Elvis' musical development. In addition to appearing on the *WELO Jamboree* radio show in Tupelo, he was quick to befriend the show's host, Mississippi Slim; Slim's brother, James Ausborn, went to the same school as Elvis, which provided the opening to an introduction. "Elvis would always say, 'Let's go to your brother's program today,'" Ausborn later recalled. "'Can you go up there with me? I want him to show me some more chords on the guitar'...a lot of times the studio would be full, but my brother would always show him some chords." As Ausborn perceptively noted, "I think gospel sort of inspired him to be in music, but then my brother helped carry it on." Eddy Arnold was a big favorite, as were Hank Williams, Roy Acuff, and Ernest Tubb.

In Memphis, Elvis was in the audience for the broadcast of country programs like *High Noon Round-Up* on WMPS. But radio also provided a gateway to other musical styles. Pop music was the easiest to find, and Elvis would listen to, and later perform, songs by Bing Crosby, Dean Martin, and Teresa Brewer. But it was hearing rhythm & blues on the radio that really opened musical doors for both Elvis and other artists.

Dewey Phillips' *Red, Hot and Blue* show on WHBQ had a big audience of both black and white listeners. Memphis was also home to radio station WDIA, dubbed "The Mother Station of the Negroes" because it not only played a steady diet of blues, R&B, and gospel but was also the first radio station in the country with an all-black air staff. Future R&B stars B.B. King and Rufus Thomas were among the station's DJs. Elvis also saw blues/R&B performers like Ivory Joe Hunter, Wynonie Harris, and Little Junior Parker at the Handy Theater; the venue was in a black neighborhood but presented "whites only" shows on Sunday nights in acknowledgement of the increasingly diverse audience the music was attracting. People of different races couldn't always attend the same shows together, but music was starting to break down those barriers.

Some might be surprised to know that Elvis also had an interest in classical music. He later recalled watching orchestras play at the Overton Park Shell in Memphis. "I listened to the music for hours," he said, adding that he also listened to the work of the Metropolitan Opera. Elvis owned records by Mario Lanza and also knew the work of Enrico Caruso—as clearly evidenced by the Neapolitan flavor in songs he later recorded like "It's Now or Never" or "Surrender."

And it's especially interesting to hear Elvis' versions of songs that made an impression on him: from the raucous R&B of "Tiger Man" to the country of "Faded Love" and seemingly everything in between.

91 An Album of Chart Toppers

A successful music act can release a greatest hits album. But it takes something special to be able to release a greatest hits collection that's solely made up of songs that topped the charts.

Elvis was, of course, one of those artists, and to prove it, *ELVIS: 30 No. 1 Hits* was released in 2002. Like the Beatles' *1* album, *ELVIS* featured songs that had reached No. 1 in either the U.S. or the UK. It's interesting to note that though Elvis always had a strong fan base in Britain, it took him a while to top the charts there; "All Shook Up," released in 1957, was his sixth No. 1 in the U.S. but his first chart topper in the UK. But Elvis also topped the charts more frequently in England; out of the 30 songs, 13 are U.S. No. 1's, while 18 are UK No. 1's.

And most of the U.S. No. 1's came during the '50s, while the UK gave Elvis No. 1's throughout his career. After "Good Luck Charm" released in 1962, Elvis had only two more U.S. No. 1's, "Suspicious Minds" in 1969 and "Burning Love" in 1972 (though the latter song didn't top *Billboard*'s chart, it's included on *ELVIS* because it did top the chart in the rival trade magazine *Cash Box*). Conversely, in the UK, Elvis had No. 1's in 1964 ("[You're The] Devil in Disguise"), 1965 ("Crying in the Chapel"), 1969 ("In The Ghetto"), 1970 ("The Wonder of You"), and 1977 ("Way Down").

There were also more songs that reached No. 1 in the UK, because Elvis had four double-sided hits there: "One Night"/"I Got Stung," "(Now and Then There's) A Fool Such As I"/"I Need Your Love Tonight," "(Marie's The Name) His Latest Flame"/"Little Sister," and "Can't Help Falling in Love"/"Rock-a-Hula." But only the A-sides of these singles appear on *ELVIS*. The sole U.S. double-sided hit, "Don't Be Cruel"/"Hound Dog," is included.

All the songs were remixed and remastered, which enhanced the overall sound. Producer David Bendeth told *Entertainment Weekly* he hesitated to use the word "remix" "because 'remix' kinda conjures up the idea that we put drums on them." He didn't; he simply brought a greater clarity and depth to the songs.

But there was controversy over the fact that "(Now and Then There's) A Fool Such As I," "A Big Hunk O' Love," and "The Wonder of You" were not the original versions of the songs. Bendeth chose to use alternate takes either because the master tape was damaged (as he said was the case with "A Fool Such As I") or that he never got the original master to begin with (as he said happened with "Wonder of You").

The album's title wasn't entirely accurate, for it really had 31 No. 1's; right before release, the newly remixed version of "A Little Less Conversation," which had been a No. 1 hit around the world (though not in the U.S.) was added to the album. *ELV1S* was released in October 2002 and became a No. 1 hit itself, topping the charts in the U.S., the UK, and more than 10 other countries.

There were three editions of *ELV1S* that featured bonus material. An edition sold exclusively in WalMart stores had a second disc with an Elvis interview done when he got out of the army. The Japanese edition had a bonus disc with an extended remix of "A Little Less Conversation" as well as the song's video. The most desirable was the two-CD edition released in 2003 that included a CD with rehearsal versions and alternate takes of 14 songs. There was also a DVD-audio only edition that featured the songs remixed in 5.1 surround sound.

ELV1S reveals that most of Elvis' No. 1's came during the first decade of his career as a major label artist; after 1965, he only had five more No. 1's on the pop charts. As such, *ELV1S* isn't too representative of the breadth of his career. For a more well-rounded overview, pick up the sequel to *ELV1S*, *Elvis: 2nd to None*, released in 2003 with 28 tracks ranging from "That's All Right" to "Moody

Blue," a remix of "Rubberneckin'" by UK producer/DJ Paul Oakenfold, and a previously unreleased track, "I'm a Roustabout."

92 The "Team Elvis" Logo

Elvis loved collecting badges, and had an impressive collection of credentials he'd received from police departments across the country (not to mention his badge from the Bureau of Narcotics and Dangerous Drugs given to him by President Nixon). So it was no surprise he created his own insignia, a logo that not only appeared on his own personal items but also items given to his friends and the people he worked with, a public declaration that they were members of "Team Elvis."

The logo first appeared on items of jewelry in the fall of 1970. The logo featured a lightning bolt with the letter "T" on the left, a "C" at the top, and a "B" on the right; TCB, standing for "Taking Care of Business." It was an expression popular in the black community during the '60s; Elvis may have heard it in Aretha Franklin's cover of Otis Redding's "Respect," when she sings, "Take care, TCB." There are differing opinions about what the inspiration was for the lightning bolt: the lighting bolt used by the "West Coast Mafia" in their insignia; the lightning bolt on patches of Elvis' battalion in the military; or the lightning bolt on the costume of comic book hero Captain Marvel (Elvis had loved reading about Captain Marvel's exploits as a child). But there was no doubt about what the bolt signified in Elvis' logo; taken all together, the message the design sent was, "Taking care of business—in a flash."

Elvis first had necklaces made with the logo, which he gave to his male friends; he later had "TLC" necklaces made for his female friends (meaning "Tender Love Care"—in a flash?). The logo then began appearing on other items: his personal stationery, his wardrobe, his guns, patches designed for the security staff at Graceland, the ID cards members of his entourage (including the musicians) carried, and the tail of his plane, the *Lisa Marie*. In the summer of 1974, he had a lightning bolt painted on the walls of the TV room.

The logo also appeared on other items of jewelry, and in 1975 he had Lowell Hays, his favorite jeweler in Memphis, design a ring for him that featured a variation of the logo. The ring, which cost $39,337.50, was an elaborate creation made out of gold and black onyx, with "TCB" spelled out in diamonds, a large diamond above the TCB, and two lightning bolts going down the sides of the ring. The diamond was later removed and set in a ring for Elvis' last girlfriend, Ginger Alden, replaced by a stone of cubic zirconium. The ring is on display at Graceland.

Elvis had great fun placing his TCB logo on different items, and today fans can buy inexpensive versions of the TCB or TLC logos on jewelry and other items like T-shirts and mugs. The logo stayed with Elvis to the end; when you visit the Meditation Garden, you'll see the TCB logo on the bottom of his tombstone.

93 The Best-Selling U.S. Stamp of All Time

On January 8, 1993, the United States Postal Service issued an Elvis Presley stamp. It quickly became the top-selling U.S. postage stamp of all time, a record it still holds today.

But it wasn't the first time Elvis appeared on a stamp. Grenada was the first country to commemorate Elvis in this fashion when an Elvis stamp was prepared for release in 1978. But the government

 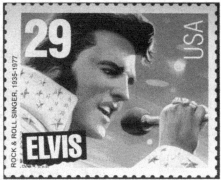

The 29-cent Elvis Presley stamps issued in 1993 accounted for 124 million stamps that have been purchased but not used, generating $36 million for the U.S. Postal Service. (AP Photo/USPS)

rejected the stamp, meaning it was never valid as postage; the first legitimate Elvis stamp was issued in 1985 by Saint Vincent and the Grenadines, an island in the Caribbean. Other countries followed, and by the time the U.S. Elvis stamp was issued, at least 14 other countries and territories had released Elvis stamps.

At the time, a U.S. citizen had to be dead for 10 years before they could be commemorated on a stamp. And from 1987 on, Elvis' name had come up before the Citizens Stamp Advisory Committee. While Postmaster General Anthony Frank had spoken in favor of an Elvis stamp, members of the Committee were opposed, generally citing Elvis' drug abuse.

The opposition was eventually overcome when it was realized how much money an Elvis stamp would bring in. Thirty designs were submitted, and the final two were unveiled on February 24, 1992, at the Las Vegas Hilton: a young Elvis in his '50s prime (designed by Mark Stutzman), and the '70s jumpsuit-clad Elvis (designed by John Berkey). Now the public was invited to help choose the final image. Specially designed postcards were available, featuring both images and a box to check for the image you liked the best ("A" for the '50s Elvis, "B" for the '70s Elvis). People were asked to mail in the postcards between April 6 and 24. More than 1 million people voted. And on June 4, in a special ceremony held at Graceland, Priscilla announced the winner: the '50s Elvis design, which received 851,200 votes to 277,723 for the '70s Elvis.

The Postal Service originally planned an initial print run of 300 million for the Elvis stamp, but by the end of December 1992, they'd increased the run to 500 million. And the image wasn't only going to be available on a stamp; it was also reproduced on numerous products, including T-shirts, mugs, hats, keychains, towels, blankets, watches, music boxes, clocks, jewelry, and other items. This meant Elvis Presley Enterprises could profit from the image as well as the Postal Service.

Some fans thought of a way to create a unique collectable. They put the stamp on a letter made out to a non-existent address; when the envelope was returned, it was stamped with the official message "RETURNED TO SENDER" (some had the additional phrase "NO SUCH NUMBER" or "ADDRESSEE UNKNOWN," the latter not exactly the same lyric as in the song "Return to Sender," but it was close enough). This created a headache for the Postal Service. You can now find these returned letters offered for sale on eBay.

The same image appeared on another set of U.S. stamps issued that year on June 14 as part of the "Legends of American Music Series: Rock & Roll/Rhythm & Blues." Elvis was one of eight artists featured in the series, which also included Bill Haley, Jackie Wilson, Ritchie Valens, Otis Redding, Buddy Holly, Clyde McPhatter, and Dinah Washington. Interestingly, while the name "Elvis" appears on the January '93 stamp, the full name "Elvis Presley" appears on the June '93 stamp.

The U.S. Elvis stamp made a lot of money for the Postal Service at the time. But because so many of the stamps were issued, you can still pick them up pretty cheaply today.

94 Frank Sinatra and Elvis

The biggest male singer before Elvis was Frank Sinatra. They were from different generations and had different singing styles, so they weren't exactly rivals. But they weren't exactly friends to begin with, either. Still, through the years they developed a clear respect for each other.

Frank was no fan of rock 'n' roll in the '50s. "Rock 'n' roll smells phony and false," he said in 1957. "It is sung, played, and written for the most part by cretinous goons and by means of its almost imbecilic reiteration, and sly, lewd, in plain fact, dirty lyrics...it manages to be the martial music of every sideburned delinquent on the face of the earth."

Reporters couldn't wait to ask Elvis what he thought of Frank's comments. "He is a great success and a fine actor, but I think he shouldn't have said it," Elvis said. "This is a trend, just the same as he faced when he started years ago." He then took the edge off his remarks by adding a self-deprecating joke; surely rock 'n' roll was noteworthy, he argued, "because it is the only thing I can do." Three years later, when Elvis left the army, Frank had no hesitation in associating himself with the King of Rock 'n' Roll, arranging for Elvis to be a guest star on one of his television specials.

Publicity for the special began the minute Elvis arrived back in the States on March 3, 1960. Frank's daughter, Nancy, was among those waiting to meet Elvis at Fort Dix, New Jersey, presenting him with two dress shirts as a gift from her father. The show, formally titled *The Frank Sinatra Timex Show: Welcome Home Elvis*, was taped in Miami on March 26. In addition to singing his new single, "Stuck On You"/"Fame and Fortune," Elvis sang a duet with Frank. The two made a very odd couple, not least because

Elvis seemed to dwarf Frank as his high-balanced pompadour made him seem even taller. Then there's the actual performance. Frank delivers "Love Me Tender" in a bright, if surprisingly bland, fashion, smiling obliviously while Elvis hilariously camps his way through Frank's hit "Witchcraft"; it's like watching a mischievous teenager sending up his straight-laced uncle. Nancy also performed in the special, singing "I may pass out!" during the opening number as she gazes at Elvis.

Unbeknownst to Frank, Elvis had a brief relationship with his girlfriend (later his fiancée), Juliet Prowse, while the two were making Elvis' first post-army film, *G.I. Blues*. In May 1967, Frank let Elvis and Priscilla use his private jet when they flew to Las Vegas to get married. The following month, Elvis began shooting the film *Speedway*, in which Nancy Sinatra co-starred; she was one of his few co-stars to sing a song of her own in an Elvis movie, performing the slinky number "Your Groovy Self."

During Elvis' first season in Las Vegas in 1969, he took out a full-page ad for Nancy's show at the International, which opened the day after his own show closed. He attended the opening show and the party afterward, hosted by Frank. Now, the two men were truly peers, and Frank continued to offer help and support over the next few years. When Elvis canceled his summer season in Vegas due to illness in 1975, Frank called the hospital, telling Elvis "not to let the bastards kill him—which Elvis took to mean not just Vegas but the whole system," according to the book *Careless Love*. And when Elvis was troubled by the publication of *Elvis: What Happened?* during the summer of 1977, Frank offered to try to stop its publication (Elvis demurred). At the end, the two even shared a song. Both performed "My Way" in concert, a song that had a personal resonance for two singers who, in spite of their differences, also had much in common.

95 King of the Road

Elvis wasn't just heralded for his innovative music. He also attracted attention with his sense of style, his clothing—and his love of cars.

Even before he made it big, Elvis sang of the lure of the automobile, changing the line "You may get religion" in the song "Baby Let's Play House" to "You may have a pink Cadillac." It wasn't just a metaphor. He bought his first pink Caddy in the spring of 1955 when he began touring. It didn't last long; on June 5, 1955, it caught on fire while Elvis and his band were in Arkansas. He replaced it the following month—only to have Scotty Moore crash it, again while driving through Arkansas. After it was repaired, Elvis had the Caddy's black roof painted white, replaced the upholstery, and presented the car to his mother as a gift. Gladys couldn't drive but proudly referred to it as "her car." The pink Cadillac became a rock 'n' roll icon, as strongly associated with Elvis as his blue suede shoes. And though Elvis regularly replaced his cars as he bought newer models, he kept his mother's 1955 Cadillac Fleetwood 60 for the rest of his life.

Cars were a sign of status and wealth to Elvis. Even before he made his first record, he told his friends that someday he'd be driving Cadillacs. "The first car I ever bought was the most beautiful car I've ever seen," he said of his first purchase. "It was secondhand, but I parked it outside my hotel the day I got it and stayed up all night just looking at it." Look through the pages of *Elvis Day By Day* and you'll see numerous entries about his cars. On July 21, 1956, he traded in a lavender Lincoln for a white 1956 Lincoln Continental Mark II. On May 19, 1965, his customized gold Cadillac was sent "on tour" around the country, displayed at theaters showing his latest film, *Tickle Me.* On October 1, 1970, he bought the very first 1971 Stutz Blackhawk made available to the public (it had been promised to Frank Sinatra, but Elvis persuaded the dealer to sell it to him instead).

And it wasn't just cars that interested him. His auto insurance policy in 1956 showed that he not only owned Cadillacs and a Lincoln Continental but also had two Harley-Davidson motor-cycles and a Messerschmitt (a unique three-wheeled German car). He kept a 1950 Chevrolet truck on hand at the time, allowing him to drive around town incognito. He also bought an array of jeeps and golf carts to ride around the Graceland grounds, even having snowmobiles refitted so that they would run on the grass.

On March 21, 1958, three days before he was inducted into the army, he bought a 1956 Ford for his girlfriend, Anita Wood. She was the first in a long line of girlfriends, friends, and complete strangers who received cars from Elvis. On one memorable occa-sion, on July 27, 1975, he bought 14 Cadillacs at once, giving away one to a woman who just happened to be window-shopping at the dealership. There's even a film about his generosity in bestowing cars on lucky recipients, the 2003 documentary *200 Cadillacs*.

It seems fitting that the last known photograph of Elvis shows him driving through Graceland's gates, waving to fans from behind the wheel of a 1973 Stutz Blackhawk III, purchased on September 6, 1974. At time of writing, the car was on display at the Automobile Museum at Graceland, which opened in 1989. Yes, Elvis had so many cars and other vehicles that they needed a museum to display them (and what you see is just a portion of what he actually owned). You'll see his mother's pink Cadillac there, too.

96 Home on the Range

Not everyone knows that Elvis was a ranch owner for a brief period—a period that only lasted a few months but resulted in one of the biggest spending sprees of his life.

It all began in December 1966, when he gave Priscilla a horse as a Christmas present. He also bought one for Jerry Schilling's fiancée, Sandy, so Priscilla would have someone to ride with. When he saw how much they enjoyed riding, he bought a horse for himself then decided everyone in his entourage needed one. By the end of January 1967, Elvis had purchased nearly 20 horses, all of which had to be outfitted with proper riding equipment—as did their riders.

The barn at Graceland was used as a stable for the horses initially; Elvis' own horse, a golden Palomino, was named Rising Sun, leading him to jokingly rename the barn the House of the Rising Sun. Part of Graceland's grounds were also bulldozed to create a larger riding area. Elvis and his friends would occasionally ride down to Graceland's front gate, thrilling the fans who perennially hung out there, especially when he lingered to chat, pose for photos, and sign autographs.

But as the number of horses he owned grew, it soon became apparent that more room was needed for them. While driving around the area one day, Elvis and Priscilla found a ranch located outside of Walls, Mississippi, which was just 10 miles from Graceland. Twinkletown Farm was a 160-acre working cattle ranch; Elvis was also suitably impressed with the 65' white cross that was located by a lake on the property (which was actually a landmark for a local airport). When Elvis learned the ranch was for sale, he quickly bought it for $437,000 and renamed it Circle G (later Flying Circle G). The "G" was for Graceland.

There was only a small house on the property, and Elvis wanted to have his friends around him, so he began buying a number of mobile homes and trailers where his entourage could live. A high fence had to be constructed around the ranch to give them some privacy. Everyone needed their own pickup truck, of course, and Elvis also purchased plenty of new equipment, like tractors and horse trailers. By the end of February, Elvis had spent close to $1 million on his new hobby. When his father begged him to cut back, Elvis told him, "I'm having fun, Daddy, for the first time in ages."

Days were spent in a leisurely fashion, riding around the ranch, skeet-shooting, having picnics. Elvis became so relaxed, for the first time in his career, he was less enthusiastic about getting back to work—and this at a time when his spending spree had made it more necessary for him to do so. When he couldn't put off recording any longer, he showed up for a recording session in Nashville in February fully attired in cowboy regalia. And when he flew home, he had the pilot circle over the ranch to admire it from above.

What prompted such extravagance? Certainly Elvis had fleeting interests—he'd spent a lot of time using a slot-car racing track he had built at Graceland before it was permanently moved into storage—but they usually didn't end up consuming so much money. It's been speculated this was a last fling before Elvis' upcoming marriage in May and/or a way of dealing with his unhappiness about his career. And certainly his disinterest in getting back to work was another sign of his unhappiness.

But that need to work necessitated his return to L.A. in March to begin work on *Clambake*, after which his interest in the ranch began to fade. By August, his father began selling off the mobile homes and equipment, and eventually he put the ranch itself up for sale (it initially sold in 1969, but the buyers defaulted; a new buyer was found in 1973).

Elvis' days as a gentleman farmer were over. But in the summer, you can tour the barn at Graceland, and there are efforts underway for Circle G to be restored so fans can visit it, too (check circlegfoundation.co.uk for updates).

97 Hitting the Charts, Charting the Hits

Elvis' recordings hit the record charts from the very beginning of his career. And with so many records, and so many different record charts, there are a lot of chart statistics to keep track of.

"Blue Moon of Kentucky" (1954) was Elvis' very first record to hit the charts, reaching No. 3 on *Billboard*'s Country & Western Territorial Best Sellers charts in August 1954. Elvis' records performed strongly on the country charts, particularly at the beginning and end of his career. The first national chart (as opposed to a territorial or regional chart) that he landed a record on was a country chart, when "Baby Let's Play House" (1955) reached No. 5 on the country chart for Most Played by Jockeys and No. 10 on the Best Sellers in Stores. His first No. 1 also came on a country chart, when "I Forgot to Remember to Forget" (1955) topped the country charts for Most Played in Jukeboxes and Best Sellers in Stores. His first album to hit the country charts was *From Elvis In Memphis* (1969), which peaked at No. 2. And Elvis' first live album to top the country albums chart was *Aloha From Hawaii Via Satellite* (1973).

"Heartbreak Hotel" (1956) was his first single to top the pop charts; "Suspicious Minds" (1969) was the last pop No. 1. His debut album, *Elvis Presley* (1956), was the first to top the pop charts. His last studio, non-soundtrack album to top the pop charts was *Something For Everybody* (1961).

The Fans' Choice

In 2012, Elvis fans were asked to help make the selections for an Elvis compilation called *I Am An Elvis Fan.*

The fans weren't given totally free rein. They could only vote for three songs from pre-determined categories: '50s, '60s, Country, Movies, Love Songs, Gospel, and In Concert.

The final lineup had four songs from the '50s ("Heartbreak Hotel," "Don't Be Cruel," "All Shook Up," and "Jailhouse Rock"). There are three movie songs ("Blue Hawaii," "Can't Help Falling In Love," "Viva Las Vegas"), two religious songs ("[There'll Be] Peace In The Valley [For Me]," "How Great Thou Art),") and two songs from the Comeback Special ("Memories," "If I Can Dream"). Other '60s studio tracks include "Guitar Man," "In The Ghetto," "Suspicious Minds," and "Kentucky Rain."

With the exception of "Always On My Mind," the '70s songs are live tracks: "Welcome To My World," "An American Trilogy," "Burning Love," and "Suspicious Minds" (all from the *Aloha From Hawaii* show), and "The Wonder of You." There was no previously unreleased material; it was simply a fun release for the fans.

The album was released at the end of July 2012, and it reached No. 137 on the pop charts, No. 27 on the country charts. It's a pretty good representation of Elvis' music, but it would have been interesting to see what kind of album would have resulted from an open vote not restricted to specific categories.

"Heartbreak Hotel" was Elvis' first single to enter the Rhythm & Blues singles chart, peaking at No. 3. His first No. 1 R&B single was "Don't Be Cruel"/"Hound Dog," which was also his first single to top the pop and country singles charts. There were three other singles that also topped all three charts: "All Shook Up," "(Let Me Be Your) Teddy Bear," and "Jailhouse Rock" (all 1957). The last single to reach the R&B charts was "Bossa Nova Baby" (1963), which peaked at No. 20.

An EP, or "extended play" record, is the same size as a single (7") but has four to six songs. The format was phased out during the 1960s, but it was still around when Elvis began releasing records. His first EP, released in March 1956, was titled *Elvis Presley*. Confusingly, a two-disc EP set of the same name was released the same month, and a second single-disc EP with the same title was also released in June. But that first EP was the first to enter the national charts, reaching No. 24 on the singles charts. The *Heartbreak Hotel* (1956) EP was the first to enter the EP charts, peaking at No. 5, while *Loving You Vol. 1* (1956) was first to top EP charts. *Follow That Dream* (1962) was the last record to chart on the EP charts, peaking at No. 5; the last EP to chart at all was *Easy Come, Easy Go* (1967), which peaked on the pop singles chart at a lowly No. 70.

As for film soundtracks, the *Loving You* (1957) album was the first soundtrack to top the pop charts; *Roustabout* (1964) was the last film soundtrack to hit No. 1. And the last soundtrack to reach the Top 40 was *Clambake* (1967), which peaked at No. 40, unless you count the documentaries; then it was *That's The Way It Is* (1970), which reached No. 21.

Elvis' first live album to chart was the *From Memphis to Vegas/ From Vegas to Memphis* (1969) set, which reached No. 12 on the pop charts, while *Aloha From Hawaii Via Satellite* (1973) was the first to top the chart. *Elvis As Recorded Live on Stage in Memphis* (1974) was the last live album released during his lifetime, reaching No. 33.

Elvis' very first box set was the four-album set *Worldwide 50 Gold Award Hits Vol. 1* (1970). It reached No. 45 in the pop charts.

"Way Down" was the last single released during Elvis' lifetime, peaking at No. 18 pop, No. 1 country. *Moody Blue* was the last album released during his lifetime; in the wake of his death, it went to No. 3 pop, No. 1 country.

98 Elvis in Print

There are so many Elvis books out there, there's even a book that's nothing more than a listing of all the other Elvis books that have been published—at least up to that point (Mary Hancock Hinds' *Infinite Elvis: An Annotated Bibliography*, published in 2001). So there's no shortage of books available if you want to learn more about Elvis. Along with the books I've mentioned throughout the text, here are more for you to consider.

Elvis never wrote an autobiography, but collector Jerry Osborne compiled a book of Elvis quotes from throughout his career, *Elvis: Word For Word.*

A number of Elvis' family members have written books about him, including Elvis' uncle Vester Presley, first cousins Gene Smith, Donna Presley Early, Edie Hand, and Harold Loyd (who worked as a guard at Graceland). Vernon's second wife, Dee Presley, and her children from her first marriage, Bill, David, and Rick Stanley, co-wrote the book *Elvis: We Love You Tender*, and the Stanley brothers have also written other Elvis books. In addition to her autobiography, Priscilla and Lisa Marie shared more family anecdotes (and plenty of photos) in *Elvis By The Presleys.*

Just about everyone in Elvis' inner circle has written a book about him, including Joe Esposito, Charlie Hodge, Marty Lacker, Jerry Schilling, Alan Fortas, and Larry Geller (some of whom have written more than one book). There are also books by Ed Parker (Elvis' karate instructor), June Juanico, Joyce Bova, and Barbara Leigh (Elvis' girlfriends), Jonnita Brewer Barrett (daughter of Elvis' girlfriend, Anita Wood), Becky Yancey (Elvis' secretary), Nick Adams (an actor friend of Elvis'), Marion Cocke (Elvis' nurse), Dick Grob (Elvis' bodyguard), and Mary Jenkins and Nancy

Rooks (Elvis' cooks). Most of these memoirs don't take more than a surface look at the subject.

Elvis and the Memphis Mafia (originally published as *Elvis Aaron Presley: Revelations from the Memphis Mafia*) is especially fascinating. It's an extensive oral history by Lamar Fike, Marty Lacker, and Billy Smith that runs more than 700 pages, and while highly subjective, no other members of the inner circle have spoken at such length about Elvis' entire career.

A number of musicians who worked with Elvis have also written books about their time with him, including Scotty Moore (*Scotty & Elvis: Aboard the Mystery Train*), D.J. Fontana (*The Beat Behind the King*), bassist Jerry Scheff (*Way Down: Playing Bass with Elvis, Dylan, The Doors and More*), and singer Kathy Westmoreland (*Elvis and Kathy*).

Memphis reporter Bill Burk wrote a number of books about Elvis. His three-volume series *Early Elvis* (*The Tupelo Years, The Humes Years, The Sun Years*) features a lot of first-person accounts you won't find anywhere else. In *Elvis: A 30 Year Chronicle*, Burk compiles original stories that ran in the *Memphis Press–Scimitar*.

Lansky Brothers: Clothier to the King (Betsy Holt) is a very entertaining book about the clothing store where Elvis (and other stars) shopped, with plenty of photos of '40s- and '50s-era Memphis, giving you a good idea of what the city was like in Elvis' pre-fame days. *Elvis Presley: Writing for the King* (Ken Sharp) is an oral history about the many songwriters who wrote songs for Elvis. Of the books on Elvis' movie career, *Elvis Presley: Silver Screen Icon* (Steve Templeton) is the best illustrated, though a bit light on critical evaluation. *The Elvis Atlas: A Journey Through Elvis Presley's America* (Michael Gray and Roger Osborne) takes a unique look at the places where Elvis lived and worked. Ernst Jørgensen's *Elvis Presley A Life In Music: The Complete Recording Sessions* is the best book on the subject, and the book he co-wrote with Peter Guralnick, *Elvis Day By Day*, has lots of rare photos from

Graceland's archives. *Elvis: The Illustrated Record* (Roy Carr and Mick Farren) is a good critical overview of Elvis' music, and *The Rough Guide to Elvis* (Paul Simpson) is a concise overview of Elvis' life, music, and films. Simpson is also the author of *Elvis Films FAQ*, the companion to *Elvis Music FAQ* (Mike Eder); at time of writing, both books were due in 2013.

If you'll indulge me, I'd also like to recommend my own *Return of The King: Elvis Presley's Great Comeback*, an in-depth look at Elvis' career during the years 1967–70.

99 The First Career Documentary

This Is Elvis was the first feature-length documentary film about Elvis, telling his story through vintage film clips and re-enactments.

Though much of the film's performance footage can now be found on DVD or YouTube, it was quite exciting to see when *This Is Elvis* was first released in 1981. The infamous "Hound Dog" performance from *The Milton Berle Show*, scenes from *Jailhouse Rock* and *King Creole*, performances from the '68 Comeback Special and the 1970 shows in Las Vegas—*This Is Elvis* made it easy to understand why Elvis became such a major figure in music.

Where the filmmakers lacked real footage, they filled in the gaps with re-creations, primarily covering Elvis' early years, and interspersed throughout the rest of the film; at times, it's difficult to tell which are the real film clips and which are re-enactments. It's also somewhat eerie hearing "Elvis" apparently narrating the film (Elvis' voice was actually provided by Ral Donner), as if he's looking back on his life from the Great Beyond.

Adding to the surreal atmosphere, some real people from Elvis' life provide narration, though while Joe Esposito is both heard as a narrator and seen as "himself" in a re-enactment, Linda Thompson only provides narration, while she's portrayed by an actress (Cheryl Needham) in the re-enactments. Knox Phillips portrays his father, Sam, during the Sun Studio era, and bluesman Furry Lewis makes a cameo during Elvis' childhood years—as a bluesman. At the film's beginning, there's also brief footage of Graceland's second floor, an area off-limits to the public.

The film has a largely positive outlook, even when considering the less upbeat periods of Elvis' life; "Elvis" self-deprecatingly admits he sure made some "silly movies" and addresses his worsening health by stating, "If only I could've seen what was happenin' to me, I mighta done somethin' about it." There are a few more controversial sequences. Elvis is seen in a limo bragging that he spent the previous night "buried in a beaver," and when it's pointed out that a film crew is shooting in the limo, he easily segues into singing the hymn "What A Friend We Have In Jesus..." Another backstage sequence shows him enthusing about a woman he was with who "gave great head."

There's even mention of drugs. Sonny West and Dave Hebler are shown at a press conference discussing Elvis' drug use while promoting their book *Elvis: What Happened?* The subject isn't mentioned again, but it's tellingly followed by a tired, sweaty, and overweight Elvis painfully making his way through "Are You Lonesome Tonight?" during his June 21, 1977, concert in Rapid City, South Dakota, completely losing his way during the song's spoken-word section and mumbling gibberish.

These sequences were altered when the film was released on home video in 1983. The "beaver" line was cut, and through over-dubbing Elvis now is now heard saying that the young woman he'd spent the night with "could raise the dead." "Are You Lonesome

Tonight?" was also cut, substituted by a livelier performance of "Love Me" from the June 19, 1977, concert in Omaha, Nebraska, with Elvis strolling across the stage as he sings, distributing scarves to the faithful. But the video cut is also 40 minutes longer, with a lot more performance footage, making it a more comprehensive look at Elvis' career.

To date, *This Is Elvis* is the last Elvis documentary that has had a theatrical release. Subsequent documentaries have not only been limited to video or DVD, they also tend to cover a specific period of Elvis' life; the landmark year of 1956, for example, or his time in the army. *This Is Elvis* offers the best overview of Elvis' life and career. In 2007, a special-edition release contained both the theatrical and home-video edits of the film.

100 Awards

Elvis won numerous awards and honors during his lifetime, so many that he set up a "Trophy Room" at Graceland to display them. He's also received a number of posthumous honors.

And the Trophy Room isn't the only place at Graceland to see Elvis' awards. The Racquetball Building also has a very impressive display of Elvis' gold and platinum records. There are 150 awards for U.S. record sales and another 100 commemorating foreign record sales. These awards are continually being updated.

Elvis was nominated for a Grammy Award 14 times during his career. But ironically, though he's known as the King of Rock 'n' Roll, his Grammy wins were for his religious recordings: Best Sacred Performance for the album *How Great Thou Art* (1967), Best Inspirational Performance for the album *He Touched Me*

(1972), and Best Inspirational Performance (Non-Classical) for his live version of "How Great Thou Art" from the album *Recorded Live On Stage In Memphis* (1974). In 1971, he also received the Bing Crosby Award—today known as the Lifetime Achievement Award—from the organization.

Six of his recordings have also been inducted into the Grammy Hall of Fame: "That's All Right," "Heartbreak Hotel," "Hound Dog," "Don't Be Cruel," "Are You Lonesome Tonight," and "Suspicious Minds."

Elvis was unsurprisingly one of the first performers inducted into the Rock and Roll Hall of Fame in 1986. But his versatility is such that he's also been inducted into the Country Music Association's Country Music Hall of Fame in 1998 and the Gospel Music Association's Gospel Music Hall of Fame in 2001. In 1984, the Memphis-based Blues Foundation gave Elvis the W.C. Handy Award in honor of his "Keeping the blues alive in his music—rock 'n' roll."

One of the honors Elvis was proudest to receive during his life was when he was named as one of the Ten Outstanding Young Men of Year by the Junior Chamber of Commerce (the Jaycees) for 1970. The Jaycees announced the winners on January 9, 1971, with the award ceremony held a week later on January 16, in Memphis.

Elvis was thrilled to play host to the other winners on the day of the ceremony. Following a prayer breakfast at the Holiday Inn Rivermont and a luncheon at which then–UN ambassador (and future U.S. president) George H.W. Bush gave a speech, Elvis hosted a cocktail reception at Graceland. He then arranged a lavish formal dinner at the upscale Four Flames restaurant.

The award ceremony itself was held at Ellis Auditorium. Elvis had worked carefully on his speech, which began by referencing the incredible journey he'd taken in his life: "When I was a child, ladies and gentlemen, I was a dreamer. I read comic books, and I was the hero of the comic book. I saw movies, and I was the hero in the movie. So every dream I ever dreamed has come true a hundred times."

He ended by not only touching on his accomplishments but also the inspiration for those accomplishments, referencing the lyrics of "Without a Song," performed by Roy Hamilton, one of his favorite singers: "I learned very early in life that without a song, the day would never end, without a song, a man ain't got a friend, without a song, the road would never bend—without a song. So I keep singing a song. Good night. Thank you."

Sources

Print

Anka, Paul with David Dalton. *My Way: An Autobiography*. New York: St. Martin's Press, 2013.

Ann-Margret with Todd Gold. *Ann-Margret: My Story*. New York: G.P. Putnam's Sons, 1994.

Barrett, Jonnita Brewer. *Once Upon A Time: Elvis and Anita*. Jackson, Mississippi: BrewBar Publishing, 2012.

Bartel, Pauline. *Reel Elvis! The Ultimate Trivia Guide to the King's Movies*. Dallas, Texas: Taylor Publishing Company, 1994.

Barth, Jack. *Roadside Elvis: The Complete State-by-State Travel Guide for Elvis Presley Fans*. Chicago: Contemporary Books, 1991.

Braun, Eric. *The Elvis Film Encyclopedia: An Impartial Guide to the Films of Elvis*. London: B.T. Batsford Ltd., 1997.

Brown, Peter and Pat Broeske. *Down at the End of Lonely Street: The Life and Death of Elvis Presley*. London: Arrow Books Ltd., 1998.

Burk, Bill E. *Early Elvis: The Tupelo Years*. Memphis: Propwash Publishing, 1994.

Burk, Bill E. *Early Elvis: The Sun Years*. Memphis: Propwash Publishing, 1997.

Burk, Bill E. *Early Elvis: The Humes Years*. Memphis: Propwash Publishing, 2003.

Burke, Ken and Dan Griffin. *The Blue Moon Boys: The Story of Elvis Presley's Band*. Chicago: Chicago Review Press, 2006.

Cotton, Lee. *All Shook Up: Elvis Day-By-Day 1954–1977*. Ann Arbor, Michigan: Popular Culture, Ink., 1993.

Escott, Colin and Martin Hawkins. *Good Rockin' Tonight: Sun Records and the Birth of Rock 'n' Roll.* New York: St. Martin's Press, 1991.

Gaar, Gillian G. *Return of the King: Elvis Presley's Great Comeback.* London: Jawbone Press, 2010.

Gaar, Gillian G. *Elvis Remembered: 1935–1977.* London: Carlton Books, 2012.

Geller, Larry with Jess Stearn. *The Truth About Elvis.* New York: Jove Books, 1980.

Goldman, Albert. *Elvis.* New York: McGraw-Hill, 1981.

Goldman, Albert. *Elvis: The Last 24 Hours.* New York: St. Martin's Press, 1991.

Gray, Michael and Roger Osborne. *The Elvis Atlas: A Journey Through Elvis Presley's America.* New York: Henry Holt, 1996.

Guralnick, Peter. *Last Train to Memphis: The Rise of Elvis Presley.* New York: Back Bay Books, 1995.

Guralnick, Peter. *Careless Love: The Unmaking of Elvis Presley.* New York: Back Bay Books, 1999.

Guralnick, Peter and Ernst Jorgensen. *Elvis Day By Day: The Definitive Record of His Life and Music.* New York: Ballantine Books, 1999.

Hazen, Cindy and Mike Freeman. *Memphis Elvis-Style.* Winston-Salem, North Carolina: John F. Blair, 1997.

Hopkins, Jerry. *Elvis In Hawaii.* Honolulu: Bess Press, 2002.

Hopkins, Jerry. *Elvis: The Biography.* London: Plexus Publishing Ltd., 2007.

Jørgensen, Ernst. *Elvis Presley: A Life in Music.* New York: St. Martin's Griffin, 1998.

Jørgensen, Ernst. *Elvis: A Boy From Tupelo The Complete 1953–55 Recordings.* Denmark: FTD Books/Follow That Dream Records, 2012.

Klein, George with Chuck Crisafulli. *Elvis: My Best Man.* New York: Crown Publishers, 2010.

Leiber, Jerry and Mike Stoller with David Ritz. *Hound Dog: The Leiber & Stoller Autobiography*. New York: Simon & Schuster Paperbacks, 2009.

Maguire, James. *Impresario: The Life and Times of Ed Sullivan*. New York: Billboard Books, 2006.

Morgan, Todd. *Elvis Presley's Graceland*. Memphis: Elvis Presley Enterprises, 2009.

Nash, Alanna. *The Colonel: The Extraordinary Story of Colonel Tom Parker and Elvis Presley*. New York: Simon & Schuster, 1993.

Nash, Alanna. *Baby Let's Play House: Elvis Presley and the Women Who Loved Him*. New York: !t Books, 2010.

Nichopoulos, George with Rose Clayton Phillips. *The King and Dr. Nick: What Really Happened to Elvis and Me*. Nashville: Thomas Nelson Inc., 2009.

O'Neal, Sean. *Elvis Inc.: The Fall and Rise of the Presley Empire*. Rocklin, California: Prima Publishing, 1996.

Pierce, Patricia Jobe. *The Ultimate Elvis: Elvis Presley Day By Day*. New York: Simon & Schuster, 1994.

Pirzada, Joseph, Rhonda Marsden, and John Michael Heath. *Elvis Presley's Graceland Through The Years 1957–1977*. Boxcar Enterprises/Entertainment Holding Inc., 2012.

Pirzada, Joseph and Joseph Tunzi, Steve Barile. *Elvis Aloha Via Satellite*. Boxcar Enterprises-Entertainment Holding Inc./JAT Publishing, 2013.

Presley, Priscilla Beaulieu with Sandra Harmon. *Elvis And Me*. New York: G.P. Putnam's Sons, 1985.

Ritz, David, ed. *Elvis By The Presleys*. New York: Crown, 2005.

Romine, Linda. *Frommer's Nashville & Memphis* (10th edition). Hoboken, New Jersey: John Wiley & Sons, Inc., 2012.

Schilling, Jerry with Chuck Crisafulli. *Me and a Guy Named Elvis: My Lifelong Friendship with Elvis Presley*. New York: Gotham Books, 2006.

Sharp, Ken. *Elvis Presley: Writing For The King*. Denmark: FTD Books/Follow That Dream Records, 2006.

Simpson, Paul. *The Rough Guide to Elvis*. London: Rough Guides Ltd., 2004.

Tunzi, Joseph A. *Elvis No. 1: The Complete Chart History of Elvis Presley*. Chicago: JAT Productions, 2000.

Tunzi, Joseph A. *Elvis Sessions III: The Recorded Music of Elvis Aron Presley 1953 to 1977*. Chicago: JAT Productions, 2004.

West, Sonny with Marshall Terrill. *Elvis: Still Taking Care of Business*. Chicago: Triumph Books, 2007.

Yancey, Becky and Cliff Linedecker. *My Life with Elvis*. New York: St. Martin's Press, 1977.

Yenne, Bill. *The Field Guide to Elvis Shrines*. Los Angeles: Renaissance Books, 1999.

Websites

www.bigelvislasvegas.com

circlegfoundation.co.uk

www.elmiro.de

www.elvis.com

www.elvis.com.au

www.elvis-history-blog.com

www.elvis-in-concert.com

www.elvisinfonet.com

www.elvispresleybirthplace.com

elvissightingsociety.org

kangrhee.com

www.lasvegaselvisfestival.com

lauderdalecourts.com

www.mariancocke.com

www.nudiesrodeotailor.com

www.orionjimmyellis.com
www.sergent.com.au/elvis
simplycilla.com
www.sunrecords.com
www.sunstudio.com
www.thekingsransom.com
www.tupelo.net
www.vegaselvis.com
www.welovetupelo.com

Thanks also to Sue Mack of Mike's Memphis Tours.